O9-BTN-583

7/04

ALSO BY BILL BUFORD

Among the Thugs

HEAT

HEAT

An Amateur's Adventures
as Kitchen Slave, Line Cook,
Pasta-Maker, and Apprentice
to a Dante-Quoting Butcher
in Tuscany

Bill Buford

Alfred A. Knopf 🐎 New York 2006

THIS IS A BORZOI BOOK

PUBLISHED BY ALFRED A. KNOPF

Portions of this work previously appeared in *The New Yorker.*

Knopf, Borzoi Books, and the colophon are registered
trademarks of Random House, Inc.

Library of Congress Cataloging-in-Publication Data

Buford, Bill.
Heat : an amateur's adventures as kitchen slave, line
cook, pasta-maker, and apprentice to a Dante-quoting
butcher in Tuscany / Bill Buford.
p. cm.
ISBN 1-4000-4120-1 (alk. paper)
1. Cookery, Italian—Tuscan style. 2. Food—Italy—
Tuscany. I. Title.

TX723.2.T86B83 2001
641.59455—dc22   2005057868

Manufactured in the United States of America
Published June 6, 2006
Reprinted Two Times
Fourth Printing, July 2006

For Jessica

. . . che move il sole e l'altre stelle.

Contents

DINNER WITH MARIO

A human being is primarily a bag for putting food into; the other functions and faculties may be more godlike, but in point of time they come afterwards. A man dies and is buried, and all his words and actions are forgotten, but the food he has eaten lives after him in the sound or rotten bones of his children. I think it could be plausibly argued that changes of diet are more important than changes of dynasty or even of religion. The Great War, for instance, could never have happened if tinned food had not been invented. And the history of the past four hundred years in England would have been immensely different if it had not been for the introduction of root-crops and various other vegetables at the end of the Middle Ages, and a little later the introduction of non alcoholic drinks (tea, coffee, cocoa) and also of distilled liquors to which the beer-drinking English were not accustomed. Yet it is curious how seldom the all-importance of food is recognized. You see statues everywhere to politicians, poets, bishops, but none to cooks or bacon-curers or market gardeners.

—GEORGE ORWELL, *The Road to Wigan Pier*

THE FIRST GLIMPSE I had of what Mario Batali's friends had described to me as the "myth of Mario" was on a cold Saturday night in January 2002, when I invited him to a birthday dinner. Batali, the chef and co-owner of Babbo, an Italian restaurant in Manhattan, is such a famous and proficient cook that he's rarely invited to people's homes for a meal, he told me, and he went out of his way to be a grateful guest. He arrived bearing his own quince-flavored grappa (the rough, distilled end-of-harvest grape juices rendered almost drinkable by the addition of the fruit); a jar of homemade *nocino* (same principle, but with walnuts); an armful of wine; and a white, dense slab of *lardo*—literally, the raw "lardy" back of a very fat pig, one he'd cured himself with herbs and salt. I was what might generously be described as an enthusiastic cook, more confident than competent (that is, keen but fundamentally clueless), and to this day I am astonished that I had the nerve to ask over someone of Batali's reputation, along with six guests who thought they'd have an amusing evening witnessing my humiliation. (Mario was a friend of the birthday friend, so I'd thought—why not invite him, too?—but when, wonder of wonders, he then accepted and I told my wife, Jessica, she was apoplectic with wonder: "What in the world were you thinking of, inviting a famous chef to our apartment for *dinner*?")

In the event, there was little comedy, mainly because Mario didn't give me a chance. Shortly after my being instructed that only a moron would let his meat rest by wrapping it in foil after cooking it, I cheerfully gave up and let Batali tell me what to do. By then he'd taken over the evening, anyway. Not long into it, he'd cut the *lardo* into thin slices and, with a startling flourish of intimacy, laid them individually on our tongues, whispering that we needed to let the fat melt in our mouths to appreciate its intensity. The *lardo* was from a pig that, in the last months of its seven-hundred-and-fifty-pound life, had lived on apples, walnuts, and cream ("The best song sung in the key of pig"), and Mario convinced us that, as the fat dissolved, we'd detect the flavors of the animal's happy diet—there, in the back of the mouth. No one that evening had knowingly eaten pure fat before ("At the restaurant, I tell the waiters to call it prosciutto bianco"), and by the time Mario had persuaded us to a third helping everyone's heart was racing. Batali was an impressively dedicated drinker—he mentioned in passing that, on trips to Italy made with his Babbo co-owner, Joe Bastianich, the two of them had been known to put away a case of wine during an evening meal—and while I don't think that any of us drank anything like that, we were, by now, very thirsty (the *lardo*, the salt, the human heat of so much jollity) and, cheered on, found ourselves knocking back more and more. I don't know. I don't really remember. There were also the grappa and the *nocino*, and one of my last images is of Batali at three in the morning—a stoutly round man with his back dangerously arched, his eyes closed, a long red ponytail swinging rhythmically behind him, an unlit cigarette dangling from his mouth, his red Converse high-tops pounding the floor—playing air guitar to Neil Young's "Southern Man." Batali was forty-one, and I remember thinking it had been a long time since I'd seen a grown man play air guitar. He then found the soundtrack for *Buena Vista Social Club*, tried to salsa with one of the women guests (who promptly fell over a sofa), moved on to her boyfriend, who was unresponsive, put on a Tom Waits CD instead, and sang along as he washed the dishes and swept the floor. He reminded me of an arrangement we'd made for the next day—when I'd invited Batali to dinner, he'd reciprocated by asking me to join him at a New York Giants football game, tickets courtesy of the commissioner of the NFL, who had just eaten at Babbo—and then disappeared with three of my friends, assuring them that, with his back-of-the-hand knowledge of downtown establishments open until five, he'd find a place to continue the evening. They ended up at Marylou's in the Village—in Batali's description, "A wise guy joint where you can get anything at any time of night, and none of it good."

It was daylight when Batali got home. I learned this from his building superintendent the next morning, as the two of us tried to get Batali to wake up—the commissioner's driver was waiting outside. When Batali finally appeared, forty-five minutes later, he was momentarily perplexed, standing in the doorway of his apartment in his underwear and wondering why I was there, too. (Batali has a remarkable girth, and it was startling to see him clad so.) Then, in minutes, he transformed himself into what I would come to know as the Batali look: the shorts, the clogs, the wraparound sunglasses, the red hair pulled back into its ponytail. One moment, a rotund Clark Kent in his underpants; the next, "*Molto* Mario"—the clever, many-layered name of his cooking television program, which, in one of its senses, literally means *Very* Mario (that is, an *intensified* Mario, an *exaggerated* Mario)—and a figure whose renown I didn't appreciate until, as guests of the commissioner, we were allowed onto the field before the game. Fans of the New York Giants are so famously brutish as to be cartoons (bare-chested on a wintry morning or wearing hard hats; in any case, not guys putting in their domestic duty in the kitchen), and I was surprised by how many recognized the ponytailed chef, who stood facing them, arms crossed over his chest, beaming. "Hey, Molto!" they shouted. "What's cooking, Mario?" "Mario, make me a pasta!" At the time, *Molto Mario* was shown on afternoons on cable television, and I found a complex picture of the working metropolitan male emerging, one rushing home the moment his shift ended to catch lessons in braising his broccoli rabe and getting just the right forked texture on his homemade orecchiette. I stood back with one of the security people, taking in the spectacle (by now members of the crowd were chanting "Molto, Molto, Molto")—this very round man, whose manner and dress said, "Dude, where's the party?"

"I love this guy," the security man said. "Just lookin' at him makes me hungry."

MARIO BATALI is the most recognized chef in a city with more chefs than any other city in the world. In addition to Batali's television show—and his appearances promoting, say, the NASCAR race track in Delaware—he was simply and energetically omnipresent. It would be safe to say that no New York chef ate more, drank more, and was out and about as much. If you live in New York City, you will see him eventually (sooner, if your evenings get going around two in the morning).

With his partner, Joe, Batali also owned two other restaurants, Esca and Lupa, and a shop selling Italian wine, and, when we met, they were talking about opening a pizzeria and buying a vineyard in Tuscany. But Babbo was the heart of their enterprise, crushed into what was originally a nineteenth-century coach house, just off Washington Square, in Greenwich Village. The building was narrow; the space was crowded, jostly, and loud; and the food, studiously Italian, rather than Italian-American, was characterized by an over-the-top flourish that seemed to be expressly Batali's. People went there in the expectation of excess. Sometimes I wondered if Batali was less a conventional cook than an advocate of a murkier enterprise of stimulating outrageous appetites (whatever they might be) and satisfying them intensely (by whatever means). A friend of mine, who'd once dropped by the bar for a drink and was then fed personally by Batali for the next six hours, went on a diet of soft fruit and water for three days. "This guy knows no middle ground. It's just excess on a level I've never known before—it's food and drink, food and drink, food and drink, until you feel you're on drugs." Chefs who were regular visitors were subjected to extreme versions of what was already an extreme experience. "We're going to kill him," Batali said to me with maniacal glee as he prepared a meal for a rival who had innocently ordered a seven-course tasting menu, to which Batali added a lethal number of extra courses. The starters (all variations in pig) included *lonza* (the cured backstrap from the cream-apple-and-walnut herd), *coppa* (from the shoulder), a fried foot, a porcini mushroom roasted with Batali's own *pancetta* (the belly), plus ("for the hell of it") a pasta topped with *guanciale* (the jowls). This year, Mario was trying out a new motto: "Wretched excess is just barely enough."

Batali was born in 1960 and grew up outside Seattle: a suburban kid with a solid *Leave It to Beaver* upbringing. His mother, Marilyn, is English and French Canadian—from her comes her son's flaming red hair and a fair, un-Italian complexion. The Italian is from his father, Armandino, the grandson of immigrants who arrived in the 1890s. When Mario was growing up, his father was a well-paid Boeing executive in charge of procuring airplane parts made overseas, and in 1975, after being posted to Europe, to supervise the manufacturing close-up, he moved his family to Spain. That, according to Gina, Mario's youngest sibling, was when Mario changed. ("He was already pushing the limits.") Madrid, in the post-Franco years (bars with no minimum age, hash hangouts, the world's oldest profession suddenly legalized), was a place of exhilarating license, and Mario seems to have experienced a little bit of everything on offer. He was caught growing marijuana on the roof of his father's apartment building (the first incident of what would become a theme—Batali was later expelled from his dorm in college, suspected of dealing, and, later still, there was some trouble in Tijuana that actually landed him in jail). The marijuana association also evokes a memory of the first meals Batali remembers preparing, late-night *panini* with caramelized locally grown onions, a local cow's-milk Spanish cheese, and paper-thin slices of chorizo: "The best stoner munch you can imagine; me and my younger brother Dana were just classic stoner kids—we were so happy."

By the time Batali returned to the United States in 1978 to attend Rutgers University, in New Jersey, he was determined to get back to Europe ("I wanted to be a Spanish banker—I *loved* the idea of making a lot of money and living a luxurious life in Madrid"), and his unlikely double major was in business management and Spanish theatre. But after being thrown out of his dorm, Batali got work as a dishwasher at a pizzeria called Stuff Yer Face (in its name alone, destiny was calling), and his life changed. He was promoted to cook, then line cook (working at one "station" in a "line" of stations, making one thing), and then asked to be manager, an offer he turned down. He didn't want the responsibility; he was having too good a time. The life at Stuff Yer Face was fast (twenty-five years later, he still claims he has the record for the most pizzas made in an hour), sexy ("The most booooootiful waitresses in town"), and very buzzy ("I don't want to come off as a big druggy, but when a guy comes into the kitchen with a pizza pan turned upside down, covered with lines of coke, how can you say no?"). When, in his junior year, he attended a career conference hosted by representatives from major corporations, Batali realized he had been wrong; he was never going to be a banker. He was going to be a chef.

"My mother and grandmother had always told me that I should be a cook. In fact, when I was preparing my applications for college, my mother had suggested cooking school. But I said, 'Ma, that's too gay. I don't want to go to cooking school—that's for fags.' " Five years later, Batali was back in Europe, attending the Cordon Bleu in London.

His father, still overseeing Boeing's foreign operations, was now based in England. Gina Batali was there, too, and recalls seeing her eldest brother only when she was getting ready for school and he was returning from his all-night escapades after attending classes during the day and then working at a pub. The pub was the Six Bells, on the King's Road in Chelsea. Mario had been bartending at the so-called American bar ("*No idea* what I was doing"), when a high-priced dining room opened in the back and a chef was hired to run it, a Yorkshire man named Marco Pierre White. Batali, bored by the pace of cooking school, was hired to be the new chef's slave.

Today, Marco Pierre White is regarded as one of the most influential chefs in Britain (as well as the most foul-tempered, most mercurial, and most bullying), and it's an extraordinary fortuity that these two men, both in their early twenties, found themselves in a tiny pub kitchen together. Batali didn't understand what he was witnessing: his restaurant experience had been making strombolis in New Brunswick. "I assumed I was seeing what everyone else already knew. I didn't feel like I was on the cusp of a revolution. And yet, while I had no idea this guy was about to become so famous, I could see he was preparing food from outside the box. He was a genius on the plate. I'd never worked on presentation. I just put shit on the plate." He described White's making a deep green puree from basil leaves and then a white butter sauce, then swirling the green sauce in one direction, and the white sauce in the other, and drawing a swerving line down the middle of the plate. "I had never seen anyone draw fucking lines with two sauces." White would order Batali to follow him to market ("I was his whipping boy—'Yes, master,' I'd answer, 'whatever you say, master' ") and they'd return with game birds or ingredients for some of the most improbable dishes ever to be served in an English pub: *écrevisses* in a reduced lobster sauce, oysters with caviar, roasted ortolan (a rare, tiny bird served virtually breathing, gulped down, innards and all, like a raw crustacean)—"the whole menu written out in fucking French."

According to Batali, White was basically illiterate, but because he was so intuitive and physical—"a beautiful specimen, perfect, a classic body, like a sculpture, with broad shoulders, narrow waist"—he could do things to food that no one else had done before. "He made a hollandaise by beating the sauce so vigorously that it began to froth up and became something else—it was like a sabayon." He was forever chopping things, reducing them, and making Batali force them through a sieve— "which was no bigger than a fucking tea strainer, because it was a pub and that was all he had, and I'd spend my whole day crushing some chunky shellfish reduction through this tiny thing, ramming it over and over again with a wooden spoon."

White's term of choice was "navvy." "You know, we're just two guys in the kitchen," Batali recalls, "and I'm not cooking the fries right, according to him, or the zucchini, or whatever it was, and he tells me to sauté the snow peas instead, while he's over in the corner doing some dramatic thing with six crayfish, and suddenly he calls out, 'Bring me the snow peas *now*,' and I duly bring them over. 'Here are the snow peas, master,' but he doesn't like the look of them. 'They're wrong, you arsehole. They're overcooked, you fucking moron. You've ruined them, you goddamn fucking navvy.' But I'm an American, and I didn't understand what 'navvy' meant, and I'd say something like 'Navvy this, navvy that, if you don't like my snow peas then make them yourself,' which made him even angrier." He threw a risotto into Batali's chest. He beat up an Irish kid who washed the dishes. "He was intimidating," Batali recalls. He stuck it out for four months—"I was frightened for my life, this guy was a mean motherfucker"—then dumped two handfuls of salt into a beurre blanc and walked out.

"I will never forget him," White said, when I met him in London. "He has fucking big calves, doesn't he? He should donate them to the kitchen when he dies. They'll make a great osso buco. If he walked in today, and I saw only those calves, I'd know it was Mario." According to White, Mario wasn't taking his calling seriously. "The sleeping thing killed him." He would have been a perfectly competent chef, White said, if only he'd got up when his alarm went off. He recalls dispatching Batali to buy tropical fruit. "He came back with four avocados. He was worn out. He didn't know what he was doing. He'd been out until four in the morning. He was wild. Hard core. Joy Division was his favorite band, and that says it all." White put his finger to his nose and sniffed. "Know what I mean?" White shook his head. "Would it be fair to say that, in those days, his enthusiasm for gastronomy was considerably greater than his talent? Is that a fair comment? Has his talent caught up?"

In White's kitchen, Batali was a failure, and you can tell that he'd like to dismiss the experience but can't: after all, White was the first person to show Batali what a chef could be. As a result, White is both loathed by Batali and respected. Even now, twenty years later, you hear in Batali's account a nagging irritation at his failure to charm or work with someone who understood so much about the potential of food—that "it was a wide-open game." From White, Batali learned the virtues of presentation, speed, stamina, and intense athletic cooking. And from White he acquired a hatred of things French. Batali has an injunction against reduced sauces, the business of boiling a meat broth until it is reduced to an intense syrup. ("If you can run your finger through it and it leaves an impression, then it's not me, we won't serve it, it's too French.") And a prohibition against tantrums. ("It's so old school, so made for the movies.") But mainly Batali learned how much he had to learn.

Provoked by White's command, Batali embarked on a grand tour of the grandest restaurants in Europe, tracing White's skills back to their origins like someone following a genealogical line: the Tour d'Argent in Paris; the Moulin de Mougins, in Provence; the Waterside Inn, outside London, then regarded as the best restaurant in Britain. "In four months, you learn the essentials of the place," Batali told me. "If you want to learn them properly, you have to stay a year, to cook through the seasons. But I was in a hurry." Most of the time, Batali was stuck doing highly repetitive tasks: squeezing duck carcasses, night after night, using a machine designed to get that extra ounce of juice to go into a duck stock, which, in turn, would be reduced into one of those "sticky, gummy" sauces for which Batali was developing such a distaste. "You learn by working in the kitchen. Not by reading a book or watching a television program or going to cooking school. That's how it's done."

That's what I wanted to do—to work in the Babbo kitchen, as Mario's slave.

KITCHEN SLAVE

~~~~~~~~~~~~~~~~~~~~~~~~~~~~~~~~

Serendipitously, I found that a man cooking turned out to be seductive. I'd invited a woman over for dinner—let's call her Mary Alice. I put on some Erroll Garner, then some Miles Davis, then "Moonglow" and the theme from *Picnic*, the most romantic music I know from the most romantic love scene ever filmed, and brought out the first course which I'd made beforehand—shrimp Rothschild, which is hollowed-out loaves of bread sautéed in clarified butter, then filled with shrimp braised in fish stock for just a couple of minutes, the stock then reduced practically to a syrup, topped off in the oven with some Gruyère and a slice of truffle. I brought it to her.

"Oh," she said and followed me back to the kitchen where I put together the tournedos Rossini—small filets of beef topped with foie gras, a truffle slice, and a Madeira reduction.

"Ah." She began asking very detailed questions about what I was doing and who I was.

What cinched it was a spectacular creation called Le Talley-rand. You make it with canned cherries of all things and ground almonds and sugar, cover them with a meringue, and in the meringue you put half an empty eggshell, bake it, and for the spectacular part you turn off the lights, ignite a little kirsch or rum, pour it into the eggshell when it comes out of the oven all browned, and it looks like a small volcano—which is where things can get very moist.

Mary Alice's eyes were limpid and beseeching. "You're the deepest and most complex man I know, and I love your knowledge and your fingers . . . but I made another date tonight at ten." And off she went to spend the night with another guy. All my work went to benefit him! And he never even called to thank me.

—JONATHAN REYNOLDS, *Dinner with Demons*, 2003

1

I WAS ACCEPTED "inside" on a trial basis. "The question is space," Mario said. "Is there room for another body?" There wasn't. There wasn't room for the people already there. But somehow I squeezed in. To start, I'd do a night or two plating pasta plus Fridays in the prep kitchen, preparing food for the evening. Mario then invited me to attend a Saturday morning kitchen meeting. It was January 26th, 2002.

Twenty people showed up, gathered round a long table upstairs, Mario in the middle. In April, *The Babbo Cookbook* would be published, and its publication, he said, had a number of implications. "We'll come under more scrutiny. There'll be television crews, bigger crowds, and, most importantly, the critics will be back." Babbo was a three-star restaurant and, according to Mario, was now likely to be reassessed to see if it still deserved its stars. What he really meant was that the new *New York Times* restaurant critic hadn't written about Babbo, and he might use the occasion of the book's publication to pay a visit, and Mario wanted everyone to be ready. "What's more," Mario said, "because the book will reveal our secrets, we're going to have to change our menu." He invited ideas for dishes and suggested that his cooks read through old recipes, looking for a traditional thing that can be made new. He then reminded everyone of the three essential principles of the kitchen: that we were there "to buy food, fix it up, and sell it at a profit—that's what we do"; that consistency was essential ("If someone has a great dish and returns to have it again, and you don't serve it to him in exactly the same way, then you're a dick"); and that the success of Babbo, "the best Italian restaurant in America," had arisen from its style: "More feminine than masculine. People should think there are grandmothers in the back preparing their dinner."

When Mario was finished, Andy Nusser, the executive chef, the one running the kitchen day to day, brought up a labor issue: kitchen rage. Andy was forty-one, Mario's age, but wholly different in appearance, Apollonian to his boss's Dionysian. He was six feet with a swimmer's broad shoulders and boyish good looks, his age betrayed only by the fact that his big head of hair had started to gray. He'd been at Babbo since it opened. His manner (austere, unfrivolous, in a hurry) conveyed discipline and a military-like respect for the rules. A cook, Andy announced, had just been fired because he couldn't control his temper. He had banged pots, thrown utensils, "poisoned the kitchen with his anger." The behavior, Andy said, wasn't to be tolerated. Mario interrupted to make suggestions: take a break before the service starts, because otherwise "the stress will enter your cooking and we'll taste it." He offered strategies for the week: even though you might have to work thirteen, fourteen, possibly fifteen hours on "your first day, because the first day back is always brutal, your second day is easier, and the last day of your week will be a breeze. You can show up at two o'clock." A shift ends around one in the morning; even if you start at two in the afternoon, your day was still a lazy eleven hours long.

"Be patient," Andy added. "Stick it out. I know most of us are here because we want to be running restaurants of our own."

I looked round the room. The average age was thirty-something. Most of the people were men. They were pale and unshaven. Many spoke English badly. Were they all here because they hoped to be running their own restaurants?

THE FOLLOWING FRIDAY, at seven a.m. I presented myself to the prep chef, a handsome, athletic woman in her forties named Elisa Sarno. I was eager, hopeful, utterly ready. But Elisa didn't seem all that happy to see me.

I put on an apron and jacket, and was given a tour. One corner of the kitchen was taken up by the "walk-in," a refrigerated closet about the size of a small truck with floor-to-ceiling shelves. That week's New York Times restaurant review was pasted on the door, as was the custom—a reminder of the competition and of the importance of Babbo's three stars (very few restaurants, you learned, got even two). Another corner was given over to dishwashing. Pots, pans, and various plastic containers were stored overhead. Elisa was describing each one according to its size, but I was distracted by the dishwasher, a young angry man (I wasn't introduced but later discovered his name was Alejandro) who was assaulting a pot the size of a suburban trash can with a high-pressured gadget that was spraying water powerfully in unpredictable directions. "These are the one-quarts," Elisa was saying meanwhile, "and here are the two-quarts, four-quarts, six-quarts, and eight, all with their own color-coded lid. Hotel pans and half hotels are there, along with sheet trays and half-sheet trays." The containers, I learned, were the medium of the prep kitchen—everything you did went into them so that it could be fetched later in the evening—and great weight would be expressed in questions such as: "Is *this* (chicken feet, say, or a quantity of beef cheeks) to be put in a six-quart, or will it fit into a four?" I was already thinking about the private autistic language of the kitchen, in which everyone around me was so demonstrably fluent—is this what you learn in cooking school, what a hotel pan is?—when Elisa stopped suddenly. "Where did you put your knives?" she asked.

"My knives?"

"You don't have knives?"

"I'm meant to have knives?"

"Oh, my God. Okay. Bring them next week." She muttered to herself: "God, I hate lending people my knives."

She led me into the walk-in, talking very fast now, wanting to get on with her day. "This is where we put stuff for the grilling station"—she pointed to a shelf packed with green-lidded containers, indistinguishable from all the other shelves, also packed with green-lidded containers. "This is the pasta shelf. This, the pantry shelf. This, the sauté shelf. Oh, yes, and this is the masking tape. Everything is labeled and dated. Where's your pen? You didn't bring a pen?"

Vegetables were in the back—crates of carrots, celery, white onions. Fish had been stacked on the floor, delivered before I arrived, some silver Mediterranean monstrosity.

"Time to bone the ducks. Come."

There were four boxes of ducks, six in each box.

"Wipe the counter, wet a cloth—do you remember where the cloths are?—get a cutting board" (Where are they again? I asked, panicking), "an eight-quart and two four-quarts, a hotel pan" (which ones were the

hotel pans?) "and parchment paper. You get sheets from the pastry station. The four-quarts will be for the gizzards. Here, take one of my
knives. Will you bring your knives next week?"

Yes, yes, of course.

"Unpack the duck from the top, so you don't get blood all over
you. Remove the gizzards. Liver goes in one container, kidneys in the
other. Remove the legs to make a confit, but first chop off the knobby bit
at the bottom with a chopper—here, use this," she said, handing me a
giant tomahawk, "—and then remove the breast. You do know how to
bone a duck, don't you?"

"Well, I think, yes, I do. I mean, I've done it." But when? I seem to
recall a dinner party. Was that in 1993?

"And you know about the oyster of meat?"

"The oyster?" I asked, and my mind did a simple calculation. Duck,
an animal with wings: fowl. Oyster, molecular thing without wings:
mollusk. Ducks don't have oysters; oysters don't have ducks. "The oyster?" I repeated.

"Yes, it's the nugget of meat you don't want to lose. It's here," she
said, swiftly cutting the breast in half and whipping her knife round the
thigh. She had an appealingly easy manner with the knife, which
seemed to involve no effort, and the meat instantaneously cleaved in
two. I was thinking, I want to learn how to do that, and ended up not
quite getting the location of the duck oyster—was it in front of the
thigh or behind?—when she was off. A delivery man had appeared,
bearing boxes of meat.

I looked around the kitchen. The pastry chefs were beside me, two
guys cutting up pineapples. In front of me was a wall of stoves, with vats
of something boiling on top. Behind me two guys were making pasta.
On the floor was a giant mixer, rhythmically knocking around a large
mound of dough. It was seven-fifteen in the morning.

I picked up a duck, removed the wings, and hunted around for that
oyster. I felt an obligation to honor this bird in my hand by ensuring
that its thigh oyster found its way onto the plate. But where was the little fucker?

I slowly got through my first ducks and stacked their parts on my
cutting board. The idea was that you should whip through each one,

slice, slice, slice, just as Elisa had done—the knife doing that effortless trick, all edge, no pressure, the meat opening up like magic—and drop each bit into its appropriate container. But I wasn't sure I was getting it right. I piled my thighs on one corner of my cutting board, burying my first hacked-up experiments under some of the better examples, just in case Elisa came round to inspect my work.

Meanwhile, she was opening up the meat boxes. ("*Frozen* pig cheeks," she was saying to the delivery man, "frozen is no good for me.") The delivery man didn't reply. He was staring at me. ("Did you count these lamb shanks?" Elisa was asking him. "It's never the number you say—I can't run a kitchen if I don't know the number of lamb shanks.") What was wrong with this delivery guy? His stare was making me very self-conscious. Don't you have better things do? You think it's entertaining to watch a guy ruining twenty-four entrées because he can't find the oyster?

I looked across to one of the cooks, who seemed to be boning quails, a much more challenging operation. And he was doing it at staggering speed. The delivery man hadn't moved. Was he actually shaking his head?—when, somehow, I dragged the blade of Elisa's knife, smoothly and delicately, across the top of my forefinger—from behind the first knuckle to the nail. There was a moment: did I just do what I think I did? Yes. And the top of my finger erupted in a gush of red blood.

"Did you just slice yourself?" Elisa asked, breaking off her lamb-shank count and in a tone that said, You've been here half an hour, and this is what you've done?

"Yes," I said, "but not to worry," as I wrapped my hand up in a meaty, soiled cloth. "I do this all the time. You should look at my fingers. A road map of scars and nicks. I think I need to wear glasses. Nearsighted. Or farsighted. Both, actually. Really, it's what I do."

"Do you need to go to the hospital?" It sounded like an accusation.

I shook my head, a little worried by her worry. There was a lot of blood.

"Band-Aids are in the refrigerator," she said. "You'll need to wear a rubber glove. The Band-Aids won't stay dry."

I retreated to the dining room, crunched up the wound with a criss-crossing of Band-Aids, wrestled my finger into a surgeon's glove, and returned. It was nearly nine o'clock, and my cutting board had a modest square of about five inches of work space. The rest of it was stacked with pieces of duck.

I resumed. Chop, trim, twist, pop, thwack. I cleared my board. And, as I did, the Band-Aids started to work themselves loose, and the clear synthetic surgeon's glove started to expand and droop, filling up like a water balloon with my blood. The truth is, I am always slicing off little bits of me, but I could see that if I sliced off a little bit of this glove it was going to be a mess. I was falling behind, and Elisa was looking at me.

She picked up a thigh. To me, it looked like I'd got the oyster. In front and back, wherever the thing was, there was plenty of meat. That wasn't the problem.

"There's too much fat," she said, trimming it off, and added, as if she'd failed to mention a crucial instruction, "you *are* aware that these are going to be served to people."

I CAME TO REGARD the prep kitchen as something like a culinary boot camp, especially during my first weeks, where I was being taught basic techniques of being a cook, especially knife skills. It seemed that I'd been using a knife for years without knowing how to use one. On that first morning, I paused to sharpen my knife—well, Elisa's knife, actually— and she stopped what she was doing and stared: I was doing it backward (ergo, I had always been doing it backward). Then, there was the rocking thing. The idea is that, when you're chopping food you want to leave the tip of your knife in place, on the cutting board: you end up rocking the knife back and forth, and the blade then slides effortlessly, and with much more control, through whatever you're chopping. Everyone who cooks probably knows this, but I didn't.

Some techniques seemed fussy. Carrots were a trauma. Long-cooking meat broths have carrots in them, along with celery, onions, and herbs, which soften the meatiness of a meat liquid. This was something I knew, or at least I thought I did. I'd made broths at home—soups, chicken stocks, that sort of thing—and I'd simply tossed in my carrots, chopped up or not: what did it matter if they were going to cook for hours? Wrong.

Evidently, there are only two ways to prepare a carrot: rough cut and fine dice. Rough cut meant slicing the carrot in half lengthwise and then—chop, chop, chop—cutting it into perfectly identical half moons (which, to my eye, had nothing rough about them).

The nightmare was fine dice, which meant cutting every bit of the carrot into identical one-millimeter-square cubes.

A carrot is not shaped like a cube, and so you first had to trim it up into a long rectangle, then cut it into thin, one-millimeter planks, and then take your one-millimeter planks and cut them into long, one-millimeter slivers, and then take your perfectly formed slivers, and, chop, chop, chop, cut them into one-millimeter cubes. I seemed to have done my first batch almost right—either that or it was late and everyone was in a hurry and no one looked too closely at the geometric mishmash in the container I'd filled. My second batch involved thirty-six carrots. It took me a long time to cube thirty-six carrots. Normally, Elisa popped round to make sure I wasn't mangling what I was working on, but she must have trusted me with the carrots—after all, what can you do to a carrot?—so when she finally looked in I was almost done. She shrieked, "I said fine dice! This is not a fine dice! I don't know what they are, but they're wrong." I had been cutting carrots for two hours, and then, like that, they were tossed; they were *that* bad. I wanted to weep. It took me three days before I could tell anyone about the experience ("She threw away my carrots—all of them!"), and even then I could hear the quiver of indignation in my voice. It was a month later that I finally succeeded in getting the carrots right, although the achievement—"Wow," Elisa said, picking up my four quart and dumping the contents into a braising liquid, "these are good"—was secretly marred by my having covertly eaten several hundred imperfect little squares.

I cubed pork for a ragù (only after my first batch was returned— "These are chunks, I asked for cubes") and learned how to trim the fat off a flank of beef. Jointing rabbits, I was taught how to tie up the loin with a butcher's looping knot and was so excited by the discovery that I went home and practiced. I told Elisa about my achievement. "I tied up everything," I said. "A leg of lamb, some utensils, a chair. My wife came home, and I tied up her, too." Elisa shook her head. "Get a life," she said and returned to her task.

I became captivated by the kitchen's smells. By midmorning, when many things had been prepared, they were cooked in quick succession, and the smells came, one after the other, waves of smell, like sounds in music. There was the smell of meat, and the kitchen was overwhelmed by the rich, sticky smell of wintry lamb. And then, in minutes, it would be chocolate melting in a metal bowl. Then a disturbing nonsequitur like tripe (a curious disjunction, having chocolate in your nose followed quickly by stewing cow innards). Then something ripe and fishy— octopus simmering in a hot tub—followed by what seemed like overex- tracted pineapple. And so they came, one after the other—huckleberries, chicken broth, the comforting chemistry of veal, pork, and milk as someone prepared a Bolognese ragù.

Until now, my cooking had been based on what I got from books. I was a home cook, always longing to do more than a simple supper, although my meals, especially when prepared for friends, tended to be stressful affairs, distinguished by two incompatible qualities: their ambition and my lack of experience. My friends would do a calculation, trying to figure out just how late they should show up, because they knew what they'd see if they got it wrong: their host bespattered, in a panic, unbathed, and wishing they'd go away. Once, guests arrived at the height of a modest conflagration, a black cloud billowing out of the kitchen, as I stood at the door, paralyzed, unable to remember how to put out a grease fire.

I hadn't worked in a professional kitchen and had always respected those who did. They knew something I didn't. Now I was among them. Once I mastered some basic skills, I discovered that I stopped feeling self-conscious. I was a member of a team of cooks, closed away in this back room, people's knives knocking against cutting boards in the same rhythmic rocking way, mine as well: no windows, no natural light; no connection to the outside world; no idea, even, what the weather might be; only one phone, the number unlisted; unreachable—a great comfort, surrounded by these intense associations of festive meals.

2

CALIFORNIA. In the spring of 1985, Mario returned from Europe and went to San Francisco. He'd been hearing about a Bay Area food revolution and wanted to join up. ("What's cooking in cooking," began an article in *Life* entitled "The New American Cuisine," published the month before Batali moved out west, "is nothing less than the rediscovery of America.") The revolution was distinguished by a radical use of local ingredients, but, in Batali's first job, working for a large catering firm, he saw little that was radical or local. At an Apple Computer office party for seven thousand people, held in a baseball stadium, Batali was in charge of the shrimp; he pushed it out in a wheelbarrow and served it with a shovel ("I mean, really, how much fucking fun is that?"). His brother Dana had moved down from Seattle, and the two rented a Victorian house in the Haight Ashbury district, an arrangement that was not without its predictable stresses. Dana's job (in computer animation) was across the bay, in Oakland, a forty-minute commute, and he regularly woke to discover a party in its last throes: his brother along with any number of strange, smelly chefs in various stages of collapse on the living room floor—the house cloudy with smoke, empty bottles everywhere, the stereo on loud.

Six months later, Mario found work at a Four Seasons hotel, the Clift, and, six months after that, was made sous-chef, his first senior position since the days of Stuff Yer Face. This was a more representatively Californian experience, and the kitchen, like so many at the time, was experimenting with all kinds of unlikely combinations (chilies and lemongrass and Chinese black beans, neo-Latino meets Asian fusion meets the lady next door selling apples). Much has been written about the California Revolution; much fun has also been had at its expense: a post-modern moment in food, united by a Bay Area commitment to an anything-goes improvisation, including outright goofy inventions. I was living in Berkeley as a student until 1979 and now appreciate that the revolution had begun only a few blocks away at Chez Panisse, the famous restaurant run by Alice Waters. I had two meals there and two recollections: a vague one of a dish distinguished by its outlandish deliberateness (homegrown snails, perhaps, in a kiwi Jell-O adorned with edible flowers—something, in any case, that was saying "Admire me" very loudly); and a specific one of Leonard Michaels, a fiction writer and English professor, eating at the next table. Michaels had grown up on New York's Lower East Side, had an urban, jaded manner, and was refreshingly suspicious of wacky California enthusiasms. But on this occasion, Michaels, surrounded by three rapt disciples, was holding forth with uncharacteristic animation on a piece of food—an asparagus spear. He was holding it between his fingers and addressing it as if it were no mere green vegetable but a matter of great urgency—a manuscript by Milton, say, or Susan Sontag. Dinner had become an intellectual issue. In America, food had never been intellectual. In this asparagus was a revolution.

One of the revolutionaries was Jeremiah Tower, the restaurant's executive chef. By the time Batali arrived, Tower had left Chez Panisse and opened Stars. He was among the cooks featured in *Life* magazine. ("Those Nubian goats," a caption quotes Tower as saying as he gazed upon the animals with amorous intensity, "how I love their looks.") Tower describes his cooking as Franco-Californian: French techniques with American ingredients and a New World sense of play, or "new-old food in a new-new setting." In his autobiography, *California Dish— What I Saw (and Cooked) at the American Culinary Revolution,* you'll find recipes for a marijuana consommé (the stems and seeds are toasted before being steeped in chicken broth), his interpretation of Chinese spring rolls (a fatty fish skin instead of a pastry), and a sea urchin soufflé served with eels simmered in their own blood. He has a famously energetic sexuality ("What about a hand job in my Mercedes out back," Batali recalls being asked by Tower when the two first met), a self-destructive knack for the occasion (brainlessly serving suckling pig at a Jewish social event), and a commitment to dinner as theatre ("I commanded each cook to down a glass of champagne and pick up two huge sauté pans," he wrote, recalling a press lunch in 1983, marking the moment when California cuisine was first widely recognized). "On a signal from me, they filled the pans with mixed tropical fruits, raspberries, and passion fruit sugar syrup; then all of us in unison tossed the fruit compote up in the air like master omelet makers. That got a standing ovation.") For Batali, Stars, in San Francisco's Civic Center, was "the perfect resto of the moment." Steve Crane, a friend then working as a waiter, remembers that he and Mario ("a clown on a Suzuki 1100 painted to look like a zebra") spent their after-hours there because "it was *the* place"—all the chefs went to Stars when their shifts were done. "Tower made lively, stylized food with attitude and energy," Batali says. "In short, much of the inspiration for everything I have done since."

Batali's recollections make me think of something from another era—a bookstore or a literary café rather than a restaurant: like City Lights, from twenty years before. "It was at Stars, during the California explosion, that I first met chefs who wanted to talk about their craft, and where I learned that the palate is a very individual thing." Intensified flavors, strong contrasts—these qualities (these *extreme* qualities) characterized much of the cooking: citrusy vinaigrettes and brightly colored salsas, raw seafood and intensely marinated shellfish. This, according to Batali, was where he developed an appetite for vinegars and lemons. "Since then, my food has always been on the upper edge of acidity, which is where I naturally like it. I tune things up with acidity. I fix things with acidity. A lot of flawed food made by these French guys would be brightened up with just a touch of acidity—to get you salivating."

AFTER TWO YEARS at the Clift, Mario was invited to work at the Biltmore in Santa Barbara, a stately old Spanish colonial hotel the Four Seasons had just bought and wanted to revitalize. Mario was brought in for all the obvious reasons ("energy, edge, fire, youth," according to Brian Young, the manager who hired him), was given his own restaurant, La Marina, and became, at twenty-seven, the highest-paid young chef in the company. Andy Nusser, a computer designer at the time, met Mario at a late-night druggy party (Batali drinking tequila from a goatskin *boda* bag, the liquor splattering all over his face). Someone had brought foie gras but didn't know how to serve it, and, rising to the challenge that a good cook should be able to make a meal with whatever is to hand, Mario prepared a sweet, vinegar-like reduction of Orange Nehi soda and Starburst fruit candies. ("First you remove each Starburst fruit gum from its wax-paper wrapper and put the candies in a saucepan, where, over a low heat, you melt them slowly until you have a bright-colored syrup, and then, separately, you cook the soda, until it's reduced by half.") Nusser insists that the result was very good, and was so impressed that he decided then and there to become a chef.

At the end of that year, the Four Seasons management asked Mario to run a more exclusive restaurant, in Hawaii, at an even higher salary ("they begged me, they were desperate"), but Batali turned down the offer; then he quit. He was bored: by Santa Barbara, by the Four Seasons, by "human resource types in suits." After the heady time in San Francisco, he had stopped learning but couldn't stop playing. He has trouble recalling a single menu from his own restaurant—"some weak pastas, a smoked veal rack, a grilled lobster with fried artichokes"—and is then vague. "The truth is, I do not have too much memory of the time. The truth is, I was staying out late. I was staying out very, very late." He couldn't account for his salary. "I wasn't buying clothes. I had nothing to show for it. Where did all the money go? You know what I mean—where did it go?" It had become imperative that he leave. He thought about going to Italy. He wanted to learn how to cook like his grandmother Leonetta Merlino Batali.

Leonetta Merlino had grown up working in the first Italian import store in Washington state—Merlino's, which her parents had opened in Seattle in 1903. The store was sold in the late 1960s, and it has been a nagging source of regret to Mario that his father didn't take it over ("They lost it. They fucked it up"). Everyone in the family has powerful memories of visits to Leonetta's house for lunch, which featured her handmade ravioli. (Her husband, Armando, who died when Mario was six, had looked after the meats, raising his own pigs to make prosciutti, black pudding, head cheese, and sausages, and bartering with Native Americans from a nearby reservation for deer and elk.) Although Leonetta made large batches of ravioli, a thousand, twelve hundred at a time, using a family recipe from Abruzzo (calf's brains, pork sausage, chicken, Swiss chard, parmigiano and Romano cheeses) and rolling out the dough with a long pole, prized for the texture it created ("rough, like a cat's tongue"), she allowed the children only six pieces each. They still talk about it. "We knew there were more!" Gina Batali recalls. "We could see them!" But Leonetta was determined to teach them to eat a family meal in an Italian way, with pasta coming after antipasto—a plate of *salume* and marinated vegetables—and before the *secondo,* a roasted meat, often lamb, always cooked with rosemary, always well done. The ravioli recipe is still in the family—Mario's brother prepares it on Christmas Day. Leonetta, having made the ravioli so often she had no idea how she did it, was filmed by a cousin, who prompted her with questions. Other recipes are preserved on two thousand three-by-five cards: a pasta sauce made from spare ribs (with, Mario recalls, "this kind of red pinky piggy flavor"); tripe; and, a feature of New Year's Eve, a salty *baccalà* (dried codfish, rehydrated with milk), served with hot polenta poured out onto a wooden board.

Armandino Batali sent me copies of the recipes. I found the stack of cards surprisingly moving, a kitchen conversation between the dead and the living. I've often thought that food is a concentrated messenger of a culture, compacted into the necessity of our having to eat to survive, and I felt this powerfully as I read these mementos from another generation and listened to Armandino's children talk about the eccentric-seeming recipes of their grandmother, who had learned them in the back room of a food store in Seattle from her mother, who, in turn, had learned them from *her* mother in a house in a village in Abruzzo.

Mario phoned his father. Did he know of a place in Italy where he might work with a matronly Italian cook in exchange for room and board? He didn't, but some friends might know. He wrote five letters. He got one reply, from a trattoria above a town where airplane parts were made for Boeing. Room and board for the son of Armandino? A sous-chef at a Four Seasons restaurant? When can he start?

3

L IKE MANY New York restaurants, Babbo accepts "externs," cooking school students who work for no pay and then write a thesis about the experience—often the final requirement in a cooking degree. The United States has two hundred and twenty-nine officially recognized cooking schools, which produce 25,000 graduates a year, including older ones (not unlike me) who always wanted to cook but didn't know how. The Harvard and Yale is the Culinary Institute of America, the CIA, two hours north of New York City on the Hudson River, which offers a four-year degree course for an annual tuition of $20,000, including knives and aprons. Not cheap, but most Babbo cooks had gone there. I now understood that, when Mario took me on, I was filling a spot left by the last extern, and I felt lucky to have it. One morning, I read his thesis, which included a recipe for preparing sheep intestines for seventy-five people and the quantities of flour, eggs, and goat cheese needed to make 1,500 pieces of tortelloni—not without use, I reflected, if I found myself crossing the Atlantic on the *Queen Mary,* say, and the whole kitchen staff suddenly died and word went round that a guy on board had mastered two recipes from the Babbo kitchen bible (a blue notebook containing instructions for every dish in the history of the restaurant, kept on a shelf between a juicer and a machine that pulverizes beef cheeks into a muddy-looking goo), and hundreds of passengers, fearful of going hungry, huddled together and urged me into the ship's galley, where, after searching through the cupboards and a small walk-in, I found a sufficient quantity of sheep's intestines to put my knowledge to a practical purpose.

Elisa was routinely greeting chefs-in-training at seven in the morning and telling them how her kitchen worked. Every three months or so, that's what she did. They needed her, to complete their studies, and she, I was starting to learn, needed them to complete all the things she had to do in a day. The difference between them and me was obvious and accounted for my continuing testing time. She kept thinking of me as someone who should know what he was doing. One morning, she instructed me to run to the basement for twenty-five oranges and fifty lemons. "Use your apron," she said, and then, noting my confused look, sighed and gathered the two corners of hers like a hammock, by way of illustration. When I returned, she held up a zester. It's the thing you use to peel a citrus fruit. "You *do* know how to use a zester?" she asked with such poorly disguised irritation that I understood her to be saying, "Don't tell me you're so ignorant you don't know what this is." I then became very reluctant to admit that the zester she gave me wasn't zesting—it was so dull it was mauling the fruit—until my cutting board was a sticky battlefield of maimed oranges and lemons, and I hesitantly suggested that maybe this zester wasn't one of the kitchen's better zesters.

The trickiness of my role was confirmed one Friday, always a long, stressful day because you're preparing food for not only that evening but the whole weekend. I was in the walk-in, trying to find a place for a tray of morel mushrooms. There was no place. Elisa was on the floor, transferring chicken stock from a twenty-quart container into a twelve-quart container, because she needed a twenty-quart container and none was to be found. (Chicken stock was the only acceptable meat stock—one made from anything else would be too French—and every morning a pot was filled with the feet and water and boiled for hours. Chicken feet are a vivid sight—like human hands without a thumb, curled up and knuckly—and the first time I saw them, bobbing in their giant vat, they looked as though they were attached to the arms of so many people, clawing at the churning water, trying to climb out, the bubbling pot a portal from Hell, there in the back of the kitchen, against the wall, the hottest place.)

Andy was in the walk-in as well, devising what he called a "walk-in special," a feature of the weekends, to clear out an ingredient that wasn't selling before it went off. "Crispy branzino" was a walk-in special, because "we've bought enough branzino for twenty a night but have been doing only nine, and it's nearly Sunday, so we've got to move it or toss it, and there's some porcini, which hasn't been moving either, I don't know why, and there's always pancetta, so let's reinvent our fish dish with porcini and crunchy pancetta on top and sell the hell out of it."

Gina DePalma was in the walk-in, too, and she was the problem. Gina was the pastry chef—an executive role, like Elisa's—and the two women ran the morning kitchen. Elisa arrived at six and started on a long list of foods that needed preparing for the evening. Gina got in two hours later and made the desserts. Although they had many things in common—both had grown up with big Sunday lunches with their Italian grandparents, for instance—they couldn't have been more different.

Elisa was thin and sporty. On her days off, she trained for marathons and sometimes ran to work in the dawn, about six miles. ("There's no point in arriving clean and fresh, is there?") Her hair was graying, and she had a narrow, high-cheekboned face. Gina didn't exercise. She had thick black hair, and was distinctly rounder, as you'd expect her to be, tasting syrups, chocolates, and creamy batters all day. She was the only person with a cell phone—in the kitchen, private calls were forbidden—partly because she looked after her own ingredients and did her own ordering, but also because she didn't want to cross the kitchen to use the phone located on a wall where Elisa works. (The issue wasn't the distance but the company she'd have to keep when she got there.) Besides, Gina was a talker and couldn't be without a phone.

Elisa wasn't chatty. Mornings would pass without her saying a word. Everything—her manner, the efficiency of her movements, her face, with its firm, no-nonsense look—said purposefulness. She was capable of sulkiness ("When she's in one of her moods, the whole kitchen knows about it," Gina complained), but you never learned why: you didn't know much about Elisa's private life. You knew too much about Gina's. You knew when, last year, she'd had a date, and what had happened, and what his name was, and then she'd wonder aloud if she'd ever date again.

"Don't you have a flight to catch?" Gina asked me. She knew this from the morning's chitchatty exchanges. "You should leave. I mean, *really*, the way we treat our externs: it's not as if you're getting paid."

I nodded sympathetically, wanting to make nice, a little confused, because I didn't yet understand the extern concept. (Externs answer to Elisa, I now understand, and the real issue for Gina was her belief that

Elisa was a dour, unfriendly slave driver. Or maybe Gina was jealous that she didn't have any slaves of her own.)

Gina continued to stare at me. I stood dumbly with my tray of morels.

"Really, you need to go. *Now.*"

She shrugged and walked out. Andy, satisfied by his branzino count, followed her. It was just me and Elisa.

"You do *not* answer to that woman," Elisa said in a low, angry voice. She was still on the floor; I was still holding my tray of morels. "Do you understand me? You leave when I say you can leave. I am your boss. I tell you when you can go. Have I made myself clear?"

I stuttered pathetically. It was four o'clock—when the prep kitchen is normally finished—but I could see there was still a lot to do.

I returned to the kitchen, bearing my tray of morels, and thought about what had taken place. The outburst had surprised me, although it shouldn't have: I was familiar with what I regarded as the shoulder-rubbing edginess of the kitchen. I'd seen it between Elisa and Memo Trevino. Memo was one of the two sous-chefs—a big man with a disproportionately big head of wiry black hair, and, at twenty-eight, emphatically in possession of an authority of someone many years older. If Memo accidentally knocked you, the blow came from the torso, not because his belly was so big but because he always led with the groin. More than once a picture popped in my head—no idea from where—of Memo with a spear and headdress. His was the swagger of a tribal chief.

I'd been in the prep kitchen three weeks when Memo took me aside, wanting to know what I thought of Elisa's cooking. I was so unprepared for anyone's soliciting my opinion I didn't know what he was talking about.

"It's not exactly perfect, is it?"

"What's not perfect?" I asked.

"The food."

I didn't understand.

"Ever notice how much food she burns?" He was whispering.

No, I hadn't noticed, although, it was true, there'd been a tray of burnt beef cheeks.

"Precisely. It's unacceptable. Ever notice the dullness of her knife?"

I pondered the question. Actually, I'd experienced her knife firsthand and had not found it dull.

"Let me put it this way. Ever notice her sharpening it?"

"Sure," I said. "A few times." By then I knew the knife rituals. Frank Langello was especially proud of his. Frankie was the other sous-chef. He was about the same age as Memo, an Italian American, with wavy black hair, preternaturally long eyelashes, and the skinny good looks of one of those crooners from the forties and fifties, like a young Sinatra in the Hoboken years. Frankie and Memo had worked together at Le Cirque, a four-star restaurant then run by the famously fanatical Sottha Khunn, and they both felt they were among the few people at Babbo who understood the importance of kitchen discipline, which, evidently, included knife care. Frankie used only cheap ones, because he whipped them so ruthlessly against a sharpening steel that the blades wore out. Every now and then he used a whetstone, for even more edge: he tested the sharpness by shaving his forearms. ("When the hair grows back, I get out the whetstone again.")

Memo was shaking his head. "That's my point—a *few* times. You've seen Elisa sharpen her knife a *few* times. Trust me. Her knife is a stick. The problem is this—she lacks the dedicated, serious approach. Great chefs," he explained, "are born, not made. It's in your blood, or it's not: the *passion.*"

I didn't know what to say. It was a pretty small space for such strong positions. Memo didn't like Elisa because she wasn't serious enough. Gina didn't like her because she was too serious. And Elisa didn't like Gina because *she* wasn't serious enough. ("Most restaurants have pastry chefs who actually work," Elisa said most mornings when Gina was chirpily chatting on her cell phone.)

The walk-in episode was illuminating in another way.

When I'd started, I'd jokingly referred to myself as a kitchen slave. Now I had a new understanding. I *was* a kitchen slave. That was the role: morning kitchen slave. In effect, I had entered into a contract: I was indentured. In the mornings, I gave Elisa my time, and she gave me instruction, and the instruction was precious enough that it entitled her to my time, exclusively, and the Ginas of the kitchen had better watch how they talked to me.

Others showed me how to do things as well. ("I am a great teacher,"

Memo told me after showing me how to bone a wild boar shoulder, "and people always tell me this is what I should do, teach, but I have one problem—impatience.") But most of my instruction was from Elisa. To my astonishment, she took me seriously. I was a project; I was being educated in how to be a cook.

The truth is, I was grateful for the run-in in the walk-in, Gina and Elisa squabbling over me: there was so much work that even *I* was needed. I wanted to be needed. I longed for a day when my presence would make a difference. Ever since that first kitchen meeting, I'd imagined my putting in so much time that I'd be trusted to cook on the line—maybe to cover for someone in an emergency or during an unexpected crunch. I didn't share these thoughts with Mario or Elisa or Memo, if only because I was still the guy who didn't know how to cut an onion without slicing into the palm of his hand. And yet I was being taken seriously: I wasn't allowed to leave.

Or maybe the truth was much simpler: Elisa needed help, and instead she had me.

SOMETIMES ELISA startled me. I'd be working at top speed, nervously waiting for her to appear and ask if I'd finished the five things she'd asked me to do so she could give me something else (and, invariably— and I *mean* "invariably"—I was still at work on the first one), when, out of nowhere, she'd give me a cup of hot chocolate or a piece of meat. "Wow! Thank you!" If she was preparing skirt steak for the evening— the cheap cut from the belly or "skirt" of the cow, needing to be cut thin and cooked hot and fast—she might keep back a few strips, season them aggressively, throw them onto the flattop, and put them out on a platter. (A flattop is a flat piece of steel that sits atop the gas burners of an oven—welded on, so little heat escapes: you can crowd more things onto a flattop than a conventional stove, and it gets very hot—a skirt steak cooks in seconds.) Once she boned a turkey and rolled it up with dandelion greens and goat cheese. Her dishes were high in protein and very salty. When making them, she got a slightly distracted look, as if a tune were playing in her head. These moments seemed important and were the only times Elisa relaxed. She didn't smile—she never got that comfortable—but you could tell that she was thinking of smiling.

Making food seemed to be something everyone needed to do: not for the restaurant, but for the kitchen. There was the family meal, of course—bountifully served around four in the afternoon—but food was almost always being made by someone at some time all day long. The practice seemed to illustrate a principle I was always hearing referred to as "cooking with love." A dish was a failure because it hadn't been cooked with love. A dish was a success because the love was so obvious. If you're cooking with love, every plate is a unique event—you never allow yourself to forget that a person is waiting to eat it: your food, made with your hands, arranged with your fingers, tasted with your tongue.

One Saturday, when neither Andy nor Elisa was around, Memo took me aside again. "Let me show you how to cook with love." He suddenly wanted to make an impromptu family supper. He'd found some beef tongues in the walk-in, which I suspect had been intended for a special: no matter, they were his now. He poached them, grilled them, and sliced them, then mixed the meat in a bowl with his own spicy hot sauce. "*This is how you make tacos*," he said, assembling his concoction on a platter: tortillas stacked on top of tortillas, along with several pounds of tongue and great quantities of tomato and lemon zest. It was my first five-story taco. It bore no resemblance to any taco I'd seen before—in fact, towering so, with gobs of cream cheese spread along the side, it looked more like a wedding cake—but it remains the best taco I've eaten.

You can't really cook like this when you're in a busy kitchen, but somehow everyone, at some point, made the time to prepare something intimate. It seemed to be at the heart of why you were a cook. Elisa once told me that in her ideal life, she would "cook only at home, with my friends at my table." Gina put it more forcefully: "I invite you to my house, spend all day preparing your meal, watch your face as you eat it, bite by bite, and you tell me I'm wonderful? Whoa! That's awesome!"

One morning Gina came up with a new dessert. "Does that have too much almond in it?" she asked, feeding it to me by hand.

I thought: she's not interested in my opinion. "No, Gina, it's perfect."

"Does this have too much almond?" she asked a guy delivering artichokes, putting a slice in his mouth, while he stood awkwardly, unable to use his hands, while Gina brushed a crumb off his lower lip.

"Hmm . . . " he said, talking through the food, "this is delicious."

"Does this have too much almond?" she asked Andy, seconds after he showed up just after noon. Andy waited for Gina to put the piece in his mouth, leaning forward, his lips puckered as though for a kiss.

"Gina, you're a genius."

And so it went, ten different people, each one fed by hand.

I find myself thinking of Mrs. Waters's seduction of Tom Jones, in the Henry Fielding novel. Actually, I see the movie version with the young Albert Finney, where "passions and appetites" blur and Mrs. Waters's soft sighs commingle with Tom's energetic consumption of a vast piece of roast beef. Food has always had erotic associations, and I suspect that cooking with love is an inversion of a different principle: cooking to *be* loved. The premise of a romantic meal is that by stimulating and satisfying one appetite another will be analogously stimulated as well. How exactly does Tom Jones's appetite for a rib medium rare stimulate a craving for Mrs. Waters? Fresh pasta cooked in butter, Mario once told me, illustrating how these things seem to conjoin, "swells like a woman aroused." Marjoram, he said on another occasion, has the oily perfume of a woman's body: "It is the sexiest of the herbs." Lidia, Joe Bastianich's mother, was more explicit. "What else do you put in another person's body?" she asked me rhetorically when I met her for lunch one day. "Do you understand?"

4

PORRETTA TERME, 1989. The small restaurant of La
Volta was perched high above the town of Porretta Terme, on a hill
overlooking a mountainous valley between Bologna and Florence.
Mario arrived by train on a Monday afternoon in November, bearing
golf clubs, even though there was no golf course for a hundred miles,
and an electric guitar with a small boom-box amplifier ("total fuzz at
volume three"), in the hope that when he ran low on money he could
cover his expenses by busking. He was wearing pajama-like pantaloons
and red clogs. But there was no one to meet him ("I arrived alone at the
train station of bumfuck"). He didn't know how to use the phones and
couldn't speak Italian. When Roberto and Gianni Valdiserri finally
tracked him down, they were astonished by what they saw. He did not
look like the highest-paid sous-chef from the Four Seasons; he looked
like an Albanian peasant, Roberto told me when I visited during a break
from my time at Babbo.

The "terme" in Porretta Terme means "baths" and refers to the local
sulfur springs. On my first morning there, I was woken by an instructor
on a loudspeaker leading an exercise class of overweight senior citizens
in one of the pools. Italians are entitled to two annual visits, paid for by
the government, and can have a number of irrigations (nasal, rectal,
vaginal) to deal with bowel troubles, infertility, hot flashes, and creaky
knees. In an older part of town, the buildings are from the eighteenth
century, when affluent Bolognese families used to come here on summer holidays to escape the heat of the plains: grand rooms, high ceilings,
tall windows with wooden shutters painted an orange-yellow evocative
of Hapsburg Vienna. Many are abandoned; so, too, is the old rail station,
built in an imperial style, carved into the side of a mountain. For nearly

two centuries, the train, the best way of crossing the Appennines, stopped in Porretta (a "Porretta box" was sold on the platform—a prosciutto *panino*, a piece of fruit, a chunk of parmigiano, and a half bottle of Lambrusco). Now tourists arrive on charter buses, wearing bathing caps. I couldn't find Porretta in any travel guides, although I located a first edition of Faith Willinger's *Eating in Italy*, published the year Mario arrived. There was nothing about the town, but La Volta, in the nearby village of Borgo Capanne, was cited as "the rising star on the road known as the Porrettana" (the old highway at the bottom of the valley). "Giovanni Valdisseri presides in the rustic dining room, and his wife and sister-in-law work together in the kitchen," Willinger wrote. "The salumi are local, and the pasta is hand rolled, freshly made, not to be skipped."

Borgo Capanne is six miles above Porretta. You reach it on a zigzaggy road of ferocious ascent. The first mile is nothing but sheerness until you come upon a church just before a village called Pieve. *Pieve* is old Italian for "country church." After another mile, the land flattens out briefly, and you enter a village surrounded by small vegetable plots. This is Orti. An *orto* is a small vegetable farm. Poggio is next, resting atop a hill. *Poggio* means "hilltop." Finally you reach Borgo Capanne. A *capanna* is a mountain hut; a *borgo* is a village: village of mountain huts. And if you climb the hill just above it you discover, predictably enough, stone ruins of the first habitations, sheltered in the woods. The modern part of the village has a wide view of the valley and the mountains (with volcanic cartoon peaks, like pyramids, covered by dense woods). Borgo Capanne is a cluster of interconnecting houses, everything adjoined honeycomb style, as though for protection—from the wild, from wolves, from whatever unknown thing might come up the road. To enter the honeycomb, you pass under a stone arch. In Italian, an arch is a *volta*. This is where you find the restaurant. Above the restaurant is an apartment: this was Mario's new home.

La Volta was closed the day Mario arrived, but a seasonal supper was prepared for him ("I am, like, holy fucking shit, family meal, and we're having white truffles!"), and everyone introduced themselves. Roberto was the expediter, after he finished his day job (he was an engineer at a factory that had been making airplane parts since World War II, when Mussolini came up with the idea of hiding the manufacturing of his air force in the mountains nearby). Roberto's brother Gianni managed the place. His wife, Betta, was the cook. Her father, Quintiglio ("Quintiglio Canario, the fifth son of the canary, a beautiful name for a beautiful man"), was the forest forager, truffle scavenger, and mystic gardener, and he and Mario struck up an instant rapport: "So tickled to have an American in the village."

The next morning, Mario reported for duty. Betta didn't show up for two more hours and then rolled out a giant sheet of pasta by hand. "It was the first food I saw," Mario recalls, although he wouldn't be allowed to touch the dough for two weeks. He took notes and embarked on a six-month apprenticeship in what he calls the "ladies' trick of handmade pasta." Betta went on to make stricchetti, small bow ties, served with porcini mushrooms and little red onions cooked in olive oil. She made a different pasta the next day and a different ragù, one made from guinea-hen legs, roasted until the bones fell out and the meat dissolved into a sauce. It was a month before anyone prepared a Bolognese, the traditional meat sauce of Emilia-Romagna. "They'd gotten bored of it," Mario said, "but then they taught me how to make it, and that became my weekly task: veal, pork, beef, and pancetta, cooked slowly with olive oil and butter. Just browning and browning, although it never turns brown because of the fat that seeps out of the meat—which you leave there, it's part of the dish—and add white wine and milk, and, at the end, a little tomato paste, so that it's pink-brown."

He accompanied Quintiglio ("a salt-of-the-earth dude with big feet, strong hands, a deep voice, floppy Italian ears, and a buttoned-up shirt and jacket") when he went looking for berries and mushrooms. He had rules about porcini and picked only the ones near oak and chestnut trees—the ones under the pines and poplars were inferior. His real talent was for finding truffles. When Armandino visited Mario the following year, he said, "It was as though God had arrived in town just before me—truffles were on everything."

In time, Mario and Quintiglio fell into a habit of having breakfast together: a glass of red wine and an egg baked in olive oil with a slice of fontina cheese. For Christmas lunch, Quintiglio showed Mario how to make a classic *brodo*, the holiday broth served with tortellini. It required an old chicken (one no longer producing eggs), some beef bones, a bone left over from a prosciutto, an onion, and a carrot—the vegetables left whole to keep the broth clear. In the spring, they ate from Quintiglio's garden, planted according to a lunar schedule (lettuce during a waxing moon; beets and parsnips during a waning one). Quintiglio took Mario to the Reno River for a "weird little watercress that grew there," wild onions, and a bitter wild dandelion, which he boiled for forty-five minutes and served with olive oil and balsamic vinegar. Today, Mario's greens are cooked in the way Quintiglio taught him. ("Much better to boil the shit out of them and *then* sauté them in olive oil and garlic—you can then actually chew the fuckers.") For Mario, Quintiglio was the first proponent of finding what is made by the land and feasting on it, of recognizing that you are eating something that you can enjoy only now, here, during this day in this season, grown in this dirt.

But the first months were not easy. Dana Batali recalls them as a time when Mario was forced to learn humility and "the things he wanted to cook were scoffed at," although, from what I can tell, the dishes Mario prepared (raw scampi, a leek soufflé, grappa-cured salmon) were done to establish his credentials and remind his hosts that he had been, until recently, highly regarded as a chef. But Mario's father picked up an uneasiness in his son's letters as well. "The experience shook him up a bit." For his part, Mario remembers it as the last lonely time in his life, a sustained pleasurable period of melancholy, "a happy sadness." At the end of dinner, he'd go up to his room, light a candle, put on headphones, playing mainly Tom Waits during his ballady, self-pitying, hey-buddy-can-I-have-another-drink phase, read (working his way through the novels of Faulkner), looking up to take in the view—the mountains, the Reno River—and longing for company but recognizing he was better off without it. "It was a great rush. I knew, that first week, once I saw the food, that I'd made the right move. This wasn't a food I knew. It was traditional. Simple. No sauces, no steam tables, no pans of veal stock, none of the things I had learned to do."

Italy changed Mario, his father said. "When he arrived, he was still a wild guy. He drank a lot, smoked, chased girls. He had no idea what he was going to do with the rest of his life. Italy focused him. It gave him his culture."

Jim Clenenden, the owner of Au Bon Climat vineyards in Santa Barbara and one of Mario's former late-night friends, described the change more prosaically. Clenenden visited Mario at La Volta five months after his arrival. "What happened? When I saw him last, he was a West Coast guy with a New Jersey accent. Look at him: that red hair, that pale complexion. Does he look Italian to you? He could have been Mark Battle. Suddenly he was Mario Batali! The change was stupefying." Clenenden's visit was stupefying in other ways: eleven dishes, eleven bottles of wine, a meal that finished at four in the morning, a brutal hangover, and all the time "Mario speaking in Italian—although still American enough, *just*, to tolerate a visitor from California." Batali hadn't mastered the menu yet, Clenenden recalled, but was in the middle of a tremendous transformation. "He wasn't even close to reaching a plateau. Any moment he was going to discover the next big thing—you could tell." This was April. By the summer, the metamorphosis was complete.

ON THE LAST NIGHT of my visit, I had dinner with Gianni and Roberto, prepared by Betta—a doll-like woman in her forties with jet black hair and very pale skin—and served by her two children, Emiliano, twenty-eight, and Mila, now sixteen and remembered by Mario as an infant in a straw basket on the kitchen floor. I was joined by Joe Bastianich, who happened to be in the country on business. Mario's time in and around Porretta has figured so large in the story he tells of himself that Joe, too, wanted to see the place firsthand. I didn't know Joe well. At Babbo, he worked the front of the house—the service, the wine—and you rarely saw him in the kitchen. You also didn't see him much during the day, because he found the Babbo office intolerable. Compared with Mario, Joe was quiet in manner, with a guardedness that might be mistaken for shyness. But he wasn't shy, just less outgoing than his often outrageous partner, with whom he had the good sense never to compete for attention or recognition. ("Joe needs me," Mario confessed one night. "He couldn't do any of this without me." "Mario is the cook," Joe explained to me on another night. "I'm the waiter.")

Gianni and Roberto were intrigued by Joe. Gianni is a soft man. He has thick wrists, big hands, and an elastic middle that betrays a life lived without the slightest expense of exercise. But he eats with joy, and since he eats abundantly and without inhibition he seems almost always happy. He has a handsome face with thick expressive eyebrows that are always coming together in a quizzical look, like that of a confused forest animal.

Roberto, his brother, seems more grounded. He is stocky and has a square head, a square body, and a solid manner. Unlike Gianni, who is bald, Roberto has plenty of hair, which is stiff and straw-like and sits squarely on his head, not unlike a helmet. You could imagine Roberto in a suit and tie, although tonight (befitting the enduringly wintry weather of the Appennines) he was wearing a dark wool sweater with a cotton shirt underneath.

Both brothers are dedicated food romantics. Mario had told me about long trips the three of them routinely took in quest of some meal of indisputable regional authenticity—a four-hour drive to Mantova, say, for the perfect ravioli filled with autumn squash—only to have one bite, realize that the pasta had been made by a machine rather than by hand, and walk out in protest, their hunger dealt with by emergency *panini* grabbed in a bar on the drive back home. To this day, Roberto is still indignant that a spaghetti alla carbonara, prepared by Mario, had been served with the eggs on top rather than mixed in the pasta. "I saw it with my own eyes! They were on top! It was scandalous!"

Joe Bastianich was not a romantic. He grew up in immigrant restaurants in Queens and has a nitty-gritty matter-of-factness about money. He was impatient with Gianni and Roberto. His manner said, "Mountains schmountains, restaurants are a business: Why are you guys such fuckups?" Joe is the son of Felice and Lidia Bastianich, both immigrants, who were running their own restaurant, a thirty-seater called La Buonavia, the year Joe was born, in 1968. (Lidia now has a television show, cookbooks, and her own restaurant in midtown.) Joe's childhood memories are dominated by "the not-so-pleasant realities of preparing food for a living"—cleaning the grease traps, sweeping up the insects after the exterminator visits, the pervasive smell of shoe polish, and the stink of a changing room crowded with "sweaty, fat Italians and Croats reading the racing forms," where Joe did his schoolwork and slept on tomato cases until he was carried home. To this day, he can't stand bay leaves. "Three times I've pulled a leaf out of the throat of someone choking on it, including my grandmother when I was nine years old, and for what? Do you think the flavor is so important?" Chicken makes him

shudder, the result of accompanying his father in the car to the wholesale market to pick up cheap poultry, "the *cheapest* poultry," piled high
with ice to keep it from spoiling, and when the ice melted it became a
pink "chicken water" that slopped down Joe's back. Joe never wanted a
restaurant; he wanted money and became a Wall Street trader, only to
discover he hated it. He recalls waiting for his first bonus, counting the
minutes, cashing it, and returning to the office to resign on the spot:
then he went straight to JFK and bought a ticket to Trieste. He remained
there a year, living out of a Volkswagen bus, working for chefs and
winemakers, needing to understand this thing that, he now appreciated,
was going to be his life.

Joe is eight years younger than Mario but has the gravitas of someone twelve years older. His head is shaved. He is big, although not
portly, and his bigness conveys power. He has a boxer's waddle—legs
apart, hands to his side, at the ready—which, when I attended a Bastianich family christening, I noticed his four-year old son was already
imitating. Over the course of a dinner prepared by Betta—a white pizza,
followed by green pappardelle with a quail ragù, then tortellini in thick
cream—Gianni and Roberto speculated on how Joe worked with Mario.

"You must be the salt," Roberto suggested, "and Mario would be the
pepper."

"You're the money man," Giovanni clarified. The idea was that Joe
must have brought Mario under control and tamed him.

Joe shrugged and turned to me. "How do you say 'whatever' in
Italian?"

Roberto and Gianni continued to press their point. For them, it was
inconceivable that the man in pantaloons whom they'd picked up at the
train station in 1989 would have left them to become a famous chef,
without the help of someone much more worldly. Mario had been the
clown of the town—or at least its most sybaritic spokesman. He had
appeared in an annual Porretta talent show ("The other contestants
were fourteen-year-old girls," Roberto said) with a three-piece band, the
barber on drums, the headstone carver on sax, and Mario on electric
guitar, playing a long, loud version of Jimi Hendrix's "Hey, Joe." He had
been the wild dancer at the disco, returning home with Bruno, the post-
master, to sing harvest songs until dawn. Mario had drunk more than
anyone had ever seen before.

"Fifteen whiskies in one sitting," Roberto said. "Can you imagine?"

"It was twenty," Gianni said. "I used to count."

He was the fat man with a dozen girlfriends who all seemed to be named Jennifer. "Even the Italian ones were Jennifer," Roberto said.

"Why is a fat man so attractive to women?" Gianni asked.

"Is he fatter now or then?" Roberto asked by way of reply.

"You know," Joe whispered to me across the table, "I don't think I can take any more of this." He hummed an opera aria.

After three years, Mario left Italy, and things became difficult for Gianni and Roberto. It was as though Mario's leaving and the decline in the Valdiserris' fortunes were connected. Mario returned to America to make money, just as Gianni and Roberto started losing it.

The restaurant had always been expensive, they said. Then, in a matter of months, there was less money in town. The year, 1992, marked the beginning of a Europe-wide recession, although neither Gianni nor Roberto had any understanding of what was going on elsewhere; they knew only that one month they'd been busy, the next month they weren't. Orders at the factory where Roberto worked had fallen, and executives from abroad visited less often. Fewer families came from Bologna, and their vacation homes were not being rented: Who wants to go to the mountains and eat the spaghetti you can eat at home, when, for the same price, you can be on a beach in the South Pacific? There were deaths: Gianni's mother, Betta's father. There were gambling debts—casinos were Gianni's secret affliction. La Volta was sold. Today there is a restaurant in the same place, but it has a French name and serves fish, and the two times I visited it was closed. It took Gianni nine years to come up with funds to open a new place, La Capannina, a pizzeria, located in a park by the river, where you could eat outside on a hot summer night. But the summer had been harsh, and business was poor. This was where we had our dinner, but it was too cold to sit outside, and the other customers—five of them, all workmen—were eating pizza and drinking beer. You could see unease in the mournful crinkles around Gianni's eyes. Borgo Capanne, the little village on the hill, was now dead, his daughter Mila said, giving me a tour of it the next day. *Più bestie che persone.* There were more pets than people.

Mario left before the decline, with the help of his best friend from Rutgers, Arturo Sighinolfi. Arturo had visited Mario in Porretta. The two shared an understanding about Italian cooking. Arturo's father was about to retire; for twenty-five years, he'd run Rocco, an Italian-American restaurant off Bleecker Street, in the "red sauce zone." Arturo invited Mario to run the restaurant with him as a fifty-fifty partner—Arturo in the front, Mario in the kitchen. There was an apartment upstairs where Mario could live. The new Rocco, inspired by La Volta, would have a powerful Italian menu.

5

T HE BABBO KITCHEN was actually several kitchens. In the morning, this small space—the work area is about twenty-five feet by ten—was the prep kitchen and run by Elisa. In the evenings, the same space became the service kitchen and was run by Andy. But between the hours of one and four-thirty, the different kitchens (more metaphors than places) overlapped.

Andy was the first to show up, calculatedly a minute or two after noon, respectfully not wanting to disturb the a.m. authority structure. Memo, the senior sous-chef, arrived an hour later. Frankie, the junior sous-chef, was next. And then the others, one after another, late risers all, buzzing with their first coffee, smelling of soap, their hair still wet. The last was Nick Anderer, the "pasta guy." Nick was tall, lean, a tennis player's build, a blue bandanna always tied round his forehead, with the dark-haired, brown-eyed features of a Eurasian. Nick's father was of German ancestry, and his mother was Japanese-American, and so he was called "Chino" (even though, in a better world, he would have been neither a Chino nor a Jappo, but just plain Nick). His station was the easiest to set up but the most demanding to run. Just about everyone orders pasta. By the time Nick arrived, between two and three, the kitchen got very busy.

By now, there were eighteen to twenty people in the kitchen. During this time, the prep people were frantically completing their tasks, while the line cooks were getting their stations ready, terrified that they wouldn't finish before the first orders. In many ways, these afternoons were exaggerated expressions of something that was characteristic of both New York (where, with so many people concentrated onto a little island, space is precious and its value inflated) and the restaurant business (in which the size of the kitchen and the dining room are financial calculations, and a small kitchen meant more tables). The space concern was extreme. There was no lunch service because the metaphoric prep kitchen was still working at lunchtime. There was also no lunch service because so much of the restaurant's equipment—tablecloths, cutlery, plates, glasses—was stored underneath the banquettes where a lunch crowd would sit: every morning, the restaurant was taken apart; every afternoon, it was put back together. The so-called Babbo office was two chairs and a computer in whatever basement cranny presented itself at the time. It seemed like an extension of the plumbing, jerry-built. When a hot-water tank exploded—for several days, the water for the dishes was boiled—the "office" was removed to get to the tank. The desk of Mario's assistant was underneath a slop sink, gurgling with the food-stuffs swirling into it. The smell was pervasive.

In the afternoon, there was a hierarchy about space. Mario had warned me of this after I mentioned that I must have been sticking my butt out because I kept getting bumped. "They bump you because they can—they're putting you in your place." The next day, I counted: I was bumped forty times. Space was Andy's first concern; when he arrived, he went straight to the walk-in to see if he could shift things from large containers to smaller ones. If he couldn't, the work being done by the prep kitchen would have no place to be stored. Once, I helped him prepare a herb salad by destemming the herbs to concentrate their fla-vors. We started in the dining room, because there was no space in the kitchen. We moved to the dark coffee station in front of the kitchen doors, when tables were being set up, until finally we were backed up against the ladies' room.

In the afternoon, if you can get a perch in the kitchen, you don't leave it. You don't answer the phone, run an errand, make a cup of coffee, have a pee, because if you do you'll lose your space. Around two o'clock, trays of braised meat came out of the oven, but there was no place to put them, so they sat on top of the trash cans. Trays were stacked on top of those trays. And sometimes there were trays stacked on top of those.

Mario flits between the shifts, unpredictably. He no longer runs the kitchen—he sneaks up on it to see that it's functioning properly or sim-ply visits it when the spirit moves him—but the public expectation is that he's there every night, preparing every dish, an idea that he reinforces, flamboyantly rushing out plates from the kitchen to special customers. The year after Babbo opened, he had a brain aneurysm, alarming his family. "I thought, Oh my God, here it comes," his brother Dana recalls. "Mario's Marilyn Monroe moment, having burned up both ends of the candle." It also alarmed Babbo customers, who canceled their reservations. "The only time anyone could walk in and get a table," Elisa remembers.

One afternoon, Mario showed up to make a special called a *cioppino*. He'd prepared the dish the night before but had got only four orders. "This time, the waiters are going to push it, and if they don't sell out I'll fire them," he said cheerfully. *Cioppino* is a contraction of *"C'è un po'?"*—is there a little something?—an Italian-immigrant soup made from leftovers and whatever "little thing" a member of the household was able to beg from fishermen at the end of the day. On this occasion, the "little thing" would be crabmeat, and, true to the ideology of the dish, Mario roamed the kitchen, collecting whatever was on hand— tomato pulp and liquid, left over from tomatoes that had been roasted, carrot tops, a bowl of onion skins, anything. He would charge twenty-nine dollars.

Mario took over a position normally occupied by Dominic Cipollone, the sauté chef. Dominic had been at Babbo for two years; it was his first restaurant job. ("Whatever he is," Mario said, "we made him.") He has a heavy, saturnine manner and a Fred-Flintstone-in-need-of-a-shave look, and, at one point, in his lugubrious way, he turned and ran into Mario.

"Dom, you just bumped me," Mario said.

Dominic apologized. His tone was ironic; it said, Of course I bumped you. You're a big guy and you were in my way.

But Mario was not appeased. "Dom, don't ever do that again."

Dom was unsure how to respond. Was it a joke?

"I do not want to be bumped by you," Mario continued. "You see this counter? I own it. You see this floor? I own it. Everything here I own. I don't want you to bump me."

I discovered Dominic in the walk-in. "I've got Mario at my station. I'm cleaning up after him, and he's bumping me. I'm staying here."

(In the event, thirty-four *cioppini* were sold that night. "The waiters came through," Mario told me when I showed up the next morning and found him reclining on a banquette, drinking a whiskey. "I'm very happy.")

Once Mario left the kitchen, you never knew when he was coming back. Elisa recalled the trepidation that had surrounded his departures in the early days, especially during a Chinatown phase, when he'd return with purchases he felt should be served as specials. Duck feet, say, or duck tongues. "Very, very small, with a tiny bone in the back which was almost impossible to get out." Or jellyfish, which, in the tradition of preparing local ingredients in an Italian way, were cut up into strips, marinated with olive oil, lemon, and basil, and served raw as a salad. "It was disgusting," Elisa said. It was equally unnerving when Mario returned with nothing, because then, with no distractions, he started rooting around in the trash. The first time I witnessed the moment—a peculiar sight, this large man, bent over and up to his elbows in a black plastic sack of discarded foodstuffs—I was the unwitting object of his investigation. I had been cutting celery into a fine dice and was tossing away the leafy floret heads (after all, how do you cube the leaves?). The florets have the most concentrated flavor, and I knew it couldn't be right to be throwing them away, but that's what I was doing: I had a lot of celery to dice.

"What the hell is this?" Mario asked, when he appeared, holding up a handful of my celery leaves, before plunging back into the plastic bag to see what else was there to discover—which was, of course, more celery florets, hundreds of them. He pulled them out, shaking off whatever greasy thing was adhering to their leaves (they'd be served that night with steak). "What have you done?" he asked me in astonishment. "You're throwing away the best part of the celery! Writer guy—busted! Remember our rule: we make money by buying food, fixing it up, and getting other people to pay for it. We do not make money by buying food and throwing it away." I witnessed the garbage routine several more times, involving kidneys ("Elisa, we don't throw away lamb kidneys"), the green stems of fresh garlic ("Frankie, what are you doing? These are perfect in soup"), and the rough dirty tops from wild leeks ("Somebody talk to the vegetable guy—he's killing me"). Anything vaguely edible was thrown out only if it was confirmed that Mario wasn't in.

· · ·

IN THE EVENINGS, I started plating pasta.

"Like this," Mario said. He took my tongs before I could plate a spaghetti and dropped it slowly from up high. "You want to make a mound of pasta and give it as much air as possible." And, later, with the tortelloni: "You want only a splash of sauce. It's about the pasta, not the sauce"—a maxim I would hear over and over again, distinguishing the restaurant's preparation from an Italian-American one. (In red sauce joints, the dish is less about the pasta and more about the sauce, as well as the ground beef in the sauce, plus the meatballs or the sausages or both the meatballs and the sausages as well as the peppers, the pickled onions, and the chili flakes.) Mario took my spoon—the tortelloni break up if you use tongs—and told me how to hold it. "You're not a house-wife. Don't use the handle. Seize the spoon, here, at the base of the stem. You'll have more control. It's only heat." (Foolish me, I thought, and had a sudden fantasy, occasioned by my embarrassment, of a futurist cutlery, including a post-modern spoon, all spoon and no handle, except, possibly, a half-inch spur on the side for the wusses who needed one.) Later, Mario explained the components of the tortelloni. The tortelloni was a soft, pillowy pasta, stuffed with goat cheese and served with dried orange zest and a dusting of fennel pollen, which was like an exaggerated version of fennel. Fennel pollen was a discovery of food writer Faith Willinger, an American living in Florence who had some secret source there: on trips to the States, she stashed the fennel pollen in her suitcase, shrink-wrapped in a smuggler's hundred-gram plastic bag. And the orange peel? Because orange and fennel are a classic combination. They also give some bite to a soft, unacidic dish.

I stepped back to take in the kitchen and how different it was at night. White tablecloths had been taped over the counters, where Andy was checking dishes before they were run out into the dining room. The long work area in the middle had changed as well. During the day, this was where I had put my cutting board, as had two of the Mexican prep cooks, Cesar Gonzalez and Abelardo Arredondo. Now it had become "the pass." Andy, the man running the kitchen, was on one side, calling out the orders and receiving dishes that the line cooks "passed" to him. Behind them was the "line," a wall of cooking contraptions. In one corner was the ornery pasta monster, a bubbling hot-water machine, obscured by steam. In the other corner was a grill, a steel square of yellow-blue flames. In between were three cookers in a row, each with an oven, turned up to five hundred degrees Fahrenheit. It was a lot of heat. I was standing next to Andy and could feel it. When I stepped closer, as when I peeked over to see how a dish was being put together, I felt the heat with much more intensity—a hit of heat, like a cloud, both a physical fact (it was in the roots of my neck hair) and an abstraction. But it was real enough: a hot wall, even if invisible, and I was happy to be on the other side.

Nick was working over the pasta cooker—his face in the steam, sweat pouring off it—and was heating sauces in pans on a flattop. This was the pasta station. Dominic was at the stove and reheating things in the oven below. This was the sauté station. Between sauté and the grill was the swinger, the person who swings between the station on his left and the one on his right, helping out each cook, plating their dishes, on call in case of a meltdown. Mark Barrett was at the grill. He'd only just started. He was tall, bespectacled, watchful, unshaven, and, with rumpled wavy hair, looking like a very late sleeper who hadn't been awake long.

He was different from the others; so was Nick. They both came from affluent, professional families. They didn't have to be cooks. I sometimes thought of them as middle-class interlopers, always having to explain their careers to concerned parents who regarded a job in a kitchen as tantamount to joining a circus. Nick had studied art history at Columbia University, where his father was a professor of Japanese literature. He had learned Italian, because mastering it was a requirement of his degree, and had spent a year in Europe, mainly in Rome. When he returned, he was no longer interested in the foundations of classic architecture or Renaissance painting or whatever it was he was supposed to have studied during his expensive, paid-for-by-his-parents year abroad. He had discovered pasta; he wanted to be a chef. Mark also has an accomplished father (a dermatologist), a liberal arts degree (English literature), and an analogous career epiphany disrupting an intellectual itinerary—in his case, a trip to Dublin, where he'd gone to see streets once walked by Joyce, Yeats, and Beckett and found instead the intense flavors of small-dairy-farm milk, cream, butter, and eggs, having subsidized his stay with a job in a café kitchen. When Mark returned, he abandoned Irish literature and went to cooking school.

Mark had grown up in Ohio and had a small-town aw-shucks wonder of the world. Today, his face was covered with bandages and gauze. On his day off, he'd attended a rock concert and broken his nose when he threw himself into a mosh pit. This, too, seemed in character—of course that's what a college-educated son of a dermatologist would do on his weekends.

Until now, I had thought I was acquainted with the Babbo menu; I could recommend dishes: the pappardelle—to die for; or the so-called Two Minute Calamari, Sicilian Lifeguard Style—spicy, don't miss it. I knew nothing. In the blue Babbo bible, I counted fifty pastas. I'd had no idea there were so many. There were sixty entrées. There were forty starters. I stared at the menu. It was pasted in front of Andy, above the pass and just below a shelf crowded with Italian clutter—a double magnum of *vino rosso da tavola*, a bottle of olive oil, some balsamic vinegars: a still life of an Italian kitchen, as though depicted in a travel magazine, and the only thing customers saw when they peered through the portal windows of the swinging kitchen doors on their way to a toilet. (Ah, the romance of Italy, the still life said to anyone peering through the windows, even though the wine had gone brown from the heat, the olive oil was rancid, and the real kitchen, which didn't seem either Italian or romantic, was out of view.) The menu was four pages long "Humungous," Andy conceded. The line cooks were moving so fast I couldn't follow what they were doing. Orders were coming in on a ticker-tape machine, a long paper stream, one after another, Andy calling them out, and, without my knowing when or how, I became aware that everyone had simultaneously increased the speed of their preparations. There was a new quickness in their movements, an urgency. At the end of the evening, I wouldn't be able to say what it was I had seen: a blur and food being tossed in the air and radically different ways of being—an aggressive forthrightness as cooks dealt with the heat and fire, long flames flaring out of their pans; and then an artistic-seeming delicacy, as they assembled each plate by hand, moving leaves of herbs and vegetables around with their fingers and finishing it by squirting the plate with colored lines of liquid from a plastic bottle, as though signing a painting. It amounted to what? Something I didn't understand. I could have been on Mars.

I was at a go-forward-or-backward moment. If I went backward, I'd be saying, Thanks for the visit, very interesting, that's sure not me. But how to go forward? There was no place for me. These people were at a higher level of labor. They didn't think. Their skills were so deeply inculcated they were available to them as instincts. I didn't have skills of that kind and couldn't imagine how you'd learn them. I was aware of being poised on the verge of something: a long, arduous, confidence-bashing, profoundly humiliating experience.

MARIO, MEANWHILE, was examining the plates going out. It was one of his surprise visits.

He eyed a skirt steak and addressed Mark. "Grill guy, your salsa verde is breaking up. You've got too much oil in it, and the plate is too hot. Replate." Mark replated the dish, his movement miraculously accelerated, like a video on fast forward. "I'm counting. Ten. Nine. Eight. Seven . . . If I can hear you talking, you are talking too loud." The kitchen was like a library. Mario studied a dish from the sauté station, the duck, stuck his finger into it, and tasted. "Dom, take down your sauce." It was too salty, needed diluting. "And the duck," he said, picking up a slice of the breast. "You want to give the fatty side an extra minute. The meat is fine." It was verging on rare. "But render more of the fat." For fifteen minutes, I'd been watching Dominic's cooking the breast over a low heat, the fatty-skin-side down. This was what Mario was asking Dominic to do a little longer, so that the skin would be especially crispy.

Then, flustered by the attention, Dominic let a plate slip, and it fell into his sauces and dropped to the floor and broke. There were sweetbreads in the tomato sauce, and tomato sauce in the chicken stock, and broken glass on the floor. Dominic tried to scoop out the sweetbreads, but in his haste he fumbled them, and they fell into another sauce. Mario said nothing but squared up in front of Dominic, spread his legs, and crossed his arms and openly stared. "Dom takes criticism very personally," he said to me. Dominic was sweating. The open stare, I would learn, was Mario's way of expressing concern—in other places, you'd hear shouting. (Memo, coming from a French kitchen, recalled a practice called "plating"—when the chef takes a plate from your hands and throws it onto the floor, usually during the busy service, and you're meant to clean it up and prepare a new plate. It was, Memo said, "the most humiliating moment in my life, and it didn't happen again.")

An orecchiette was returned from the dining room, half eaten, the plate borne into the kitchen by the maître d', John Mainieri, who explained, "There are not enough florets on the broccoli." Five people gathered around the plate and started eating from it. "He says that the last time he ate here the broccoli had more florets." Everyone picked out a floret and stared at it closely.

"It's true," Mario said. "We've had larger florets, but nature isn't making big florets at the moment." A new pasta was prepared, and Mario handed it to one of the runners. "When you give this to him, please pistol-whip him with your penis."

Half an hour later, another return from the same table—this time, from a woman. A steak. It was chewy. "She doesn't want a new dish. She wants steak, properly prepared." The cooks assaulted the meat, indignantly tearing off pieces with their hands, and turned to one another, saying, "Chewy?"

The steak came back. Now, evidently, it had been overcooked. And there was also a chop. It, too, was not satisfactory.

"For fuck's sake. Find out their names. They're not coming back." Mario paused. "What are they drinking?"

"A Solaia 1997." A bottle was $475.

"Forget it," Mario said and ordered another round of entrées.

6

NEW YORK, 1992. The dishes Mario prepared at the new Rocco read like episodes in an autobiography; each one is so intimately associated with a specific moment in his life that the menu is almost more literary than culinary—cooking as memoir. Ravioli stuffed with brains and Swiss chard is his grandmother's recipe. A review in *New York* magazine singled out an "old-fashioned tagliatelle in a ragù Bolognese"—the very ragù Mario had prepared at La Volta. A stricchetti with porcini and cremini mushrooms is a variation on what Betta made on Mario's first day in her kitchen. The leek soufflé (with grappa-cured salmon) was the dish he had cooked for his first Christmas lunch in Italy. Mario had finally arrived in New York City and had a lifetime of cooking to express.

In his second month at Rocco, Mario met Susi Cahn, his future wife, who sold organic vegetables and goat cheese to downtown restaurants. (The cheese was made by her parents; the vegetables were grown by Susi on their land in upstate New York.) Two weeks later, she took her parents to Rocco for dinner: it was her birthday, and the restaurant seemed the right place to celebrate. Mario's family happened to be in town, also to celebrate a birthday, his mother's. The dinner didn't finish until three. For Susi, it was a drunken, energetic blur of festivities, Mario's rushing back and forth from the kitchen, returning each time with a surprise—another course, another bottle of wine, another grappa, and, finally, an accordion, which his father played, leading everyone in Italian drinking songs. Cahn, who is so many things Mario isn't—petite, dark-haired, East Coast, Jewish to his lapsed Catholic, early-to-bed to his out-until-early, reserved and deliberate to his outgoing and impulsive—illustrates the kind of person Mario probably gets on best with. "I'm *very, very* different," she said, when we met to talk, as though to say "Get real. Mario could not live with another version of himself." Arturo, his new business partner, was, it seems, not so different, and nine months into the enterprise, their partnership collapsed.

They weren't getting customers. Even Dana Batali was perplexed. "The food was good. I don't know why no one came." Whatever it was, it confused the regulars. "I asked Mario to start slowly," Arturo told me on the phone after I tracked him down in Miami, where he is now a bartender. "I've been to Italy. I know what's good. I didn't like the old style of food, either. But no, for Mario it was his way or the highway. This was my father's restaurant. I'd known the customers for twenty-five years. They looked at the menu and said, 'What's this shit?' and walked out." There were squabbles about money. Mario was always giving people extra dishes, even whole meals, and not charging for them. "Most of the grappa he drank himself."

The parting was acrimonious. "I can't watch the Food Network because I don't know if he's going to be on," Arturo told me. "Last night, I had people over for dinner, and they mentioned *Molto Mario*. How could they do that to me? And you," he said, suddenly quite angry, "how could you phone me out of the blue and mention this guy's name. You've ruined my evening."

Mario was now unemployed and homeless. Armandino invited him to Seattle to open a restaurant together—a longing born out of the enduring regret Armandino felt for having lost his family's store. Mario didn't take up the invitation because, finally, he'd found a venue, an abandoned Indian restaurant, with an especially low rent because the tenants had left in the middle of the night and the landlord was distraught. Batali had no money but borrowed some from Cahn ("There was never a moment's doubt that he was going to succeed," she told me) and invited Steve Crane, his friend from San Francisco, to be his partner. Pó opened six weeks later, at the end of May 1993, quietly, because they were short on cash (and therefore on many ingredients), had no liquor license, and couldn't afford air-conditioning during what turned out to be the second hottest summer in the history of the city. But they were in business, and at the end of August a *New York Times* food critic, Eric Asimov, wandered in and was overwhelmed by the food's unapologetic Italianness. It was, Mario recalls, heartening to find, at last, that "what I wanted to make in New York City was what New York City wanted to eat." (In the aftermath, Armandino, inspired by Mario, quit his executive job at Boeing and, at the age of sixty-one, went to Italy to be an unpaid apprentice to Dario Cecchini, one of the country's most famous butchers—like son, like father.)

Pó is like a teenage Babbo—thirteen tables, plus another two on the sidewalk, and a menu that borrows heavily from La Volta. For Steve Crane, the first two years were the best. He was in the front, Mario in the kitchen ("like an athlete"), and in no time the place was a late-night haunt of chefs, the result, Crane recalls, of Mario's pressing his card into the hands of the people he met, building up a business by word of mouth, consolidating it by treating invited customers as VIPs. (The practice has been refined at Babbo, and the only times I've seen Batali red-faced with anger involved the neglect of VIPs. He rarely shouts, but when the maître d' failed to spot a record producer who had appeared at the bar, he exploded—"You fucking moron! You fucking motherfucking moron!"—and chased him out of the kitchen with such menace that I thought he was going to throw something. "If it's a VIP table, you prepare the order *now*," he then hissed at the kitchen staff, reinforcing his rule that VIPs get served first and fast. "You don't prepare the food when you're good and ready. You don't make a VIP wait because you're a fucking great talent and you know better. You are not some fucking artist. I am counting. Ten seconds. They must have their starters in ten seconds. Nine. Eight. Seven." And, with hysterical speed, the starters appear, the pale look on the pantry chefs preparing them being one of unmitigated fear.)

According to Crane, the problems at Pó started after an executive at the nascent Food Network saw Mario running the kitchen and asked him to an audition. Mario the celebrity chef ("How could I run the front when there were lines of people from New Jersey waiting for this guy's autograph?") produced strains between the partners. "I'd walk in, and there'd be a photo shoot I didn't know about, and the photographer would say, 'Hey, you there, get out of the way,'" Crane recalls. ("What could I do?" Mario asks. "No one was interested in the maître d'.") In 1999, Mario assigned a price to the restaurant and gave Crane a choice: pay it, it's yours; take it, it's mine. Crane paid. When the deal was signed, tears welled up in Mario's eyes. "Mario is the toughest guy I know—'Hit me with your best punch,' that's his attitude. I had never seen him cry." It was painful, Mario said. "Like someone putting his name on your first baby." He had never thought that Crane would want the restaurant, let alone pay for it. "He was shocked when I said I'd take it—he didn't think I could run it without him." Yet, curiously, Crane isn't running it without Mario, who lingers in a ghostly fashion—not only on the menu, which continues to feature his La Volta dishes, but also in the minds of the staff.

"Is Mario here?" I asked a waitress when I ate there one weekend.

"Not tonight," she said, distressed by having to answer a question put to her so often.

7

It was the second week of March, the warmest day since summer, and people were wanting a new menu. The rabbit would no longer be served with Brussels sprouts but with spring peas, pea shoots, and a bright orange vinaigrette made from baby carrots. "We're giving you not only the rabbit but what's inside his head," Mario explained. "You get to eat him *and* what he wants to eat, too!"

There was a delivery of fava beans. They were to replace the chickpeas in a duck-themed dish called Pyramids in Brodo: a piece of pasta architecture squeezed at the top like an Egyptian monument and stuffed with what was left over from boning the ducks—kidneys, hearts, gnarly bits of meat stewed into a ragù, a risotto cooked in duck stock. "No one has any idea what's inside!" Mario declared. "It could be Jeffrey Dahmer's penis, *and* it costs nothing, *and* people love it." But the broth would be made from both turkey and duck bones: duck alone was too gummy, "too faggoty French."

Wild nettles had been ordered but hadn't arrived. "This is so typical," Gina observed. "The moment it gets warm, everyone wants spring. Fava beans, berries, and English peas, and I worry about what we'll get. It won't be local, that's certain." In fact, the green market in Union Square was still barren, except for the first batch of ramps, the unequivocally local wild leeks from upstate New York. Ramps were added to spaghetti, wrapped around a pork tenderloin, pickled for the summer, or served on their own with a cow's-milk cheese from Piemonte crumbled on top. "Oh, when they're done like that, they give me wood," Mario said happily. Everyone in the kitchen ate them as well—thrown on the flattop, squirted with oil, turned once, and scooped up with tongs. The ramps were evanescently tender and had an earthy, bright green freshness: a harbinger of warmer weather.

There were changes in the kitchen. Nick was leaving. Longing to be back in Rome, and inspired by Mario's stories of Porretta, he'd decided to return to Italy. Mario was flattered—the decision was tantamount to saying "I will follow your example, master"—and openly regarded Nick as a disciple. ("Going to Italy, it's the only way to learn.") Mario was now an effervescent source of advice: about what Nick should look for ("If your objective is to run your own restaurant, pick carefully—you want a place that does the cooking you'll want to do"), about finances ("You'll need five thousand dollars and a credit card of good standing"), and where he should go ("Great cooking in the south, but no game— you'll never get laid"). This was the big question—where?—and Mario debated it loudly with himself while Nick watched silently, sitting on a bar stool, until Mario finally settled on a Roman trattoria called Checchino ("Lots of action"). Mario would phone on Monday. In the kitchen, Nick's going was a big deal, abandoning his job, his country. Everyone recognized that you could only learn so much about cooking Italian food in a country that was not Italy.

Stacie Cassarino, one of Gina's cooks, was returning to being a prep cook during the day. She'd been working the evening service on a trial basis but wasn't fast enough. "Unfortunately she's a published poet," Andy explained in a tone that said, Need I say more? "She thinks too much." The kitchen had four vacancies—not all at once, but almost all at once—and Mario and Andy had to move fast.

One position was filled immediately because the perfect candidate walked in the door. Tony Liu would be Gina's new pastry cook, a gift because Tony was overqualified but desperate to work at Babbo. He was short, with closely cropped dark hair, muscular shoulders, and a serious manner. He was from Hawaii—a surfer in the summer, a snowboarder in the winter, with an appealing athletic bounce in his step—but was often out of place in an urban kitchen staffed with pale, nervous line cooks who hadn't seen daylight in months. But he was here to learn what Babbo had to teach him—that was his mission—and seemed never to lose his focus. He never smiled, for instance, not once, although he always managed to seem friendly. When he showed up at midday, he

greeted the Latin prep workers, one by one, in Spanish—something no
one else did. Tony had been a cook at Daniel Boulud's four-star French
restaurant. He'd also lived in Spain, working at Martín Berasategui, a
Michelin three-star place outside San Sebastián. In his mind he had
mastered two European cuisines. Italian was next. He could talk the talk,
walk the walk, and was accepted as a colleague.

This was not the case with Abby Bodiker. She had been a prep cook in
the Food Network kitchen, and, the others were wary: a television stu-
dio is not a restaurant, and, in the eyes of Memo and Frankie, Abby was
underqualified, inexperienced, and both female *and* feminine—in short,
undeserving of a position on the line. Memo and Frankie could be a
menacing duo, like sinister twins with their own private language. They
scarcely spoke to each other, but were always communicating—an eye-
brow, a small nod—and were then united in whatever they had to do:
fixing a dish, tweaking a special, or hazing the newcomer. Frankie, in
particular, took exception to Abby's approach, whatever it was—what
did I know?—and the two were locked into a mutual antipathy. Abby
was quite girlie. She had blond hair, which she sometimes wore in ponytails, and was petite, with a turned-up nose and small features. Within
days of her being in the kitchen—all new cooks start at the pantry station, preparing starters—she'd grown demonstrably harder, her face
drained of expression, as though a mask.

"All women go through this," Elisa said. "It was worse before, when
the Neanderthal was the prep chef." (Elisa had become the prep chef
after the Neanderthal had moved to Pittsburgh to run a restaurant that
Joe and Lidia Bastianich had opened there.) Elisa used to complain to
Mario about the Neanderthal—"He's crude, he's sexist, he's abusive"—
along with other laments: the kitchen shorthand for broccoli rabe
("rape"), the vivid accounts of prostitute visits. But Mario told her there
was nothing he could do. "Really, Elisa. This is New York. Get used to
it." In the event, the Neanderthal didn't last in Pittsburgh and was fired.
He couldn't stop himself from talking about the waitresses' butts until
finally the waitresses started complaining.

I then witnessed what might have been a symptomatic exchange
involving sweetbreads. Elisa and Memo were trying to settle what
should constitute a portion. Elisa had recommended six ounces and
using a scale, but Memo disagreed.

"Let's call it a B-cup," he said. "Trust me, Elisa, all the boys know the feel of a B-cup," and he grabbed his own breasts to illustrate his point. "You want a B-cup portion of sweetbreads."

Elisa went deep red—"I-I-I-I really think we should use the scale"— and turned to me as a witness from the outside world. "What is it about these guys? Is it because they have to wear aprons?"

There were two other positions to fill, and Mario was anxious, because both he and Andy happened to be going away at the same time. Andy was making a much-anticipated trip to Spain, one that couldn't be postponed. Andy, Mario's number two for eight years, had watched Babbo chefs go off and, with Mario and Joe's backing, open their own places. Now it was Andy's turn. "Ultimately," he confided to me, "I only want to be a chef in order to have my own place. I pretend Babbo is mine but it's not, and what's the fun of doing this if the money isn't in my bank?" Like Mario, Andy had lived in Spain, and his restaurant, when the space was found, was going to be Iberian. This trip was for inspiration; he'd eat at forty-eight restaurants in three days.

One spot was filled by Holly Burling, twenty-eight, tall, lanky, tomboyish, with red hair and pale skin. I witnessed Mario's pretending to interview her, but I knew his mind had been made up beforehand: Holly had worked in Italy. What else did he need to know? She hadn't been there long (a few weeks at an *agriturismo*, a farmhouse with guest beds, learning how to make gnocchi and handmade pasta), but the point was she'd learned Italian and found a kitchen. "She did it. She gets it." There was also, I felt, watching the two of them talk (and seeing in Mario a determination to see Holly as a kindred spirit), evidence of his conviction that women make better cooks. Mario believed that Elisa was Babbo's best chef, "not just because she's the most experienced but because she's a woman. I know it doesn't make sense, and I don't understand it. But it is consistently the case: women are better cooks. They approach food differently." The assumption would seem to resist scientific scrutiny but was one Joe shared as well. The day after Elisa had started running the prep kitchen, Joe tasted the Bolognese sauce and nodded sagely, finding in it a confirmation of what he was looking for. "It's true," he said, "a woman cooks differently. This is much better than what the last guy used to do." The last guy had been the Neanderthal, and, in fact, he hadn't prepared the Bolognese. It had been made by the kitchen's principal prep whiz at the time, Miguel Gonzalez.

Holly was offered a job. It paid five hundred dollars a week, with five days' vacation starting in her second year. There was no mention of sick pay because it was understood you didn't get sick, which I'd already discovered in the chilly silence that had greeted me when I'd come down with the flu and phoned Elisa to say that I wasn't coming in that day because obviously she didn't want an ill person in the kitchen. Nothing of the sort was obvious. Memo explained this to me later, after he refused to go home when he had a fever and was sneezing and wiping his nose on his sleeve. "When I made the decision to be a chef, I accepted I would never claim a sick day for the rest of my life. It's one of the sacrifices of my calling."

The trouble was the final hiring. There wasn't the budget to hire the experienced cook Andy wanted. He then wondered if he could use Marcello, "one of the Latins," who worked mornings, making the pasta. But Andy wasn't sure he wanted a Latin working service.

"I don't know if it's appropriate. We had them at Pó. But Babbo is different."

People talked about "the Latins" in this way (in quotes because, after all, Latin America is a big place). Even so the remark was curious. Because three-star restaurants don't like Mexicans making their food?

"No, no, no. It's just a bigger kitchen, and I don't want to stop and translate." It's true, Marcello's English was rudimentary, and when Mario interviewed him he spoke Spanish.

Are you ready to work evenings? Mario asked him. You know you'll be the only Latin? Can you take the pressure?

Marcello—his forearm wrapped in thick gauze (he'd slid it across a chef's knife that had been sitting blade out)—listened carefully and answered, Yes, he can do this. Marcello was like a miniversion of his boss: short and compact, with red hair gathered into a ponytail, a thick neck (in American football, you could imagine his playing center on a junior varsity team), and a round, warm face. His manner was deferential, polite, attentive. He confessed to me afterwards that the interview had made him very anxious. The anxiety had been wholly observed by Mario, who had a salesman's gift for registering the physiological symptoms of discomfort: "I love it when they're nervous. It makes me feel so gooooood."

Mario asked Marcello if he was working elsewhere. Many "Latins" had two jobs.

"Yes," Marcello said. He mentioned the hours, the pay.

"How much are we paying you?" Mario asked. He looked at Andy. Andy didn't know.

"Three hundred and seventy-five a week," Marcello said.

"From now on, you work nowhere else. Your salary will be five hundred and fifty dollars a week."

This was a tremendous change. Implicit in it was a new designation: now, Marcello was being told, you are one of us. He returned to the kitchen. He looked solemn but had a distinctly lighter gait. He could have been walking on water balloons.

I HAD WITNESSED a privileged moment and, in the little history of a little restaurant, a modest milestone. The "Latins" are in every New York kitchen. They bring food to your table and clean up the plates afterwards. The unspoken assumption is they're America's *gästarbeiter*, here to do the dirty work: the dishwasher routine. But they also make most of the food, while the elite positions, on the line, are reserved for white guys. Two of the most productive cooks in Elisa's prep kitchen were Cesar, twenty, and Abelardo, who was twenty-one: both "Latins." Every morning, Elisa gave them a list—sometimes thirty different tasks—and by late afternoon they'd made most of what the restaurant served in the evening. To most people, they were invisible—even to their employers (they are "Latins," like a race, rather than Mexicans, Uruguayans, or Peruvians), a pool of interchangeable laborers, few of them English speakers, living on the fringes of the city's boroughs, piled into one-bedroom apartments that no one wants to know about. Of course Mario and Andy hadn't known Marcello's salary; until this moment they hadn't been entirely aware of his existence.

"We're going to need a dishwasher," Mario told Marcello when their interview was finished. "Do you know anyone?" Mario wouldn't know where to find the next one. In this, there was a Latin chain: the current dishwasher, Alejandro, would now make the pasta, duties that had been Marcello's. "Cousins? Someone else in the family?"

I spent a Friday afternoon, paycheck day, with Jesus Salgado. Jesus, who had worked at Babbo since its second day, was the cousin of Miguel, the cook who'd prepared the feminine Bolognese. Miguel was dead. May 19th was the first anniversary of his death, and people were talking about the date with dread. I had never met Miguel but knew about him from Elisa—his knife skills, his understanding of food, his flashy dressing, his charisma: qualities that also characterized Cesar, Miguel's successor (and cousin), although Elisa insisted that Miguel had been "much sexier." It was Jesus who had proposed that the restaurant hire Cesar after Miguel died. Jesus had proposed Miguel, too. (Jesus and Miguel "had been like brothers" and shared a business card, both their names on it, which was, eerily, the same card that Jesus handed out now.) Jesus had also proposed his brother, Umberto, who cleaned the restaurant during the day, and Marco, a cousin, who worked in the prep kitchen. Jesus, having recommended them all, felt responsible for them: if they were late or didn't show, Jesus had to answer for them. For an employer, the informal system was pretty reliable, although it reinforced the distance between the "Latins" and everyone else. The only thing an employer asked for was a worker's Social Security card (no card, no job), and even after September 11th it is still possible to buy a card cheaply.

Jesus was a natural patriarch. On payday, he gathered the members of his extended family around him—Umberto was wearing a leather jacket and leather shoes; the younger Cesar and Marco were in baggy hip-hop jeans and bright red running shoes, each wearing headphones, swaying to a muffled rappy sound. Jesus had been down to the Babbo basement to pick up their weekly checks and was now leading everyone to a place on 8th Street to cash them (none of them had a bank account), Cesar and Marco following loosely behind, bobbing happily. Afterwards we found a bench in Washington Square Park. I wanted Jesus to tell me about Miguel.

Jesus came from Puebla, in Mexico, about two hours from Mexico City. So, too, did his many cousins. At Babbo, there's a view that the best pasta makers come from Puebla. The observation was first made by Joe on his realizing that the restaurant had employed three exceptional prep cooks in a row who all came from the same place. I asked Jesus: Do the best pasta cooks come from Puebla?

"Well, it's a little more complicated," he said. "*Everyone* comes from Puebla. Most of the Mexicans in New York are from Puebla." *La migra*, Jesus called it. The migration. Puebla is poor and overcrowded, and New York is a destination city on an immigrant trail simply because someone from Puebla succeeded in making the journey and others followed. "In Puebla, we don't know fast food. We know only the food we cook. There is a McDonald's, but I never ate there. I couldn't afford it. For us, it was a three-star restaurant. A hamburger was a week's pay. We all cook our food."

Jesus said that when he returns to Mexico—he hadn't been back in eight years—his grandmother will celebrate by slaughtering a goat. She'll rub it with avocado leaves—"the oil from the leaves hides the strong goat smell"—cover it with a paste made from pumpkin seeds, peanuts, chocolate, and cloves, and bury it in a hole of hot coals. "We cook a sheep's head the same way. A lot of Babbo's preparations, which are quite rustic, are familiar to us. The skirt steak—that's a Mexican preparation. Or the grill station—*la barbacoa*, we call it—that's how we cook our meat. Or braising: that's how we deal with big cuts. Or a *bain marie*: we call it *baño maría*, which we use to prepare tamales. We have much to learn when we work in a kitchen like Babbo, but we know many things already." He described a wedding he'd attend that weekend in Queens. "Everyone will bring food—a pig, a turkey, a chicken." It was the same at Christmas. "The day is spent cooking and being together." Elisa remembered conversations with Miguel. "He often talked about food he made at home. Cesar is like that as well. They have a capacity to look at a whole kitchen and understand how it works. They both always know what's in the walk-in and what needs reordering. They know more than most kids coming out of cooking school."

When Miguel arrived in New York, Jesus looked after him. They lived together, an extended family of cousins, siblings, and friends, in a three-bedroom apartment in the Bronx: three guys in a room, nine guys in all. After Miguel found work at Babbo, he began taking English lessons in a class taught by a Puerto Rican named Mirabella, and the two of them began seeing each other.

Elisa remembers her. "They had problems, and she was always phoning. She was older, and you could hear the age in her voice, but I didn't know how much older until I saw her at the funeral. Miguel was twenty-two. She was forty-two. Why would a forty-two-year-old woman go out with a twenty-two-year-old?"

Around Christmas last year, Miguel came to Jesus for advice. The relationship had been openly tempestuous, but, according to Miguel, they had sorted out their difficulties. Mirabella wanted Miguel to move in. She had an apartment in Brooklyn. They planned to marry in June.

"I'd never met her," Jesus told me. "Miguel had never brought her to the house. This puzzled me. There were other things. She always needed money. She had a heart problem and had to see a specialist. Miguel didn't have much money. He didn't have enough to be giving it to an older woman with a heart problem. Miguel asked me for my advice. I said he shouldn't move in." Miguel asked the others in the apartment. They said he shouldn't move in.

In the new year, Miguel moved in.

The fights continued. Mirabella was now calling the kitchen every day. There was an insistence in the woman's tone, Elisa felt, an imperiousness. "The others in the kitchen told me she dealt in some sort of I.D. thing—she bought and sold identities." At the time, the going rate for a Social Security number was sixty-five dollars. A green card was a little more. A passport varied: a good one could cost several hundred dollars. "None of these kids have papers," Elisa said. "Sometimes I've wondered if she gave Miguel a fright about his immigration status. And he feared that if he got in trouble the whole family would be in trouble."

The relationship didn't work out, Jesus said. "But because Miguel had asked for our advice and we'd told him not to marry this woman, he felt he couldn't come back to us. He was embarrassed. He had no place to go."

On May 18th, Miguel's last day in the kitchen, he finished an enormous amount of work, Elisa recalls. He did the prep for the entire week. "Then he put his fish knives in a plastic container and gave them to me. I didn't know what he was doing. 'Thank you,' I said. 'These are very nice.' " That night he hanged himself from a shower fixture in the Brooklyn apartment. Jesus rushed over on getting the news. It was his first time in the apartment. The police wouldn't let him see the body.

Jesus was thirty-three but looked older. He has thick black hair, which is stiff like tarred straw, a strong angular nose, and a heavy, scarred face. He has a serious air and an appealing toughness. He phoned his uncle, Miguel's father. "His grief was unbelievable. Nothing I said made sense to him."

Jesus paused. The two of us were still sitting on the park bench, surrounded by his cousins and brother, in no apparent hurry, watching us patiently. Jesus was staring fixedly, avoiding me. It seemed he didn't want me to see the tears welling up like a heavy oil along the rim of his eyes. He took a breath. After a church service, Jesus continued, he arranged for the body to be returned to Mexico. Andy wrote a letter, describing "what a hero Miguel was, because the parents don't understand what has happened. We didn't understand. We still don't."

Jesus stood up. His household stood up. "We are now very close," he said, gesturing to the others. "We don't want this to happen again. We talk. We make sure no one is alone." He walked off in the direction of the subway, the gang following behind, subdued, everyone with sad, sloping shoulders.

I phoned the police. Jesus carried the name and number of a detective who had been in charge, a Detective Lamposone. I got one of his colleagues.

"Oh, yeah, I remember that night. Mexican kid. Very ugly. Was drinking with his friends and started playing the game with a pistol. He lost. Messy."

I was horrified: was this why Jesus hadn't been allowed to see the body? "Oh, no," I blurted out, startled. "No one said anything about Russian roulette."

The detective was taken aback. "You know, you'd better speak to Lamposone. I might have the case confused with another one."

Detective Lamposone had been transferred to another precinct, in Bay Ridge. He had no recollection of the incident. I told him the details, the name, the date. Nothing. "I'm sorry. That one's gone."

One morning, about ten months later, I was working in the prep kitchen. I was making pasta with Alejandro, Marcello's successor. (Alejandro had been the dishwasher on my first day at Babbo.) Alejandro had grown up on a farm, just outside Puebla, and had left when he was sixteen. He had been in New York four years. He was a kid. (One afternoon, when the members of the entire prep kitchen were in the basement, changing back into street clothes—the routine was that everyone stripped down in a space about half the size of a very small closet—Alejandro noticed that Elisa was staring at his belly. For someone so young, the belly was remarkably soft and round. "Mexican men," he said cheerfully, slapping it with vigor. "Macho potbellies.")

I had a little Spanish. I wanted to know how Alejandro's family farm worked—what animals were raised, the vegetables, what was eaten at the family table. Alejandro, while perfectly happy to answer my questions, didn't have that "capacity to look at the whole kitchen." This was a job. He wasn't interested in talking about food, although he was a perfectly good cook. He was interested in meeting American girls. He proposed helping me with my Spanish and, yes, if I insisted, talking about farm vegetables, provided I'd take him to some clubs. Just then Marcello walked in. His wife was outside, in a car. Marcello wanted to show the kitchen his new baby, a bundle of pink miniature girl cradled in his arms, a few weeks old, conceived, I realized, not long after his interview with Mario: in the confidence conferred on Marcello by his new position, he began a family.

People who don't live in New York don't appreciate how much the city has once again become fashioned by immigrants and is where you come to become the next thing you'll be. In 1892, four out of every ten New Yorkers were born abroad. Since 1998, that has been the case again, owing to the arrival, legal or illegal, of immigrants from Latin America, Russia, the Asian subcontinent, Albania, the Baltic states. Both of Joe's parents are immigrants, ethnic Italians who were living in Istria when it was incorporated into Yugoslavia by Tito: the Italians, long resented since the war (most had been Fascists), were told to assimilate or get out. Joe's father hopped on a ship and arrived in New York illegally. He was fifteen. Lidia had a marginally more conventional passage and was granted political asylum. "Restaurant work," Joe observed, "is the lifeline of immigrants in this city." His father's first job was in a restaurant; his first home was above a bakery (run by an immigrant). Thirty-five years later, their son, now a co-owner of his own venture, was providing a lifeline for another generation. He employed Marcello, an émigré from Argentina (and not, for all his pasta-making gifts, from Puebla).

And now Marcello was secure enough in his new country to begin a family. Someone had died; someone was born.

I ONCE ASKED Mario what I could expect to learn in his kitchen.

"The difference between the home cook and the professional," he said. "You'll learn the reality of the restaurant kitchen. As a home cook, you can prepare anything any way anytime. It doesn't matter if your lamb is rare for your friends on Saturday and not so rare when they come back next year. Here people want exactly what they had last time. Consistency under pressure. And that's the reality: a lot of pressure."

He thought for a moment. "You also develop an expanded kitchen awareness. You'll discover how to use your senses. You'll find you no longer rely on what your watch says. You'll hear when something is cooked. You'll smell degrees of doneness."

Once, in the kitchen, Frankie used the same phrase, "kitchen awareness," as though it were a thing you could take classes to learn. And I thought I might have seen evidence of it, in how people on the line were cued by a smell and turned to deal with what they were cooking, or in how they seemed to hear something in a sauté pan and then flipped the food. Even so, it seemed an unlikely prospect that this was something I could master; the kitchen remained so stubbornly incomprehensible. From the start of the day to the end, the place was frenzied. In fact, without my fully realizing it, there was an education in the frenzy, because in the frenzy there was always repetition. Over and over again, I'd pick up a smell, as a task was being completed, until finally I came to identify not only what the food was but where it was in its preparation. The next day, it would be the same. (By then, I was somehow managing to put in extra days in the prep kitchen, even though I was technically employed elsewhere.) I was reminded of something Andy had told me. "You don't learn knife skills at cooking school, because they give you only six onions, and no matter how hard you focus on those six onions there are only six, and you're not going to learn as much as when you cut up a hundred." One day I was given a hundred and fifty lamb tongues. I had never held a lamb's tongue, which I found greasy and unnervingly humanlike. But after cooking, trimming, peeling, and slicing a hundred and fifty lamb tongues, I was an expert.

One morning, Elisa went out to deal with a delivery, and I picked up a change in the way the lamb shanks smelled. They were browning in a large pan about ten feet away, and I walked over, trance-like, turned them, and resumed my task. My nose had told me that they were sufficiently browned and would be ruined in a minute. By the time Elisa returned, I'd removed the shanks and thrown in another batch. She looked at me, slightly startled.

It was a modest breakthrough, and I was allowed to cook. The first item, appropriately enough, was lamb shanks. They were followed by beef cheeks, both basically cooked in the same way: browned and braised in a wine-based liquid until they fell apart. Then duck thighs, rabbit ragù, beef tongue, and guinea-hen legs. Once, cooking beef cheeks, I smelled that they were cooked, even though they were meant to remain in the oven for another hour. But I didn't pull them out right away, which was a mistake and they were nearly burned, but I'd learned I could trust my senses.

8

I FOUND myself needing to understand short ribs, probably because I really didn't know what they were, even though I was now helping Elisa prepare them every week and even though I recognized their overwhelming ubiquity: just about every New York restaurant of a certain pretension seemed to have them on the menu—and, in fact, has had them on the menu for fifteen years. In this is a rarely recognized thing, that cities have their restaurant dishes, some ingredient or preparation that mysteriously self-replicates (and yet rarely emigrates—until recently, you wouldn't have found short ribs in Boston or Chicago) through the easy, professional promiscuity of chefs, always hopping from one place to another, never staying long, especially in Manhattan, which was also why Mario refused to give a job reference to anyone who left after working for him for less than a year. ("Why should I? So they can steal ideas it took me a lifetime to learn?") The short rib lends itself to being appropriated because, in each appearance, it can be so effortlessly and thematically reinterpreted. It becomes Gallic when it shows up at a four-star French establishment (the short ribs, cooked in veal stock, are served with braised celery); vaguely fusion at a fancy four-star Euro-Asian place (on white rice, with bok choy and water chestnuts); a comfort food at the down-home but two-star Americana restaurant (with mashed potatoes and gravy); a piece of exotica at the cash-only Vietnamese spot (plastered on a stick of lemongrass and served with plum sauce); and bearing an Italian signifier—polenta, invariably—when Italian. At Babbo, it was also topped with a mound of parsley, lemon zest, and horseradish (because horseradish and beef are a traditional coupling, and because horseradish also provides the requisite heat, and lemon the citrus kick, required of a Batali dish). The dish also had an Italian name, Brasato al Barolo, which means "braised in Barolo," Barolo being a hearty red wine from Piemonte in northern Italy.

A braised dish, a variation of the pot roast, is one in which meat is cooked with the lid on very slowly in liquid—wine or broth, or both—until it starts to fall apart. The meat is usually a tough cut like a leg or a shoulder, one of those gnarly, complex pieces that are chewable only if they've been hammered for several hours. In Italy, braising has long been a winter preparation, associated with house-heating wood stoves and subdued root vegetable flavors. (Braised meats, for instance, feature in the peninsula's oldest cookbook, *De re coquinaria*, written in Latin around the time of Christ by Marcus Gavius Apicius, who also recommends the same obliterating approach for wild ducks and desiccated, tough, otherwise inedible game birds.) The thing about Babbo's Piemonte version is that you'd have a hard time finding a *brasato* made from short ribs, with or without Barolo, anywhere in Piemonte, and Mario, when pressed, concedes that there might be a little invention in the dish's name. Like me, he didn't have a clue what a short rib was until he ate one on a wintry night in 1993 at a restaurant called Alison on Dominick Street, where, as it happens, it was prepared in the North African style, with couscous. In a sign of our jaded how-can-I-give-you-my-heart-when-it's-already-been-broken era, the candlelit Alison on Dominick Street—which, as recently as Valentine's Day 2002, was regarded as New York's most romantic restaurant—has closed, but I tracked down one of its former chefs, Tom Valenti. At the end of the eighties, Valenti had scored big making a dish with lamb shanks, same principle: a cheap, worked muscle (the shin) was cooked in wine and broth until the meat fell apart when tapped with your tongs, and the result was so popular, and so imitated, that Valenti found himself looking around for another meat to prepare in the same way. "I wanted to do something with beef but never liked beef stew. I found it dry and chewy. So I did some homework and came across old recipes using short ribs. I liked short ribs much more than any other beef cut: they are rich and marbled and full of so much fatty flavor that they never dry out." When he put the dish on the menu, in 1990, it was accompanied by a small fillet—"technically, a beef dish done two ways, which I did so people would have a choice in case they hated the short rib." Valenti now runs his own restaurants, and short ribs are a regular feature—except for a brief six-month period when he took them off the menu and "got lots of shit from customers." In 1990, short ribs were forty-five cents a pound; now, thanks to Valenti, they are more than five dollars.

But what is a short rib, and where do you find it on a cow? Elisa didn't know, and she'd been preparing them for four years. Even Valenti wasn't sure; his short ribs, like Babbo's, were prepared by the meat guy and arrived as a shrink-wrapped unit of three or four. So I went to my local butcher, Benny, at Florence Meat Market in the West Village, and he explained. There are thirteen bones on each rib cage, he said. Six of them—the longest and the meatiest—are prime rib: these would be your standing rib roast. (This is probably what Tom Jones was eating when seduced by Mrs. Waters—a great chunk of meat on a bone you can hold with two hands.) But three or four bones at the bottom of the rib cage and another three or four at the top, near the shoulder, are shorter. These are short ribs. And this is why they're delivered by the butcher in units of three or four: three or four from the bottom and three or four from the top, although the ribs at the top are often too fatty to use.

For all that, the ribs aren't all that short—they're about a foot long. They're also surprisingly meaty, akin to pork spare ribs, but with a lot more to eat.

You start by browning them. You remove them "from the *top* of the packaging," Elisa reminded me after I'd already slid them out from the side, "so you don't get blood all over the front of you"—because, of course, by then, I had blood all over the front of me—and then separate them, one by one, by slicing down through the meat between each rib. "Carefully," Elisa said, "*please.*" You set your ribs out on a hotel pan and season them with salt and pepper abundantly on both sides: they look freckled when you're done. (A hotel pan, I understood finally, is not actually a pan but a tray, and gets its name from being one of the largest trays that can fit on an oven shelf, the kind of very large tray that a hotel would need.)

At Babbo, they cooked up about three cows' worth of short ribs at a time, around forty-eight, but a quarter of them always turned out to be impossibly fatty and unusable, or else crooked, mutated, and very ugly—and unusable. (Christ, I found myself saying, holding up some dwarfed, battered boomerang specimen, wondering if pasture pastimes included bovine boxing, What happened to this cow?) This is the nature of the cut—some are just mutant—so if you're preparing short ribs at home you want twice what you think you need: say, eight ribs for four people. You can do other things with the bits you don't use—at Babbo, the discarded meat, shredded by hand and mixed with parmigiano, becomes a ravioli stuffing, unless Cesar gets to it first, in which case chili flakes and cayenne pepper are added to make a fiery filling for family-meal tacos, with white-flour tortillas grilled on an open flame.

By now, it is widely recognized that you don't brown meat to seal in the juices; you brown it for the flavor. The misplaced belief, in which a crunchy outside was seen as the protein equivalent of Saran Wrap, arose in the nineteenth century out of the untested speculation of a German chemist, Justus von Liebig. The theory was that a seal is created when protein coagulates at a high temperature, just as when bleeding wounds are cauterized, and it gained popular acceptance as a scientific justification for what was seen as the new cooking method of the moment: hot and fast, rather than the traditional slow and wet. Remarkably, it went largely unchallenged for more than a century, until 1984, when chemist and cookery writer Harold McGee confirmed that no such seal exists and that we brown our meat simply because we like the taste.

With meat, browning is the result of proteins breaking down under heat—the surface is caramelized (it literally becomes sweeter and more aromatic) and the texture changes—but this doesn't occur until the temperature reaches at least 340 degrees Fahrenheit. As it happens, cold-pressed extra-virgin olive oil starts smoking at 360 degrees, so I suppose, if you are scrupulous in these matters, you could find happiness inside this twenty-degree buffer zone and brown your meat in olive oil without polluting the kitchen and the lungs of your colleagues. This, alas, was not the way at Babbo, where you were told to take a big, heavy-bottomed pot—a "rondo," about three feet in diameter—place it on the flattop, and pour olive oil inside once the bottom was smoking. The first time I did this, I hesitated. I peered over the rim of the by now very, very hot rondo, a rib in each hand, like pistols about to be drawn in a game of cowboys and Indians. The olive oil had acquired a hot liquidy quality, and some molecular thing seemed to be going on, and the oil was moving around in currents. I had not seen olive oil currents before, and I didn't like what I was seeing. As I stood there, I heard a voice, a tiny one, coming from a little man residing in the back of my brain whom I'd always regarded as Mr. Commonsense. Mr. Commonsense, who also had not gone to cooking school, was telling me that I didn't want to stick my hand into the bottom of a very hot gigantic pan, so hot that it was spitting oil, did I? Of course not. So, as I made to set my ribs inside, I dropped them just before they reached the bottom. The ribs landed. They bounced, splashing in the hot oil, which then seemed (in my mind, anyway) to *roar* up the length of one of the ribs, leap off the end and explode, enveloping my knuckles. The pain was remarkably intense, and my skin responded immediately by forming globe-like blisters on the tender area between the back cuticle end of the fingernail and the first knuckle. Four of them, one on each finger. These globes were rather beautiful, not unlike small shiny jewels.

Okay, so I learned something that I'm sure every other person in the world already knew: hot oil was not for splashing in, bumpy landings strongly not advised. I had forty-six more ribs to go, and these, I concluded, would be eased down into the bottom of the pot. But there was a problem. The jewel-like globes at the ends of my fingers were now extrasensitive to the heat (not unlike an inverted case of frostbite), and the closer I brought them to the hot bottom of the pot, the more they protested. An extraordinary thing then happened: just as I was about to lay down another rib, my fingertips, like little pets that had got loose from their leash, ran off on their own and dropped the rib. Once again, it bounced. Once again, there was a splash. And once again hot oil roared up the bone, leapt off the end, and exploded, enveloping, this time, not my knuckles but the shiny jewel-like blisters that were on them. Blisters on blisters. The process was akin to what I was trying to do to the meat—break down the protein in the tissue with high heat. But this thought occurred to me only later. At the time, I had only one thought: to remove myself from the source of the pain. I became airborne. I shot straight up, ramming my maimed knuckles into my crotch (no idea why men do this—do we expect to find comfort there?) and howled. By the time I landed, I was surrounded by several Mexican prep chefs, staring at me with compassion but also with a clear message: You, señor, are actually very stupid. Cesar handed me his tongs.

Use these, he said.

Of course. Another lesson learned: use tongs.

After the browning, the rest is straightforward. Actually, with tongs, the browning, too, is straightforward. There are five remaining steps.

One. Remove the now brown and glistening ribs (using tongs, *por favor*) from the rondo and make a braising liquid, the stuff that's going to cover the ribs while they cook. In this method, the liquid is the essential ingredient, and it doesn't matter what it is as long as it's wet and plentiful (in an Irish pot roast, it's water), although the ideal liquid is both flavoring and flavorful and is made from one part wine (at Babbo, about three magnums' worth, which, as it happens, is not the Barolo of the dish's name but a perfectly acceptable, very cheap California Merlot) and one part meat broth (say, a chicken stock), plus loads of vegetables: some carrots, an onion, two stalks of celery, and five peeled cloves of garlic, all roughly chopped, which you throw back into the rondo, still hot, and stir. You add the wine, the broth, a can of tomatoes, and cook for a few minutes.

Two. Put the now-browned ribs in a roasting pan, pour the braising liquid over them, add some rosemary and thyme, put a lid on top, stick it in the oven (350 degrees), and forget about it.

Three. (Three hours later, the ribs now cooked.) Turn the braising liquid into a sauce, although the instruction itself raises an obvious question: what is a sauce? In this preparation, for instance, this is what you do: first you remove the ribs and set them aside to cool; then you pour the liquid they were cooked in through a strainer into another pot. This liquid, even before you'd begun cooking the ribs in it, had been pretty rich, being a broth that had been made from chicken feet, plus lots of vegetables, herbs, and plenty of wine. *Then* the ribs themselves had been cooked in it. (The bones of any animal, simmered slowly, make for a wet, intense expression of the meat; here you're getting a double expression, like a broth made from a broth.) Next, you take this dense, aromatic, already highly extracted liquid and hammer it: you put it back on a burner and boil it to hell. Just torch it. Full blast. Lots of yellow-frothy melted fat will rise disgustingly to the surface. You skim this off and keep boiling the thing until it's reduced by more than half, when, lo and behold, it is no longer a braising liquid or a broth: it's a sauce. The result is very, very, very concentrated. (In fact, it's really almost French.)

Four. Once the ribs are cool, you discover that the bones have loosened themselves from the meat and come right out. You also discover that what's left is really quite ugly. It consists of two parts: a muscly tendon of some kind (the texture is not unlike a baseball catcher's mitt) that is smooshed, by way of a fatty sinew, to the meat. The two parts can be pulled apart by hand. The bit that looks like a catcher's mitt is, in addition to being very ugly, entirely inedible. With great pleasure, you throw this away. The other bit is quite yummy, although you need to trim it into a rectangle, eliminating any fatty goo. But, curiously, mixed in with your good short ribs are a number of mutants. In these, for some reason, there is no distinction between the two parts, the bad and good bits (that is, catcher's mitt and dinner). They're all mushed together, and you can't pull them apart without tearing the thing to shreds, which is what you do: tear the thing to shreds to find some something, anything really, that Cesar can use to make the family meal with.

Five. Assembly. Your meat is now arranged like so many dead toy soldiers, neatly tidied up. The sauce has been skimmed of fat and reduced to something that could be described as the food equivalent of most male movie stars: dark, rich, and thick. Everything is ready. Next you want to put it away in a fashion that allows you to retrieve it quickly, blast it in an oven, and serve: say, six short ribs in a half-hotel pan (which isn't a pan, either, but a tray, and is half the size of the full hotel not-actually-a-pan-but-a-tray pan, or in normal life what you cook brownies in), pour some sauce on top to keep the meat moist, and bundle the whole thing up first with plastic wrap, then with foil, tightly, tightly, so that, once stacked on the floor of the walk-in, it can be stepped on (and in the frantic rush of service, things happen—they always happen) without short-rib juice squirting out and adhering to the bottom of your shoes, leaving a disgraceful track to the toilet when you finally get a chance to go. What you now have is a wholly typical restaurant preparation, in which most of the work is done long before the dish is even ordered (and if a restaurant can do it, why can't you?). It keeps for a week.

These steps—brown meat, make a liquid, cook meat in it, remove it, and reduce the liquid until it's a sauce—are the same for every braised dish everywhere. Lamb shanks are done this way; so, too, are lamb shoulders, veal shanks, wild boar hams, venison shoulders: it's all the same.

Then, on December 2, 2003, a modest proposal, with potentially historic implications, was made by the Babbo meat supplier, Pat La Frieda. He asked Elisa if she wanted to experiment with chuck flaps.

"What's a chuck flap?" she asked.

"It's like a short rib without a short rib," he said.

"A short rib without a short rib? You mean, you don't have any ugly ones that you have to throw away?"

"Exactly, it's like the perfect short rib—the dream short rib, the short rib from Heaven, the Platonic ideal of a short rib—but without a short rib."

And so, for the first time in five years, on the following Thursday, the Babbo winter menu didn't have short ribs on it. It had chuck flaps. The dish was still called "Brasato al Barolo" (why change now?), and, to my palate, there wasn't a lot of difference in the taste, although I've since wondered if the sauce, without the short rib bones to enrich it, hadn't lost some intensity. Of course, nobody knows what a chuck flap is or where it might be located. Even so, Tom Valenti liked it. Not long after Elisa's menu change, he dined at Babbo on his night off and was particularly taken by the chuck flap. Who knows?

And so the short rib ends with a new beginning. Or so I thought. But recently I happened upon an account, published in 1979 by the English cookery writer Jane Grigson, of her efforts to re-create dishes cited by Proust in *À la recherche du temps perdu*. The second volume of Proust's novel begins with a dinner featuring *boeuf à la mode*, what Grigson describes as a slowly braised secondary cut of beef served in its own jelly. A secondary cut is anything not fancy, and several of them work in the dish. Grigson prefers one that's shipped to her by Charles MacSween & Son in Edinburgh. This is how she describes it: "The special cut is the long lean muscle from the inside of the blade bone, known by many names, principally as the shoulder fillet, but also as the salmon cut or fish tail. I first saw it in our butcher's shop in France, and cannot understand why English butchers do not provide it." A long lean muscle from inside the blade bone? I went to Benny, my butcher, and asked if he had a name for such a cut. "Well," he said, "there are several possibilities. It could be a mush steak or a flat square or even a Scotch tender. Then again, it might be the chuck flap." A chuck flap? The implications are interesting: Babbo's Brasato al Barolo is not only made neither with Barolo nor in Piemonte: it's French.

THEN, WORKING ALONGSIDE Mario one evening, I boldly asked a question that would change my life. I recalled a suggestion he'd made, that at some point I might try being a line cook. When can I start? I asked him.

"What about now?" He addressed the grill cook. "Mark, move over. As of tonight, you're training a new person."

LINE COOK

Imagine a large kitchen at the moment of a great dinner. See twenty chefs coming and going in a cauldron of heat. Picture a great mass of charcoal, a cubic meter in size, for the cooking of entrees, and yet another mass for making the soups, the sauces, and the ragouts, and yet another for frying and for the water baths. Add to that a heap of burning wood for four spits, each one turning, one bearing a sirloin weighing forty-five to sixty pounds, another with a piece of veal weighing thirty-five to forty-five pounds, and another two for the the fowl and game. In this furnace, everyone moves with speed; not a sound is heard: only the chef has a right to speak and at the sound of my voice everyone obeys. Finally the last straw: all the windows are closed so that the air does not cool the dishes as they are being served. Thus, we spend the best years of our lives. We must obey even when our strength fails us, but it is the burning charcoal that kills us. Does it matter? The shorter the life, the greater the glory.

—ANTONIN CARÊME, 1833

Cooking is the most massive rush. It's like having the most amazing hard on, with Viagra sprinkled on top of it, and it's still there twelve hours later.

—GORDON RAMSEY, 2003

9

HE GRILL STATION is hell. You stand at it for five minutes and you think: So this is what Dante had in mind. It is in a dark, hot corner—hotter than any other spot in the kitchen; hotter than anywhere else in your life. Recently air-conditioning was installed in the kitchen, but there is none over the grill during service: how else can it maintain its consistent hot temperature? The light is bad, for no sensible reason except that there isn't enough of it, reinforcing a feeling of a place where no one wants to be—too greasy, too unpleasant. What light there is seems to come from the flames themselves: they are lit about an hour before the service starts and remain burning for the next eight hours. I hadn't thought through the implications of learning the station. I never projected myself into this corner, doing its tasks. Mario said go there; I went and crossed the wall of heat I'd once erected in my mind, feeling the sudden rise in temperature as a crackling sensation on my skin. Close up, Mark Barrett, who had been told to teach me the job, reminded me of a person from another era. His hands had a nineteenth-century griminess. His fingernails were crescent moons of black cake. His forearms were hairless and ribbed with purple burns. His eyes were magnified—he blinked distortedly behind big-framed glasses—and his nose, still bandaged from being broken, was streaked with sooty streams of grease. He could have been a nearsighted chimney sweep. He smelled of sweat.

Mark described the station. There were two cooking devices besides the grill. An oven was to your right to finish the cooking of large items, like a three-inch-thick steak (first on the grill, then in the oven), and a flattop was to the left for preparing the *contorni*—the accompaniments, the rest of the stuff that went on the plate. Mark gestured behind him, at a display of nearly a hundred different small trays of food: herbs, green beans, artichoke hearts, beets, and who knows what else—lots of red and green and yellow. I took them in and thought: never in my lifetime. I looked back at the corner. I was hemmed in by heat. "Watch your jacket," Mark warned. "If you have your back to the grill, the threads melt and stick to your skin." He proposed dividing the duties: he'd do the plating, and I could run the grill. He added that dividing them was the practice of most restaurants, anyway.

I was thrilled. Didn't this mean I would be cooking *all* the meat in the restaurant? (Didn't it also mean I wouldn't have to learn the contorni?)

Mark explained the drill. Because meat needed to rest, it was cooked the moment an order came in, even if it wasn't needed for another hour. (Later, when the order was "fired," the meat would be rapidly reheated and plated.) Orders were called out by the expediter, which was Andy five nights a week and one of the sous-chefs, Memo or Frankie, on the other nights, and the person at each station shouted them back in confirmation. "Two Chinos," Andy would say, the kitchen shorthand for the pasta-tasting menu, and Nick would answer, "Two Chinos." Or Andy would say, "Followed by Love, Sweetie, Butt," meaning that the next course was a pasta called love letters, an order of sweetbreads, and a halibut, and the pasta chef would answer back, "Love," and Dom, the sauté chef, would answer, "Sweetie, Butt"—a sequence of words which, if listened to with any detachment, seemed to constitute a narrative in their own right. Or: "Bar loser, tender," which meant that there was a person at the bar alone (the loser) who had ordered a pork tenderloin.

I shouted back and removed the pork from a "lowboy" refrigerator underneath the display of contorni. Everything was designed to minimize movement, so you could pivot like a basketball player on your planted foot. Raw meat went onto one tray, where I seasoned both sides with salt and pepper. Once cooked, the meat went onto another tray, to rest. The idea was that, at any moment, I should be able to see everything that had been ordered, cooked or not. On the floor was a large plastic bucket of hot soapy water. "Your hands will be covered with oil and fat, and you need to dip them in water to prevent food from slipping through your fingers," Mark said. "Unfortunately, it's usually too busy to change the water." After an hour or so, the water was neither warm nor sudsy. Actually, after an hour or so, the water was not something I wanted to look at, and I closed my eyes when I dipped my hands into it. By the end of the evening, I stopped: my hands seemed greasier after I washed them.

The branzino, which was regarded as the simplest item on the menu, was my first nightmare. The fish (a Mediterranean sea bass) had already been cleaned by someone in the prep kitchen and stuffed with fennel and roasted garlic. The difficulty was the cooking.

The grill was the size of an oven top, with flames coming up from long gas jets, and the fish was put on it at an angle. The angle was important: in the beginning, the fish pointed to the right-hand corner. This was the practice for the meats as well—cooked on the diagonal, always pointing northeast. Once it had cooked, you turned it ninety degrees, which gave it a crusty skin and a grill's crisscrossing hatch marks. This also helped you to know where your meat was at any moment. Stage one: pointing to the right. Stage two: pointing to the left. Stage three: flipped over, still pointing to the left. The last stage, pointing back to the right. It seems obvious, but when the grill gets busy you need the obvious. With the branzino, you did the crisscrossing turn with a pair of tongs, by slipping one tong into the opened cavity and pinching the fish with the other tong from the top (not unlike grabbing a shoe from a fire, although I hated doing it at first, feeling irrationally that I was hurting the fish). Once one side was done, you gently rolled the fish over to cook the other side. The tricky part was the last stage, when you grabbed the head with a towel, slipped one of the tongs underneath the tail, and lifted it to get the final hatch marks. Three things could go wrong. If done lurchingly, the fish broke in half. If done too soon, the skin stuck to the grill. And if done too slowly, your arms went up in flames.

On my first night, a lot of branzino was ordered. By seven o'clock, the hair on my arms had disappeared, except for one straggly patch by my elbow, which had melted into black goo. I broke many fish. Mark's calculation was that twenty-one had been ordered, but thirty-nine had been cooked. For some reason, I couldn't get the hang of diving into an open flame and grabbing a fish by its head. I panicked. I did it too slowly. Then I did it too fast. There were bits of fish flesh everywhere. Before I could go home that night, I was told to walk around the kitchen holding a branzino in my tongs. This made me feel stupid. Everyone else was very busy, and I was walking in circles with a raw fish. But by the second night I seemed to be getting it—such is the miraculous pedagogy of relentless repetition. After fifty or so branzino, even *I* figured out how to cook one.

Learning to cook meat was learning to be at ease with variation and improvisation, because meat was the tissue of a living creature, and each piece was different. In this, I was coming to recognize that there are two kinds of cooks: meat cooks and pastry cooks. The pastry cook is a scientist and works with exact measurements and stable ingredients that behave in a predictable fashion. You mix a specific quantity of milk, eggs, sugar, and flour, and you have a pastry. If you add more butter, your pastry is crumbly; another egg, it's cakey. Meat is done when it feels done. You cook a bird, like a quail or a squab, until you know from experience that it's ready (or, if you're me and don't have that experience, you split one open slightly and peek inside). You cook a steak until your "touch" tells you it's there. This can't be taught by a cookbook—this feel, a thing you're meant to learn until it's stored in your memory like a smell—and I was having trouble getting it. Conventionally, a piece of meat—a lamb chop, say—is medium rare when it has a certain softness to the touch. To illustrate, Mario would press the softest part of his pudgy palm and say that meat should have "this kind of bounce," a pillowy trampoline puffiness, which was no help, because his hands were like no one else's, great mitts of excess, squat and wide. My touch was always heavy-handed, and I burned myself and wouldn't know if it was *the* moment or not.

Then I began touching the meat not for doneness but for undoneness. I put my lamb chops on the grill—five of them, each a different shape—and touched one, even though I knew it was going to be soft and mushy. I turned the chop and touched it again. Still soft, like wet wool. I touched it, again, then again, and again, until finally one chop started to get firmer—but only just. Touched it. Firmer still. Touched it. No change. Touched it. Ready. The undone principle applied to the rib-eye steak as well: after the meat was grilled, it went into the oven, and a timer was set for five minutes. You then took out the meat to see how much it had cooked by putting a metal skewer into it, pulling it out, and putting it against your lips. The skewer was cold. You returned the meat to the oven and reset the timer. Once again, the skewer routine: still cold. Back in the oven, this time for two minutes, until, finally, the temperature changed, not a lot, but perceptibly: it was a little warmer than your lip—just above body temperature. That would be pretty rare. Back in the oven for a minute, and again the skewer routine. Now it was warmer than body temperature: that would be medium rare. A little warmer, and it would be medium. Hot, and it was well done, and your lip, alas, blistered. (Even so, I recommend the skewer technique—better than a thermometer—because you're able to see the whole cut, feelingly.)

I had been at the grill for two months when, in the kitchen's phrasing, I was "hammered." It was June, the hot beginning of a hot summer. The menu had changed again. Lamb shanks and short ribs were dropped. The duck was served not with barley but with a cherry compote and a cherry vinaigrette. Accompanying the branzino was a nine-herb salad, the same one I'd made with Andy, trimming off stems while being pushed around the restaurant: chive and chamomile flowers, parsley, chervil, oregano, lovage, celery florets, the fluffy fur from baby bronze fennel, and something called "salad burnet," an explosion of summer greenness.

It was ninety-three degrees outside. Inside? Who knew. Hotter. Once the service started, the air-conditioning over the grill was shut down. I was told to line up pitchers of water. "Get ready," Frankie said: when it gets hot, everyone orders from the grill. (Why? Because the method says "rustic, outdoors, Italian"? Or because people know that the food comes from the hottest part of the kitchen—let's make the grill guy suffer?) At five-thirty, there was the sound of the ticker machine. "Game time," Memo said. A chart prepared by John Mainieri said that nearly two hundred and fifty people were expected. It turned out to be more, and the biggest number arrived in the first ninety minutes.

One of the mysteries of a restaurant is that there is one thing that everyone seems to order, and you never know what it's going to be. One night, it was two things, duck and branzino, and Dom and I were the busiest cooks in the kitchen—there were twenty-five branzinos and twenty-three ducks. It was a hot night; I understood the appeal of a grilled fish. But why duck? One evening, it was rabbit. Then: no rabbit. Tonight, it was lamb chops, cooked medium (medium rare was easier to feel, and well done was easiest of all—you just killed it).

"Ordering branzino, two lamb medium, one lamb well done, one lamb m.r.," Andy called out.

I answered, "Branzino, two lamb medium, one well done, and one m.r." Why, I remember thinking, does one go to an Italian restaurant and order lamb chops? They're served on Jerusalem artichokes (sliced paper-thin and sautéed) and topped with red onions (cooked in beet juice for extra color), mint leaves, and lemon zest, with a spicy yogurt secreted underneath: that is, all the elements you'd expect from a Mario dish. But they were, finally, just lamb chops.

The chop has a layer of fat along the outside, and, once you've grilled both sides, you roll it onto the rib to render some of the fat away. At one point, there was so much fat that it began to pool hotly under the grill. Then it caught on fire: fat flames, hot and difficult to put out. Although you're cooking meat above a flame, you don't want a fire—the taste is black plastic—and it's imperative to put it out quickly. But there was so much fat that Memo told me to let it burn—it was the only way to get rid of it: just avoid the flames when I was cooking. The bottom of my grill, the part I was always having to lean over, was now on fire. Then the orders came, one after another.

"Ordering!" Andy sang out. "Two lamb medium, squab, tender, rib eye." I spun around, dipped into the lowboy, loaded up, spun back, dropped the meat onto the raw tray, and seasoned it. I lined up the chops on the grill in two rows of five, all pointing to the right, flopped the tenderloins into another corner, put on the rib eye, but hadn't got to the squab when I heard the ticker tape: "Ordering three branzino and two lamb medium." The same routine: another two rows of chops pointing to the right but in a different spot from the first batch (which I had turned and were pointing to the left), because these were medium rare. But what was I to do with the branzino? There was no room.

The ticker tape again. "Ordering three lamb medium, branzino, rabbit." More? I stopped what I was doing—I had to get the new orders on the raw tray to season them, at least that, because otherwise I was going to forget them with the next batch of orders, and if I fell behind I'd throw the kitchen into chaos. Uncooked meat was stacking up because there was no room on the grill. I noticed that Memo had taken up a position nearby, waiting to jump in if I got overwhelmed: what the kitchen calls "the meltdown" or "the crash-and-burn moment," when there's more than your head can remember.

Again the ticker tape. This was starting to feel like a sporting event. Sweat was running off my nose, and I was moving fast, as fast as my concentration allowed, flipping, turning, poking, being burned, one row pointing to the right, another to the left, poking again, stacking up meat here, rushing over the branzinos that had been waiting for a spot, turning, the flames in the corner of the grill still burning, fed by the fat cascading off the new orders. Again the ticker tape. My mind was at full capacity, with only one stray thought, a question, repeated over and over again: What happens if I fall behind? And still there were more: lamb medium, lamb m.r. What's wrong with these people? I was surrounded by meat. Meat on the grill. Meat on the seasoning tray. Meat on the resting tray, in big heaps. So much meat that it no longer seemed like meat. Or maybe it seemed exactly like meat. It was tissue and muscle and sinews. And still more orders. "This is the buzz," Memo whispered, still behind me. "This is what you live for," Andy said, picking up plates from the pass, adding, mysteriously, "it feels really fucking good." And the remark remained in my head for the rest of the night, and I thought hard about what I was feeling: exhilaration, fear, weirdness, some physical-endorphin-performance thing. But good? It was, I concluded, my first glimpse of what Mario had described as "the reality of the kitchen"—a roomful of adrenaline addicts.

And then, as suddenly, the evening's first cycle was finished.

It would repeat itself three more times—three "hits," the last at eleven-thirty—but now there was a break. During a slow period, someone made food: fish, because, in the heat and grease of being hit, it tasted clean and unworldly and healthy. Once everyone in the kitchen wanted the restaurant's spicy calamari preparation, and for a week that's what we had: squid in a chili-hot broth. These were surprising moments, happy collegial meals, the cooks leaning against a counter, eating off the same plate, talking in a mixture of English and Spanish. During these moments, Mark would advise me about how to behave in the kitchen—how not to be noticed, how to observe the hierarchy—and I would ask him about his strange, late-night life that always began in a few hours' time. ("Tuna grilled on skewers of lemongrass," he said once, explaining a meal he'd prepared for a woman on his day off. "It never fails: I always get lucky. But then she realizes that on every other day of the week my evenings begin at two and things don't go much further.")

I got a message that friends had appeared in the dining room, and I wanted to go out to meet them. I had to cool off first. I doused myself with ice water, put a cold towel on my head, and stood in the walk-in. Steam was pouring through my chef's jacket. I removed my headband and wrung it out. Just then, Dom walked in and hooted at the spectacle of a man standing in a hot foggy cloud, trying not to move. I changed my jacket and got a new apron. I'd been thinking about the chemical process of cooking, about transferring heat, and how, in grilling, food is placed above a flame until enough heat has been absorbed to change its molecular makeup. But I now couldn't get it out of my mind that the heat source—the agent of molecular change—wasn't a flame but the entire kitchen. The workplace was an oven. I washed my face and walked out into the dining room, filled with well-dressed civilized couples, and I asked myself, "What's wrong with them, that they all eat lamb chops?"

The transition was abrupt. Cooks don't come here normally. Except for Mario, who spends some of his evening at the bar, prominently, so that everyone sees him (for many, seeing him is a feature of their visit), cooks don't leave the kitchen. The cultures of serving and being served are too different. The cooks' hours are unsocial. Cooks work when others play; they work to allow others to play, preparing meals that they're not earning enough to purchase. It's easier to remain in the kitchen— the contradictions never surface. I saw the cooks go into the dining room only once. John Mainieri had popped in with news. "Hooker on table thirty-two," he said, and one by one all the men filed out and then debated the woman's price. Holly, the new cook and the only woman working that night, had a look of modest moral confusion. "Do I have to look, too?"

The evening service exaggerated people; it was different from the prep kitchen. In the evening, they behaved differently. More sexist, cruder, harder. I liked it. I think everyone there did; the kitchen had a blunt, unapologetic reality. But what did I know? I had survived one night of being hammered. In fact, I had done only half the job. The other half had been done by Mark, preparing the contorni and plating the dishes. I had been so busy, so frantic, so panicked, I'd never once looked at what he was doing.

I became a grill guy. During this time, Mario hadn't been in the kitchen. He was away, promoting something, and by the time he returned I'd been a grill guy for nearly a month. Maybe I'd got cocky. Maybe I needed to be put in my place, but on his first night back he fired me from the line. I'd cooked two pieces of meat incorrectly. The plates were sitting on the pass.

"Your pork is undercooked," Mario said, peeling away slices of a loin and judging them to be too rare. "Replate." He handed me the dish. "And your rabbit"—he pressed the white fleshy loin between his thumb and forefinger—"is overcooked." The pork could be fixed by putting it under the salamander, an overhead grill that is used for reheating and flash-cooking, although it wasn't ideal: the result, while no longer pink, was an unappetizing gray. But the rabbit was beyond repair and was handed to a runner and served anyway. Mario called Memo and Frankie over and spoke to them with his back to me, an inaudible mumble except for one word: "unacceptable." He then walked off in what seemed like a huff and disappeared into the restaurant. Memo, who had been previously doing something in the walk-in, came over and told me to step aside.

"It's not what I would do. It's what my boss told me to do." He then assumed the duties of my station.

There wasn't a place for me to step aside to. I was in a quandary. Should I go home? For the next hour I considered the prospect. It was a long hour. I stood as straight as possible. I was pressed up against a hot oven, the same one I'd used to complete the rib-eye steaks. I was trying to be small. Actually, I was trying to take up no space. People were hurtling past me purposefully. The pantry guy uses the grill to reheat his octopus, and I had to squish myself against the oven to stay out of his way. Finally, in an attempt to be useful, I started seasoning the meat that Memo cooked: that was my job—the salt-and-pepper guy. A little salt, a little pepper, followed by a long wait until another piece of meat was ordered. I reflected: if I walked out, it would be tantamount to saying I can't take it. I wouldn't be able to return. I seasoned more meat.

The kitchen had grown quiet. No one made eye contact with me, which I know because, without anything else to do, that's what I did: I looked around at the people who were not looking at me. The kitchen fosters feelings of comrades in arms—the hours, the pressure, the need to work in unison—and this explicit public dressing-down, the look-at-him-he-fucked-up spectacle of it all, made everyone uncomfortable: it seemed to go right to the heart of what it meant to be a member of the place. Had that been deliberate on Mario's part—to create dissonance, to remind everyone that there are no friends, only results? Had I got too chummy? Maybe Mario was in a pissy mood. Was the pork really so undercooked? I was reminded of something Mark Barrett had once told me: Mario never screams, but when he's in the kitchen he's a different person and has been known to crush people. Then Mario reappeared. (Shit. Now what?) He went to one of the flattops and began making pizzas, "griddle pizzas," the kind he intended to serve at his new pizzeria. The pizzas were his current obsession, and he wanted someone in the restaurant to taste one. He made several, topping them with gobs of white pork fat and hot chili sauce, a squishy melty concoction. Mario took a bite of one and it ran wetly down his cheek, a glistening red-hot rivulet of grease. I watched this because, again, that's what I was doing, watching. He then marched over to my corner and shoved the rest of the pizza into my mouth—quickly and with force.

"This," he said, "is the taste America is waiting for." He was inches from my face. "Don't you think this is the taste America wants?" His head was tilted back, like a boxer's, giving me his chin but protecting his nose. He had a wide, aggressive stance. The look was hard, almost sneering. He stared at me, waiting for me to agree.

"This," I said, "is what America is waiting for."

Satisfied, Mario took his pizzas out to his guests and went home, whereupon Memo ordered me back to the grill. "Mario is gone," he said, "and you have to get back your touch." It was a profoundly sympathetic act—generous, rebellious, correct—and, like that, I returned to the team.

Frankie explained. "It's happened to all of us. It's how you learn. It's the reality of the kitchen. Welcome to Babbo."

The next day, I apologized to Mario.

"You'll never do it again," he said. And he was right: I never did.

10

WHAT DID BATALI learn from Marco Pierre White? And, whatever it was, was it something I should be learning, too? I remained intrigued by the time the two of them had spent together. I then discovered an extraordinary coincidence (one that Batali wouldn't know, because he never spoke to White again): days after Batali quit, White quit, too. He walked out, locked the kitchen door, and never returned. And then, just like Batali, he embarked on a culinary education of punishing penury and duration. In effect, having become a chef, he signed up for a five-year refresher course.

For Batali, the pub had been a lark, an adventure that ended badly but one that showed him how much he had to learn. For White, the stakes were considerably higher—the pub had been his first venue, a dream, and therefore a dream that failed—but its failure was also a turning point: he, too, realized how much *he* had to learn. "There had just been the two of us, me and Mario, just little boys, serving a hundred people a night, kidding ourselves that we were doing a great fucking job. We weren't." In White's view, their just getting by confirmed how much neither one of them knew, and, within twenty-four hours of his quitting, he sought out the nearest Michelin-star restaurant, La Tante Claire, then on the Royal Hospital Road, a quarter of a mile from the pub, and presented himself to the proprietor, Pierre Koffmann: Would the chef be prepared to take him on for no pay? White was there six months. ("I knew he'd stay only long enough to steal my recipes," Koffmann said.) Not satisfied, White sought out the nearest two-star restaurant, then Le Manoir aux Quatr' Saisons in Oxfordshire, run by Raymond Blanc, where once again White presented himself to the chef and where he would remain for most of the next two years. White was about to move to Paris and work at a three-star restaurant, the next logical step, when fate intervened and he found himself with a venue once again—Harvey's, in South London.

But it was the coincidence that I found so compelling, and once I'd discovered it I couldn't stop myself from musing on just how bad life in the pub's dinky kitchen must have been: that no pay would have been more attractive—that *anything* would have been more attractive—than these two outsized, alpha males' being cooped up in that hellhole together. The coincidence was also instructive. This, it told me, is what you have to do to learn this craft: you keep having to be a slave—to not one master but several, one after another, until you arrive at a proficiency (whatever that might be) or your own style (however long it takes) or else conclude that, finally, you just know a lot more than anyone else. I needed to go to London, I concluded. I needed to learn what Mario learned. (Why didn't this process have a name—this self-education by self-abasement or what, in my case, always ended up being lessons got by making an ass out of myself?)

I made five trips. On each one, White taught me things, although they were rarely the lessons I'd expected. In the mysterious way of these matters—in which nutrition, mortality, and traditions of food unite in one continuum—Marco stopped cooking on December 23, 1999, when he turned thirty-eight, his mother's age when she died. Instead, he now teaches cooking to cooks, or invents the dishes they will serve, or tweaks their preparations, or dreams up restaurants that others put up money to run. On one visit, for instance, White and his "people" bought a small place in East London on the day I arrived and over a weekend turned it into a lunchtime brasserie. On another, they'd just bought a grand restaurant in Mayfair called Madame Prunier. Two months later, on another visit, they'd bought a casino on St. James's Street. The extent of White's interests—thirteen restaurants, plus a five-floor gambling establishment—suggests a tycoon-like figure with a staff and a techno-modern office; at the very least a fax machine and an assistant. In fact, White's life is nothing short of impulsive chaos and is a marvel to witness. He has no assistant and would have no place to put one anyway because he has no office. He can't type, has no computer, and only occasionally remembers to carry a cell phone. He has a driver—Takanori Ishii, referred to as Mr. Ishii, who is employed mainly to take White hunting and fishing. Returning from one such expedition, I was shown White's diary—Mr. Ishii keeps it—which consists of appointments to pursue a beast or bird of the forest. Business, such as it is, is conducted over a meal at one of White's restaurants.

I witnessed how this was done after an architect had been asked to draw up plans for refurbishing the Prunier place. White had been expected at the architect's office but was two hours late, which was immaterial since he'd got the venue wrong and showed up at one of his restaurants, Mirabelle. The architect, duly summoned, arrived with a gigantic model depicting the future Prunier, squeezing through the front door with great difficulty, his face saying, I can't believe you made me do this. Once there, he had to fight for White's attention. Without realizing it, White had arranged other lunches at the same time.

"Oh, Will, how good to see you," he said to William Sitwell, the editor of *Food Illustrated*. "Let's get you a good table. Who are you having lunch with?"—a question that surprised Mr. Sitwell.

"Er, well, you, Marco. I thought you and I were having lunch."

A journalist from the *Evening Standard* arrived, greeted warmly by White, who pushed tables together to accommodate him, ordering another risotto and a bottle of wine.

A lawyer arrived. White was confused. He'd had no idea that these people, too, had been counting on having lunch with him.

A journalist from the *International Herald Tribune* appeared (another wine, another risotto), followed by White's wife, Mati ("Oops!"), and then his PR guy, a close friend, Alan Crompton-Batt, whom around the fourteenth bottle White began referring to in the third person feminine—as in "She's never very good after lunch, you know."

I studied White. He was wearing Wellington boots caked with yellow mud, a bulky sweater covered with bits of straw, and a tattersall plaid shirt underneath, cut to be worn with cuff links, but with the cuffs open and extending out like flippers. He had a frenzied, unkempt look—his hair jaggedly pointing in several directions like a bird's nest—that reminded me of demonic paintings of the young Beethoven. He smelled of dirt. He'd spent the night on a gamekeeper's sofa, he explained to each person he greeted. He looked Mediterranean (dark hair, olive skin), sounded working class, and was dressed like a drunken country squire.

DESPITE THE PIERRE in his name, Marco Pierre White is not French and has spent only a day in Paris, at a racetrack. He is half English (born in Leeds), and, like Batali, half Italian: his mother came from Bagolino, near Genoa. She met White's father, Frank—a chef, fond of his drink, and capable of "starting a fight in an empty room"—when she was twenty-two, after coming to Britain for English-language lessons. The father named White's brothers Clive, Craig, and Graham. Marco was named by his mother. "It was like being called Sue. I wanted to be Tom or John. Gary—I would have loved Gary. Or Jerry. Anything, just not Marco Pierre. I used to give friends my pocket money not to use my name. In the end, people grow into their names, don't they? Know any Nigels? They all look like Nigel, don't they?"

White's mother died after giving birth to a fourth child. White was six and witnessed her collapse. Twenty-six years later, in a moment of personal crisis, he set out to recall every small-boy memory he had of her. Most pertain to summers the family spent in Italy and have, in White's telling, the quality of an old black-and-white film. The sky is white, not blue, the figs are gray, a swollen river has no color, the wooden floors the boys sleep on are cold, until finally he returns to Leeds: the green carpet where his mother collapsed, the blue sofa where his father laid her down, the National Health red blanket, the white enamel doors of an ambulance disappearing over a green hill. White's only invented dish is dedicated to his mother, a tagliatelle with oysters and caviar ("In Memoriam Maria Gallina White"), which, tellingly, is more French than Italian in inspiration: its parents are preparations by White's mentors, a "huitres Francine" by the Roux brothers and a "tagliatelle of langoustines" by Raymond Blanc. In Britain, Italian cooking had no charisma; there was no Anglo-Italian tradition comparable to the Italian-American one. It had, in White's phrase, "no rock 'n' roll," especially in 1978, when White, sixteen years old, a failure in school ("I couldn't read—I stood up in front of the class with a book and had no idea what it was saying"), was dispatched by his father to Harrogate, a spa town in the Midlands, and told to knock on kitchen doors until someone gave him a job. Someone did, as a slave at the beck and call of a butcher at the Hotel St. George. Here, studying the "old boy's use of a knife," memorizing it, then gathering up the scraps, and grinding and stuffing them into a pastry for a family meal, White discovered a knack for imitating the people around him, who, invariably, were doing a version of a French classical menu, because a French menu was what you found at the time. It was the moment White began growing into Marco Pierre, on his way to becoming one of the best French chefs outside France. "My mother couldn't have given me a better name."

Harvey's, White's first restaurant, earned its first Michelin star in 1988, the year after it opened. It earned its second in 1990. Five years later, White, cooking in new premises, earned his third star. During this time, he also earned a reputation for theatre: he was so highly strung, so unpredictable, and got himself so worked up (in 1990, he was hospitalized after a hyperventilating panic attack paralyzed his left side) that people came to his restaurant in the expectation that the unexpected would happen. When he talks about this period, he sits up in his chair, his eyes bulge, he raises his voice, and he is animated and indignant all over again. Patrons ("fat ugly bastards") who ordered meat well done were an insult to the kitchen, and on two occasions Marco ordered them to leave his restaurant before they completed their meals. ("It was ten months before I threw out my first customer," White was quoted as saying at the time, adding, with a flair for exaggeration, that, once he'd got the taste for it, he couldn't stop.) When someone ordered fried potatoes, he was so insulted he prepared them himself and charged five hundred dollars. "I used to go fucking mental." He threw things; he broke things; unhappy with a cheese plate, he hurled it against a wall, where it stuck, sliding down as the evening progressed, leaving behind a Camembert smear. When his head chef fell and broke his leg, White assaulted him. "How dare you? If you were a fucking horse, I'd shoot you." Once, frustrated by the kitchen's slowness, he ordered his cooks to stand in the corner at the height of service. " 'You want to be naughty?' I asked. 'All right, then. All of you—in the fucking corner where you will watch me do your jobs. Let your consciences talk to you.' "

I'd heard variations of these stories and, once, fifteen years ago, had witnessed a little of the show myself when I was having lunch at the Criterion, off Piccadilly, shortly after White had taken it over, and caught an earful of the famous rage when the kitchen doors opened and members of the wait-staff scurried out with stricken, pale faces, their shoulders beaten into rounded stoops of humiliation. It was a perversely satisfying thing to have seen (was it what I'd come for?). Being a chef then, White explained, with no small nostalgia, was a license to scream. People screamed at him; he screamed at others. He enjoyed being a screamer and insists that everyone else did, too, with the exception, obviously, of the person being screamed at.

White is no longer a screamer because he is no longer in the kitchen, but he is still highly volatile. At one point, narrating another misdemeanor—an account of his being provoked by a remark he'd overheard by an American diner ("They say the chef's crazy, you know")—White grew so excited that he forgot why he was telling me the story in the first place, except as an illustration of a mind that was wholly unpredictable, even to its keeper. "And so I walked up to his table, and I said, 'So you think I'm crazy? You think I'm fucking mad?' I was starting to twitch. And I said to myself, I'm going to deal with this fucker. 'Can I just say one thing in my defense?' The bloke was horrified. 'Yes,' he said, weakly. So I said, 'I may be many things, but I am not fucking crazy, do you understand? And I'm not fucking mad.' Of course, even I realized that I'd confirmed I was completely fucking crazy."

Even in modest-seeming things, Marco conveys a feeling of recklessness. In June, the two of us were having lunch on a terrace at the Belvedere, a restaurant he co-owns in Holland Park (originally a tearoom run by Lyons, the tea people—one of Marco's tricks is to pick up cherished English restaurants and reinvent them). It was a warm afternoon, and the park was busy. Marco finished a cigarette and tossed it over the balustrade. I thought: Was that wise?

A woman screamed. Then, with great irritation, the same woman shouted: "*Marco!*"

We both stood up and looked over. "Oh, fancy that," Marco said. "It's my wife, Mati. What's she doing there?" She was standing behind a baby stroller and was furious: the cigarette had landed in their child's lap. Both the mother and daughter were staring up at us angrily, the mother with her hands on her hips, the child with her arms crossed in front.

Another time, White invited me to join him on a dawn hunting expedition. We were on our way back to London, White slumped in the front seat, his boots propped up on the dashboard, when he spotted a field of bright blue flowers. They were framed by a break in a hedge and the early-morning sun, big and red and watery, and White told Mr. Ishii to go back so he could look at the field again.

"Isn't it wonderful, Bill. Look at that! They're linseed flowers. They bloomed when the sun came up. They weren't here when we drove by earlier." He then put his boots through the windshield. He'd got too excited. ("Oh, so sorry, Mr. Ishii, you're going to have to get a new one.")

I joined White on another hunt at the end of the summer, on the Lord Rank estate, a sprawling property in Hampshire, south of London. There were plenty of deer ("Look at the light—do you see how it's turning gray-brown, just like the hills, and how the animals' hides blend in with the trees, the sky, everything?"), when Marco spotted four men with greyhounds ("Oh, this doesn't look good"). They were Irish migrant workers, tough-looking—one had a crescent slash-scar across his cheek—and evasive ("We're just out for an evening's stroll"), and the dogs, on their hind legs, eagerly eyeing two does, were for coursing, an illegal blood sport: it involves chasing down a prey and keeping it "on course" until it's exhausted, when the dogs then rip it apart. "In this hand," Marco told them, "I have a cell phone. In this one, I have a rifle. With this hand, I'm phoning the gamekeeper, and if you're not off his property by the time he answers, I am shooting your dogs dead." He lifted the rifle, rested it against the opened window, and, cradling the phone between his head and shoulder, aimed at a dog. He finished dialing the number and released the safety.

"Please," I found myself whispering. "Please leave. He's really, really, really going to shoot your animals. Then he may shoot you." The men departed with gratifying haste. They were justifiably afraid. Everyone could see that White was a beat away from firing. Later I reflected: Why do I continue to accompany this man when he's armed?

But I did. And just before the light disappeared on what would be our last trip, at the end of September, we shot a young buck. "There's nothing like a deer you've shot yourself, is there, Bill? You've had this long love affair with the animal and, because you've done the killing, you can taste so much more of it." I'd persisted because this was what White now did—he chased animals—and I was interested in his views on game, the least adulterated of meats but lean and tricky to cook. This, I decided, was a subject where I'd learn something, and White had much to say, on game birds especially, which I discovered the next night, when we ate grouse in the dining room of 50 St James, the new purchase.

The British are proud of their grouse. The season opens on August 12th, the "Glorious Twelfth," and there is a ritual preparation involving a bread sauce, fried bread crumbs, sometimes rowan jelly, croutons, watercress, and a wine-based sauce, surrounding a bird that is roasted to a specific degree of pinkness. Our waiter was terrified by White and, as though infected by a degenerative disease, lost more of his coordination on each trip to our table (dropping cutlery and napkins, bumping into our chairs), until finally, when the grouse arrived, White relieved the man of his duties and carved up the bird himself. The waiter retreated and watched our table helplessly.

White had a bite of the bird (scooping up some bread sauce). I had a bite (scooping up some bread sauce) and then looked to him to see what he thought. I was probably looking to him to see what I thought, when I was happily surprised by what was in my mouth. You don't taste this kind of thing in American restaurants, where, by law, the game has to be farmed.

"Five days," he said.

"Five days?" I asked.

"Five days. It has been aged five days."

"Right," I said. "Five days."

Almost all meat is aged—aging encourages the growth of an enzyme that breaks down tissue and makes for tenderness, and, as water evaporates, the flavors are intensified. In a wild animal, the inherent gamey flavors are intensified, and in England there is a practice that involves hanging a bird on a hook until its neck grows so rotten it tears in half. This is just before the maggot stage (unless you're unlucky and it's just after). The rotten thing is then served rare with considerable bravado: You think you like game? (Chuckle, chuckle.) I've long suspected a conspiracy. Unlike the United States, where hunting is usually done by the less affluent, shooting in Britain is the pastime of people who own the land. What better way of fending off outsiders than giving them an occasional taste of what they're missing, so repellent they won't be tempted to go back for more when the landlord isn't looking?

White had another bite. I had another bite.

"I'd have aged it a bit more," Marco said, "but not much." He explained that he had experimented with aging. What he said in fact was this: "I've aged birds for one day, two days, three days, four days, five days, six days, seven days, eight days, nine days, ten days, eleven days, twelve days, thirteen days, fourteen days, fifteen days, sixteen days, seventeen days, eighteen days, nineteen days, twenty days, and twenty-one days."

"Your conclusion?" I asked.

"Twenty-one days is too long," he said.

"Pretty nasty?" I asked.

"Fucking inedible," he said.

We carried on. He had a bite. I had a bite.

"The croutons are not correct," Marco said.

I ate a crouton. Marco was looking at his as though he'd discovered an insect impaled on the tine of his fork. "It should have been darkened by the heart and liver," he said. "You make the heart and liver into a kind of paste."

He tasted the sauce. "It's not right, is it, Bill?"

I tasted the sauce. To me, it tasted of—well, sauce. But was it right? I had no idea.

"You can serve the bird with a sauce," Marco explained, "but the sauce needs to be light. Personally, I prefer the roasting juices. That's my sauce: the natural juices of the bird, and nothing else. This sauce is too fancy." He tasted it again. "It is made with a veal stock reduction, isn't it, Bill?"

I tasted it again. Maybe I wasn't very good at this. It really seemed like, you know, a sauce.

"Plus there's a little port and Madeira, isn't there, Bill? And butter at the end. You don't need this kind of a sauce. It's too intense. You can't taste the bird."

He had another bite. I had another bite.

"The bread crumbs—they're disappointing, aren't they, Bill?"

"Are they?" I asked. I duly tasted my bread crumbs. What did I know? Nothing, except that, until now, I had been enjoying my meal: erroneously, I was coming to understand.

"Well, they haven't been cooked through, have they, Bill?" He ran his fork through his bread crumbs, the disgust on his face now undisguised. "They should be golden, the bread crumbs, shouldn't they, Bill?"

He had a bite. I had a bite.

"The butter sauce," he said. "I mean, *really*. It should have been foamy. And the bread sauce—it has been overcloved. A bread sauce, with grouse, is very important," he said, sounding like an exasperated schoolteacher. "You take an onion, right?—a half, studded with a clove. You pour in your milk, bring it to a boil, and drop in your bread. But you don't make it too fancy. *One* clove, do you understand me, Bill? Just one fucking clove. You're not making a fucking dessert." He was becoming agitated. I noticed—just past Marco's shoulder—that our waiter had been joined by other members of the kitchen: you could see in their eyes that they saw the future and weren't liking it.

Marco continued. "And there were too many herbs. A bird can be ruined by herbs. You have to be careful. We're here to eat a fucking bird, are we not, Bill? Isn't that why we're here, to eat a fucking bird?" The waiters had been joined by a cook in a toque. Marco, meanwhile, was inching up to the edge of his chair, and his eyes were bulging again. "We're not here to eat a fucking herb garden. Would I have ordered grouse if I wanted to eat a salad? And the parsley. I mean—look at it. There's no fucking point, is there, Bill?" His eyes were darting round the room wildly. His eyes said: Some fucker was responsible for this, and I'm going to find out who. "I just don't know why it's there. Do you, Bill? Is there someone here who can tell me why this fucking parsley is sprinkled all over my grouse?" Marco was shouting. "If someone will tell me what it's doing there, that will be fine. But I don't have a fucking clue."

He sighed heavily. "It's all about good eating." He said this quietly. "Good smells and good eating. Very straightforward, very English. Nothing fancy, except that it's very hard to get the simple things right. What do I want? The pure taste of grouse. Not too strong. I want the gamey flavor without its being overpowering: I want to taste it here, in the back of my palate, a secondary flavor, evocative of the moors. Everything else is on the platter—the bird, the bread sauce, the bread crumbs, the gravy, and the carving of the bird, right there in front of you. It's very visual. Nature is the artist."

In normal life, "simplicity" is synonymous with "easy to do," but when a chef uses the word it means "take a lifetime to learn." I made a practice, therefore, of asking Marco about really simple things. I once asked him how he cooks an egg.

"Whoa," he said, "an egg is *very* important. Give a chef an egg, and you'll know what kind of cook he is. It takes a lot to cook an egg. You have to understand the egg in order to cook an egg, especially if it's one you want to eat."

For two days, we talked about eggs. How does he fry one, for instance?

"You start by *always* knowing the temperature of your pan—heating the butter in it, not too hot, never letting it froth—then add your egg and start touching it. And you keep touching it: you have to be on top of your temperature, *always*, waiting for the protein to firm up, not fully cooked, and at the last moment you spoon some of the butter on top."

How does he scramble them?

"In the pan, never before—that's where you whisk your eggs and then cook them *very* slowly."

I asked him about other foods. A piece of wild salmon?

"Season the pan, not the fish, and flip it once to release the juices, which you use to cook it—never add oil. Then wipe out the pan before making your sauce."

Foie gras?

"It's all in preventing a shoe from forming—you need to put paper underneath it, otherwise it cooks too fast."

How does he fry a potato?

"Know your supplier. Potatoes are grown on hilly fields. The top fields make the best chips. The bottom ones make shit chips. Soak them for two days to wash out the starch. Chip and blanch them in hot fat until half cooked—the French like *arachide* [ground nut oil] but I use beef drippings—and put them out on a tray. They will carry on cooking without coloring. If you cook them until they color, they'll be hard in the middle. Then put them back in for a second time, which makes them crispy: now they're soft in the middle."

On fat?

"Cooked fat is delicious. Uncooked fat is not. Why do you stuff a goose or duck? Chefs today don't know because they don't learn the basics anymore. You stuff the bird so it cooks more slowly. With the empty cavity, you let in the heat, and the bird is cooked inside and out, and the meat is done before your fat is rendered. Stuff your bird with apple and sage, and the fat is rendered first."

ONE DAY, I met Marco for lunch at the Drones club, his experiment in everyone's-my-friend membership dining, a narrow room, with wood-paneled walls and large paintings of large women with very large breasts. Marco thinks of the place as an extension of his home (on the mantel-piece are pictures of his children and a pair of his shoes), although it also conveys an atmosphere of a gentlemen's club: at lunch, the diners are male, with crisp white shirts and strands of long gray hair tucked behind their ears (at the table next to me, a man was negotiating a deal with someone from Tehran). It also looks like a Las Vegas cabaret bar from, say, forty years ago, done up for New Year's Eve: suspended from the ceiling are pink balloons and two disco balls, and, at night, "the suits are replaced by unbelievable birds." It's the first restaurant where Marco has permitted music—principally Dean Martin. "Don't you think it's like a New York club?" Marco asked me, calling to mind a question he'd put to me when we'd eaten at Max's, another White establishment ("It's like a Paris bistro, innit?"). Marco is terrified of airplanes and has been to neither a Paris bistro nor a New York club. The truth is that Drones was like nothing in New York. It was Marco's idea of how he likes to spend an evening.

Someone gave Marco his mail, which included a letter from Malcolm Reid, a co-owner of the Box Tree restaurant, in Yorkshire, where Marco worked after the hotel in Harrogate. ("The Box Tree turned my life from black and white to color.") Marco put the letter on the table, and I read it upside down and happened to notice how much trouble he was having reading it right side up. His face was in pain. He was stuck on the first paragraph. "It's dyslexia," he conceded. "Very bad dyslexia. I didn't find out about it until my children's teacher told me about their problems—dyslexia is often hereditary—and I thought: Wait a min-ute! This is me!" He mentioned a recent fishing trip with his boys. "We went to get a boat, but I was confused by the sign. It said, 'Mackerel fish-ing, no nemesis.' What the fuck does that mean? No nemesis? I read it again. 'Mackerel fishing. No nemesis.' I don't get it. I read it three more times. I said to my son, Marco, 'Marco, what the fuck is "No nemesis"—this posh big word, from Latin—what's it mean?' " The word was 'omnibus.' A mackerel omnibus, a shuttle boat. Marco had scrambled the letters, finding the "n" and "o" in omnibus and was unable to see the word any other way.

Dyslexia—the term is derived from the Greek to describe a difficulty with words—is a neurological disorder that disrupts the brain's ability to process language. Like most dyslexics, Marco responds best to information in a nonwritten form. He can spend an hour reading a page of *The Times* and remember nothing. "But if you read it aloud, I can recite it word for word." In a dyslexic, the brain's abnormalities at processing visual information often develop into unlikely strengths. Marco has an exceptional sense of proportion. "Those disco balls—no one believed they'd come through the door and they started to take down the frames, but I knew there was a millimeter to spare." He also has a knack for numbers ("It comes from the other side of the brain") and an uncanny visual sense. White has a photographic memory for dishes and, according to Crompton-Batt, an ability to recall every plate served to him in the last twenty years.

I found myself thinking of the way Marco insists on the visual in food preparations—there is a history of diners who have known that he was in the kitchen because the composition of their plates was so uniquely expressive—along with the quirkier moments when he'd been stopped by something he'd seen: sunrises and sunsets and the changing light. A butcher's shop in the hunting season was "a work of conceptual art—hares, rabbits, pheasants, each with their own markings and colorings, hanging on a rail in the window." In talking about his first job, working alongside the butcher, he described the older man's knife skills in exhilaratingly precise detail. "I love the way he opens a piece of meat up with his hands, using his palms and fingers, the whole thing so effortless, and how he then rides the knife through, as though it's a part of his hand. Forget the knife. It's like this. These are your fingertips, right? They just glide through. The knife is just an extension of your fingertips. *That's* knife discipline. *That's* what it's all about. And I used to stand next to this old boy—I was sixteen, and he was in his fifties—and watch him, until finally I'd learned enough that I was told I could do the turkey legs, to bone them and take out the sinews. It was my first important job, and I'd learned how to do it from hours of watching. Then I tied the legs—to get used to working with string—massaging the meat first, to even it out. It was so difficult in the beginning, you're so uncoordinated, until it becomes natural, as if someone has programmed your fingers."

When Marco talked like this, I thought, You're a freak. You're not seeing the same world I see. He's like the tall guy in school, who, because of his height, can play basketball better than anyone else. Marco has, in effect, an exaggerated facility to survive in a kitchen. At some point, Marco learned he had this gift but kept it to himself. "Early on, I realized I had a photographic memory for food but wouldn't tell the chef. I'd be at a new job, working on starters, say, but was always watching and memorizing the other stations so that when I was moved to one I knew exactly what to do. They all thought I was a genius."

Marco's genius might be nothing more than an exaggerated variation of Mario's "kitchen awareness," but it made me realize how this visual facility was not one I had developed, probably because I'm a word guy— most of us are—and for most of my life the learning I've done has been through language. Most metropolitan professions are language-driven—urban, deductive, dominated by thought, reading, abstraction, from the moment you wake and wonder how you should dress for the day and read a weather report to find out. Until now, everything I had known about cooking was from books. A different process was at work when I found myself in a kitchen for twelve hours. I wasn't reading; to an extent, I wasn't thinking. I watched and imitated. The process seems more typical of how a child's brain works than an adult's. It was like learning to throw a ball. For instance, how to bone a leg of lamb. Now I have a picture of Memo's working down the thigh bone with his knife. Or how to tie a piece of meat: there's a brain image. How to use a plastic squirter bottle to create a circle of green dots on your plate (with olive oil) or a dark one (with *vin cotto*) or a rich brown one (with a porcini reduction). How to know that your vegetables are caramelized, that your fennel is braised, that your dandelions, although floppy like a washcloth, are ready. How to recognize that a branzino is cooked because you can smell its skin turning crispy. How to toss a pan so that everything in it turns over. How to toss it so that only the things on the outer rim turn over—like ravioli, which need to be coated with butter, but gently so they don't break. How to compose a plate, how to use asymmetrical items with a sense of symmetry. How, in effect, to learn like a child.

The masochist in me regrets I never worked in Marco's kitchens. He's moved on. He has since sold both 50 St James and Drones, perhaps having discovered there's more money in real estate than in cooking. But in the end I learned some things (over and above the most obvious one, which is that chefs are some of the world's nuttiest people). I learned how much I had to learn.

11

I WENT TO ITALY, where, during my first lunch, I ate a homemade pasta, and my life, in a small but enduring way, was never the same.

I was on a brief culinary tour of the Po River valley—much of my itinerary proposed by Mario—but, at the suggestion of a friend, had made a detour to visit Zibello, about twenty miles from Parma. This was the livestock heartland of Italy. (All day, and everywhere, there was a pervasive porcine smell and invisible particles of something I didn't want to think about clinging to my hair and clothes.) The pasta was prepared by Miriam Leonardi, the fifth woman in successive generations to be running the Trattoria La Buca. Miriam, as she insisted upon being addressed, ran the trattoria in the Italian style of you-don't-cut-an-onion-until-the-dish-has-been-ordered and, after each course, waddled out and asked me what I wanted next. She had just turned sixty-two. She wore a tight-fitting, white chef's cap—more scarf than hat—and had dark eyebrows and a big, hooked masculine nose. She was a little over five feet, with a wide girth, and, moving slowly with her legs apart, had an overwhelming sense of ease and confidence: she has, after all, been making this walk from her kitchen to one of her tables and back again for forty-five years.

My friend had mentioned several dishes in addition to the pastas: eel, frog legs, tripe, and *culatello*, a specialty of the village. Culo means "ass." Culatello translates loosely as "buttness" and is made from the hindquarters of a pig—boned, stuffed into a bladder, cured, and hung for two years in the damp local cellars. The method is deemed unmodern by the U.S. Department of Agriculture, and culatello is forbidden in America. The friend who recommended Miriam's now has developed such cravings for it that he imports her culatello illegally.

I had a plate of it, served with shavings of butter on top. It was a deep red brown, with a light, soft fluffiness—no obvious fat, although obviously fatty—and a piggy intensity I'd never tasted before. Afterwards, Miriam invited me to see her operation, a *cantina* just behind the kitchen where I counted the culatelli, a hundred rows of ten, hanging from the cantina's rafters and being refrigerated by nothing more than the breezes off the Po. I breathed in deeply, wanting to enjoy the romance of what Miriam referred to as the *profumo profondo della mia carne*, the perfume of her meat, and concluded, after identifying the dank smell of aging animal and the ammonia sharpness of the mold adhering to a thousand pig bladders, that the perfume was probably an acquired taste. I mentioned I was trying to cure meats myself, under the instruction of Mario Batali (as it happened, Miriam's daughter, who will be the sixth woman to run the trattoria, had eaten at Babbo on a recent trip to New York, objecting only to the tripe, which didn't "stink enough"). For the rest of the afternoon Miriam kept referring to Mario, "the famous New York chef," and cackling. "He probably uses a refrigerator, he's so smart," she said and laughed uproariously. "What I prepare in my kitchen," she said, by way of definitive explanation, "is what my grandmother taught me. She cooked what her grandmother taught her. And she cooked what her grandmother taught her. You think I'm interested in a famous New York chef?" She said "New York" as though it were a bad taste in the mouth.

I then ate two pastas. One was tortellini, small, complicated knots of dough with a mysterious meaty stuffing. The other was giant pillowy ravioli, distinguished by their thin, floppy lightness. I'd never had anything like them. They were dressed with butter and honey and filled with pumpkin, so that when you bit into one you experienced an unexpected taste explosion. The pumpkin, roasted and mixed with parmigiano cheese, was like a mouthful of autumn: the equivalent of waking up and finding the leaves on the trees outside your window had changed color. The dish was called *tortelli di zucca* (*zucca* means "squash") and was so memorable it provoked me to find out where it came from.

Outside of Italy, you see "ravioli" more than "tortelli," but the two words seem to have been used interchangeably for centuries. Technically, ravioli are what goes inside (it's still possible to get *ravioli nudi*—naked ravioli—which look like little balls of filling, as though the chef that day had run out of flour), and tortelli are the casing. Tortelli are the diminutive of *torte*—small torts or tarts—and a torta is one of the oldest food preparations on the Italian peninsula. In the Middle Ages, the word described nothing more than a container of dough with something inside, probably more like a savory pie or tart than a pasta, although it appears to have meant both a savory pie and a pasta. Recipes for making it appear in the *Liber de coquina,* the first known Italian cookbook, written at the end of the thirteenth century. (Miriam's other pasta, the tortellini, are much smaller—they're the diminutive of tortelli—and date from a later time, probably the early Renaissance, a specialty of Bologna. According to the most common story of their origins, they were invented by a clever baker to look like the navel of a married woman he was having an affair with—done with such verisimilitude that the likeness was identified by the unhappy husband.)

At the time, my research was informal and limited because, although I was learning Italian (I'd been dutifully attending a two-hour Saturday-morning class at the Scuola Italiana in Greenwich Village, conjugating my verbs with flash cards on the subway), I couldn't read it, and most of the early Italian food books haven't been translated into English, except for one, possibly the most important, certainly the most illuminating. (Like Miriam's pasta, this, too, changed my life in another one of those small but enduring ways.) The text, written in Latin, was inspired by a fifteenth-century chef known as Maestro Martino and was called *De honesta voluptate et valitudine,* "On honest pleasures and good health." Tellingly, it had been translated into English only recently, even though, since its publication in the fifteenth century, it had rapidly appeared in almost every other European language and become one of the Continent's first international best sellers. It was also the most influential book on cooking for two centuries.

The author was not a chef but a librarian at the Vatican, a Lombard known as Platina, a scholar, a humanist (his other works include a biography of the popes, a treatise on war and one on peace, one on love and one against it), and an eater. In 1463, a year after he arrived in Rome, at the age of forty-one, he was invited by Cardinal Ludovico Trevisan, a legendary gourmand, to escape a hot summer in the city and go to the cardinal's hilltop retreat in Albano, southeast of Rome. Maestro Martino was the cardinal's cook.

The Maestro, born near Lake Como, was also a native of Lombardy and, like Platina, had only just arrived in Rome (from Milan, where the chef had cooked for the nobles of the city). The two men, probably the same age, established an immediate rapport. For Martino, Platina appears to have been one of the first non-chefs to appreciate a great chef's talents. For Platina, the Maestro's preparations were a revelation—the first time he'd witnessed cooking as "art"—and he spent the summer at the Maestro's side, learning everything he could of this new discipline. His informal study represents, in effect, the first known example of "kitchen trailing" (the lingo for a newcomer following a chef to learn his approach).

The book Platina then wrote is really two books. One is a humanist treatise on nutrition and living well, written in the style of Pliny's *Natural History* as a succession of numbered paragraphs (on sleep or salt or figs), each one ending with a salutary observation: that five almonds eaten before drinking protect you from getting drunk; that an occasional portion of porcupine meat reduces bed-wetting; or that "the testicles of younger animals are considered better for you than those of old animals," except the testicles of roosters, whose testicles are good for you regardless of the age of the bird, especially if served alongside calves' feet and spices, in the Roman style. Then, halfway through, Platina's style changes radically. "Oh, immortal gods," he declares, in the middle of describing a white sauce. "What a cook you bestowed in my friend Martino of Como!" He goes on to extol the Maestro's eloquence and to insist that, in his cooking, we are witnessing the future: an example of the "modern cooking school," where ingredients are taken seriously and subjected to "the keenest of discussion." The rest of the book is given over to the Maestro's recipes, told in a noticeably different voice—the Maestro's, I suspect. In hanging around a chef's kitchen just long enough to steal his recipes, Platina is also illustrating an early example of a modern practice (recipe theft), and, when, four hundred and sixty-four years later, a manuscript of the Maestro's recipes, written in fifteenth-century Italian, was discovered in a bookshop by an American food writer, it became obvious just how extensively Platina had plagiarized his teacher, deviating from his recipes only in error (leaving out an essential ingredient, say) or to add one of his Pliny-like medical observations, as in his addendum to the Maestro's recipe for boiled cannabis meatballs *(offa cannabina)*, a dish "to be fled from, for it nourishes badly, arouses squeamishness, generates pain in the stomach and intestines, and dulls the eyes." (There are several cannabis recipes, a dissonant detail for the modern reader, evoking what would seem to be an anachronistic picture of fifteenth-century stoners loitering in the Vatican Library.)

The Maestro, clearly a gifted chef, was also something of a show-off. When he prepares his blancmange (a sweet, meaty white sauce made from minced capon breast and almond milk), he suggests dividing it in two and adding egg yolk and saffron to one part, so you can then serve two parts together, a swirl of white and bright yellow. (I read this and thought: So Marco Pierre White's extravagant basil-and-beurre-blanc two-sauce French concoction originated in Italy after all.) On occasion, the Maestro's flashiness was too much for Platina. He dismisses the Maestro's roasted eggs, for instance, as a "stupid concoction, one of the absurdities and games of cooks." (The Maestro delicately pokes a needle through the shell of a raw egg and suspends it over the fire, turning it gently, as though the needle were a spit, until the egg is ready to eat.) There was also the Maestro's use of meat to fill his torta, which was controversial, French, and inexcusably pretentious: typical, Platina says, of "the pampered tastes of our contemporaries"—the reference is to the Renaissance practice of grand feasts—when "we are all so given over to gullet and stomach" that people now want their torta made from meat and "birds and whatever fowl they wish, not from vegetables. They are revolted by chard, squash, turnip, parsnip, borage—their native fare."

The hissy digression intrigued me. For Platina, there was already a traditional way of doing things. Your torta and your tortelli were filled with vegetables. That's how things were done. To be fair to the Maestro, most of his recipes are the established ones—established, that is, in 1465. The Maestro's torta di zucca, for instance, calls for grated pumpkin, boiled in milk and mixed with parmigiano, plus a little ginger, cinnamon, and saffron—the familiar spices of the Renaissance. Traditional then, and traditional still: this (minus the Renaissance flavorings) was what Miriam served to me in her tortelli di zucca. In fact, the impression I drew from the Maestro's recipes—and the eerie delight I got from reading them—was not only of difference (the exotic spices, the fascination with sugar, the pot suspended over a fire because there was no oven) but of overwhelming continuity. Now, when I look back at my time at La Buca, I am astonished by what I understand: versions of every dish I ate there can be found in Platina's book.

The tripe: from the Maestro, I learn that the trick is to cook it twice (Miriam's trick as well), not to use salt during the first cooking (which makes it tough), and to add a pork bone ("It will be tastier").

I ate eel. (I returned to La Buca in the evening; people had driven miles for the eel.) For the Maestro, an eel is cooked either on a spit or by braising, when it is then served with parsley and vinegar—which was Miriam's preparation, too.

The frog legs were made in the same way by both Miriam and the Maestro—he rolls his in grain, she rolls hers in bread crumbs, and then both chefs fry them in olive oil. But the Maestro's more colorful presentation, served with a salsa verde *(salsa viridi)* and fennel pollen *(ac feniculi floribus)*—the yellow-green fennel pollen on the bright green sauce—was distinguished by what I now recognize to be his greater visual flair.

"I am not creative," Miriam told me. "That's not what I do. What I do is what has been handed down to me. For ten generations—and maybe longer, I can't tell, there are no records—we've been cooking for people who weren't hungry." Her ancestors learned how to prepare the food she continues to serve in the medieval kitchens of the local nobles. The Maestro's first kitchens—the medieval kitchens of the nobles of Milan—were not far away on the culinary map. Coincidence?

12

I NEEDED TO LEARN pasta. I longed to join a tradition that had already been established and codified by the time a chef had come to Rome from Milan in the 1460s. Besides, I didn't understand how something so simple (flour, water, usually an egg, a pot of boiling water) could be so different in different hands. And by "pasta" I now meant the soft, handmade kind, like Miriam's, what in Italy is called *pasta fresca*— fresh pasta. Dried pasta, *pastasciutta*, now seemed to me an industrial food, made by a machine—not the real thing.

I went back to Babbo. I had been away for three months. "Mario," I said. "I want to work the pasta station."

"You can't," he said. "Look at you. You physically can't do it. You're in your late forties. You're too old. You have to be in your twenties. It's too fast—you no longer have the mind for it." And this same mind, thus warned, sank momentarily into a Shakespearean despair, recognizing the limits of mortality and despondently surveying the many things in life that were now, owing to its age, definitively beyond its capacities, like higher mathematics or the infinitesimal subtleties of molecular biology, until I stopped myself. The issue was boiling food in hot water. How difficult was that going to be? And Mario relented. Which wasn't the same as his agreeing: his last words were "Okay. I warned you"— not exactly an enthusiastic endorsement.

In the time I'd been away, Nick Anderer, the former pasta guy, had gone to Italy and returned. I was in the dining room when Mario and Gina were talking about him. Nick had grown lonely and missed his girlfriend. "He fucked up," Mario said. "He will never have a chance like this. He's just pissed away his future."

"But he did it for love," Gina said.

"Love? What the fuck are you talking about?"

I located Nick, now a line cook during the day at another Manhattan restaurant. ("Unbelievable," Mario said when I told him. "All that promise and he's doing lunches?") Nick had always wanted to be based in Rome and cook according to the fresh-fresh-ingredients philosophy of southern Italy, but hadn't saved enough money to work for nothing and couldn't find a restaurant in Rome that would pay him. He ended up in Milan, at a risotto station at San Giorgio e il Drago (Saint George and the Dragon). In the six months he was there, he mastered risotto. ("The received wisdom is, you don't let your rice stick to the bottom, but in fact that's how you make a good risotto. You want that rustic grinding of the rice against the pan, so that the grains almost burn and break up, releasing the starch. The point is to get out the starch.") But Milan was a modern city, rainy and cold, and very lonely.

Memo had left Babbo. Restaurant Associates, one of the largest catering corporations in America, had offered him a job as executive chef at Naples 45, a busy pizza-and-pasta place next to Grand Central Terminal, frequented mainly by lunchtime office workers. At Babbo, Memo had grown resentful. He'd taken to criticizing the food openly, which, in the military hierarchy of a kitchen, was a profound taboo. "These stuffed guinea-hen legs," he'd said to me once, removing one from the oven with his tongs as though it were a locust carcass and flinging it onto a counter. "This is not three-star cooking. It's a disgrace." (Were they really so bad? I objected silently. They'd been boned and stuffed with bread crumbs, orange zest, and parsley, which I knew because I'd made them.) "Or this poor excuse for a pizza. Look at that thing," Memo said, pointing to a flattop pizza that a pantry chef was making. Mario had been testing the preparation for the pizzeria, which now had a venue, One Fifth Avenue. The address had been cursed by so many failed restaurants that Mario and Joe decided to gut the space and name it after the cross street, which was 8th. *Otto* is "eight" in Italian. Otto was going to open in September: then, October; then, November. Now no one had any idea. A curse, it turned out, wasn't so easy to shake off.

"I don't know what that thing is, but whatever it is, it's not a pizza." The whole kitchen had gone quiet. "You guys are to blame," Memo said, suddenly very angry. "You writers and journalists, you media types, fawning all over Molto Mario. He believes it all. He thinks that everything he touches turns to gold. You haven't noticed he can't cook anymore."

But when I met Memo for lunch at his new restaurant, he said I'd misunderstood. Sure, there were disappointing dishes, but Mario was actually a great chef. "I'd work with him again in a heartbeat. What I couldn't tolerate was Andy. He was the one who didn't know how to cook. He can run a place well enough, but a chef who doesn't know how to cook can't tell you how to fix a dish. That's unacceptable." There had also been the interminable question of Andy's leaving to open a Spanish restaurant. "Mario said, 'When Andy leaves, his job is yours.' Andy was supposed to leave, and he was supposed to leave, and he was supposed to leave, and then, inexplicably, all the talk was about Otto."

Memo's executive chef job came with a big salary ("A hundred and twenty thousand a year—more than Andy was making, which Mario couldn't match because he's a cheap bastard"). But he missed Babbo. "Its flaws are its perfections—it's like a jigsaw, so small that everything is in reach, so intimate that you know the smell of each person's farts." He'd wept when he left. Now he understands that "Babbo's serious approach to dining" is actually quite rare.

"Here, I can't do what Mario calls the conceptual dishes. One day, I made a special: sliced steak served on a caponata. It didn't sell. Why? No one knew what a caponata was. For Valentine's Day, I prepared a wood-oven-roasted lobster on a lemon risotto. I had thirty-five lobsters. I didn't sell one. Valentine's Day was dead. The busiest day in New York, but, for that special meal, everyone went somewhere else. That night, I cleaned the lobsters myself. I cracked the claws with my bare hands. All thirty-five. I wanted my hands to hurt. I wanted them to bleed. Then I froze the meat. I'll make something with it later."

With Memo's going, Frankie became head sous-chef. Tony Liu, the other experienced person in the kitchen, was made the second sous-chef.

Dominic was gone. He'd been hired to run an Italian-American restaurant in the Bronx. ("Go figure," Mario said, still mystified. "Who knew he'd be able to run a restaurant?")

Mark Barrett, my grill coach, was now at the pasta station. He'd lost weight, standing in steam for eight hours. He'd also had corrective eye surgery, no longer wore glasses, and let his hair grow out, which curled prettily in the dampness of his corner. By now, he'd worked every station in the kitchen and had a swagger of sorts, arising out of this new confidence. When a woman entered the kitchen—a new waitress, say, or a stranger making a delivery—he walked over and asked for her phone number. "Hi, I'm Mark, are you married, and would you like to have dinner on Thursday?" The kitchen's long hours no longer bothered him. He'd become a natural inhabitant of nocturnal New York, forsaking daylight and enjoying a city without traffic or crowds, organized around a Lower East Side matrix of late-closing bars and clubs.

To START, Mario suggested I try my hand at making some pasta in the mornings and teamed me up with Alejandro. (At Babbo, fresh pasta is made during the day, frozen in plastic Baggies, and cooked to order in the evening. In my head, I heard Miriam's voice: "Mario Batali is so clever he owns a freezer!")

Our first task was orecchiette. *Orecchiette* is a diminutive of *orecchio*, which means "ear," and is regarded as one of the easiest pastas to make. The dough is made of nothing but water and flour (semolina, cruder than the all-purpose stuff), and you roll it out by hand until it's a white tube. You then chop the tube into bite-size segments and crush each one on a ridged piece of wood with your thumb. Like a child's magic trick, the pasta changes shape under the pressure and when it's removed it has ridges underneath and is shaped like an ear (unless it's like the one I peeled off my thumb that first day, in which case the ridges looked like a tic-tac-toe board, because I invariably had to do the thing twice, and wasn't able to line it up correctly the second time, and the ear was all large and distorted, a floppy flap of dough, more like a cartoon elephant's ear than a normal ear, because my hands were so clammy from the excitement of my finally making pasta that the damn thing wouldn't come off my thumb). At the end of the session, Alejandro showed Mario examples of what I'd produced—mine were fatter than normal orecchiette, not squished enough, and verging on mutant—to see if they could even be served that night. Mario examined them. "Oh, they're okay," he said and chuckled in a way that meant, "Bill, this is the easiest pasta to make, and yet—"

Eventually I mastered the squishing technique. I also discovered that after you've made a couple thousand or so of these little ears, your mind wanders. You think about anything, everything, whatever, nothing.

Such moments illustrate what is referred to as the Zen of making pasta, which is also a way of saying that making pasta can be very boring. I was rather earnest during this phase, so I found that when my mind wandered it tended not to stray too far from the matter at hand. Why, it asked, would anyone want to eat a thing that looks like a squashed ear? So I studied each one and thought hard about its shape. The explanation I came up with involved belly buttons. As with belly buttons, I concluded, there are two kinds of pasta: innies and outies. The innies, like ravioli and tortelli, are designed to surprise you with goodies inside: you bite and discover a juicy something previously hidden from view. The outies are designed to "hold on to" the goodies from the outside. People like to eat orecchiette because they retain a tiny cup of sauce in their ears, I decided, while ingeniously holding on to a little more on the bottom, along the ridges.

Having arrived at this illuminating philosophical distinction, I felt it was appropriate that making innies should be my next task. These were what I really wanted to make. (Miriam's tortelli di zucca were innies.) I had tried to produce my own batch once—a long-ago dinner party, another failure—which might have accounted for my overzealous interest in them. I don't know why I'd thought I could make a fresh pasta—some cookbook must have made it seem easy. Friends arrived and found me in the kitchen—a pot of boiling water fogging up the windows, walls dripping from the wetness—pleading with twelve porcini-filled ravioli to hold their shape. They were my first efforts, and after I'd put them on a wire rack their doughy casings melted and disappeared, vanishing into the humid air, until only mushroomy mounds remained, lodged in the gaps of the wire mesh.

Babbo's innies had a variety of exotic names, although I now knew that fundamentally they were all just different kinds of ravioli. Mario's version of Miriam's tortelli di zucca, for instance (which he filled with butternut squash instead of pumpkin), were cut into circles and called lune. Another pasta, one filled with dried cod, were called mezzalune: so named because they were folded over like half-moons. There were also "love letters," with sweet peas and mint, shaped to look like air-mail-sticker-size rectangles with zigzaggy ends. (The name was a poeticized mutation of a pasta called francobolli, or postage stamps.) In fact, there were so many exotic names and weird shapes that I need to pause for a moment and indulge in a bit of cultural speculation. Postage stamps, half-moons, moons, little ears, belly buttons: what exactly is going on? Or put another way: What other country serves up its national cuisine in the form of little toys? And what does that tell us, that Italians seem always to have been playing with their food? When you make tortelli, the thirteenth-century *Liber de coquina* says—and with such unrestrained glee that you're left to conclude that this food-as-a-plaything situation has been a feature of the Italian meal for a very long time— you can shape the dough into "horseshoes or brooches or rings, the letters of the alphabet, or any animal you can imagine." Is the secret appeal of pasta, the world's greatest comfort food, in its evocation of childhood? Must an Italian dinner always include a version of animal crackers? Pasta intimidated me. There was a mystery to it that I wasn't fathoming—the secrets of a nation's romper room, a too-intimate history of meddling madonnas. And, frankly, if I couldn't recognize all these shapes (I mean, really—belly buttons? postage stamps?), how would I ever learn to prepare them?

Today I feel more sanguine about the prospect, if only because I've come to suspect that Italians don't know all the shapes either. Even if you've grown up eating bow ties, guitar strings, and pens, you never learn all the pastas, because there are too many—hundreds, according to Amelia Giarmoleo, the curator of Italy's national pasta museum in Rome, the Museo Nazionale delle Paste Alimentari, where you can lose yourself for several hours marveling at centuries of food toys, exhibited like butterflies in a lepidopterist's collection. But there is a basic pasta vocabulary—that's what most Italians master—which allows them to interpret all the variations they encounter for the rest of their lives. ("Oh, I get it, it's like penne, but gigantic and with ridges.") And, if nothing else, I was determined to learn the essential lexicon.

THE SAUCE that an outie clings to is a wholly different branch of philosophy. Usually this will be a ragù, and I'll be honest in this matter: until I started working at Babbo, I didn't really know what a ragù was, except that I'd seen unappetizing jars of it on supermarket shelves. I'd had no idea it was such a serious business.

An Italian ragù and a French ragout are more or less the same thing. In any language, the process involves taking a piece of meat and, as it was described to me in the vernacular of the kitchen, cooking the shit out of the fucker. Both the term and the technique, I've since discovered, are at the heart of a centuries-long debate between advocates of French cooking and those of Italian in the we-were-there-first stakes. The rivalry, felt more acutely by the Italians, who believe they are seen by the French as a tribe of amusing primitives, might be summarized thus: In the history of European cooking, the Italian peninsula was first to establish a sophisticated high cuisine, starting with Maestro Martino in the fifteenth century. Then, Italians claim, their secrets were packed up and transported over the Alps by Caterina de' Medici when, in 1533, she married the man who became Henry II of France.

Afterwards, France underwent its own cooking renaissance, culminating in the post–ancien régime Olympian dining events of Antonin Carême—elaborate aspics, all-day sauces, architectural desserts—while Italians, having concluded that the New World fruit known to us as the tomato wasn't poisonous after all and even had promise as a sauce, sank into a two-hundred-and-fifty-year culinary depression and, in outright violation of their chauvinistic character, started imitating the French. All those *alla* constructions—risotto alla Milanese, pollo alla cacciatora, bucatini all'amatriciana—are the Italian equivalent of the French *à la* and arose out of a nervous effort to sound fancy. Other food words changed, too, including *sugo*, which became a ragù. In 1903, the now very grand cuisine of France was codified encyclopedically in Auguste Escoffier's *Guide culinaire*, which remains the seminal text of the "classical" approach. The seminal text in Italy, *La scienza in cucina e l'arte di mangiar bene* ("The Science of the Kitchen and the Art of Eating Well"), written at the same time, was a bunch of home recipes gathered by a textile merchant named Pellegrino Artusi. Escoffier, drawing on his experience as head chef of the grand hotels, tells you the two hundred ways to make a sauce. Artusi, drawing on letters from country housewives, tells you about belly buttons and tortellini. The French have become professional, scientific, and urban. The Italians are improvising amateurs, following rustic preparations handed down for generations. The Italians, it could be said, were still playing with their food.

Fundamentally, a ragù is an equation involving a solid (meat) and a liquid (broth or wine), plus a slow heat, until you reach a result that is neither solid nor liquid. The most famous ragù is a Bolognese, although there is not one Bolognese but many. Gianni Valdiserri confessed to me when I was in Porretta that when he and Betta married—Betta pregnant, sixteen years old, and still in school—he was concerned that, in their hurry, he hadn't tasted her ragù. This ragù, which she'd learned from an aunt, had been passed down through many generations of her family and would be different from the ragù that Gianni had grown up eating, his mother's, which was profound and complex and touched something deep in his soul. He also knew that he'd never be able to teach Betta to make someone else's. A ragù, he said, was a very personal thing. So imagine his happiness when he first ate a ragù made by Betta and discovered that, yes, it was different from his mother's—and better.

A Bolognese is made with a medieval kitchen's quirky sense of ostentation and flavorings. There are at least two meats (beef and pork, although local variations can insist on veal instead of beef, prosciutto instead of pork, and sometimes prosciutto, pancetta, sausage, and pork, not to mention capon, turkey, or chicken livers) and three liquids (milk, wine, and broth), and either tomatoes (if your family recipe is modern) or no tomatoes (if the family recipe is older than Columbus), plus nutmeg, sometimes cinnamon, and whatever else your great-great-great-grandmother said was essential. (The only meat in Miriam's, for instance, is sausage, cooked slowly with butter and oil, plus her own homemade tomato sauce and the slightest hint of garlic, one clove, removed before the cooking is completed.) In any variation, the result is a texture characteristic of all ragù: a crumbly stickiness, a condition of being neither solid nor liquid, more dry than wet, a dressing more than a sauce or, as Mario describes it, a "condiment," a term he uses for his American staff to emphasize that what a pasta is served with is—like ketchup on a hot dog—never more important than the pasta itself. (And yet still very important: Gianni speaks of the erotics of a new ragù as it cooks, filling the house with its perfume, a promise of an appetite that will mount until it's satisfied. Actually, what he said was the cooking of a fresh ragù *mi da libidine*—gives him a hard-on—and until he can eat some he walks around in a condition of high arousal.)

According to Betta, the Bolognese ragù made at Babbo is incomplete, which I suppose she should know since she taught Mario how to make it. "There's no prosciutto!" she told me, appalled, when I asked her about the dinner she and Gianni had eaten there on their first trip to

New York in 1998—a criticism that, when I repeated it to Mario, astonished him: "She could tell that from eating it one time!" The prosciutto-less ragù is served with pappardelle, a long flat noodle made (Betta also observed, even more horrified) "with a machine." None of this, frankly, meant a lot to me when finally I was allowed to work at the pasta station. What mattered was that pappardelle ("Pap!") was the easiest order to do, if only because there wasn't a lot that could go wrong. I put two scoops of ragù in a pan and added water, a dollop of uncooked tomatoes, and some butter—that was it. When the dish was done, I sprinkled on cheese and parsley (referred to as "chiff," for chiffonnade, to describe the feathery way it had been chopped). In fact, all the ragù dishes were fairly straightforward. The gnocchi ("Ox!") was served with an oxtail ragù (a stringy beef stew), the love letters ("Love!") with a lamb sausage ragù, and the orecchiette ("Ork!") with a pork sausage ragù plus a tongful of broccoli rabe.

From the start, the station was a test of the mind's capacity to hold many things in place without ever having to think about them. There was a cheat sheet taped to the wall. Evidently, everyone needs a cheat sheet at first, a reassuring thing to discover, and looking at this one—a page of once yellow legal paper rendered into a greasy transparency by some wild olive oil moment—I was relieved to see that my predecessor had been just as clueless as me. The ingredients for each dish were written out with a blunt pencil, along with crude diagrams. Two concentric circles illustrated the hollow bucatini, for instance (*buco* means "hole"; *bucatini*, "little holes"). A flattish oblong was linguine (*lingua* means "tongue," and *linguine* means "little tongues"). The chitarra was a thick, rough line, like the bass string of a guitar. Most were misspelled phonetic approximations. "Ork" was orecchiette, although no person, learning the station, would have known the word orecchiette, mainly because it was never used. What you heard was "ork," and you never saw a written version, because, unlike every other station, where ticker-tape printouts were tacked up along a shelf just above eye level, this one had no place to stick the little slips of paper, which would have wilted in the steam and fallen off. Besides, the orders came so fast you had no choice but to keep them in your head, however they happened to be spelled when you put them there.

The problem was the variations. To rehydrate the oxtail ragù, you added water and a half scoop of uncooked tomatoes—just as you did with the Bolognese—but no butter. Also, although you sprinkled cheese and parsley on at the end, the parsley was whole leaves, rather than the chopped-up feathery kind. Why? I didn't know why. I still don't know why. To fuck with my head—that's why. And to the lamb sausage ragù that went with the love letters you added a little water and butter, just like the Bolognese, but this time no tomato, although you then finished it with cheese, like the others, but with mint leaves rather than parsley—after all, the love letters were stuffed with mint and peas. What didn't make sense was the red chili flakes: you were meant to add these, too. Can you imagine—chili flakes in your love letters?

"There's no chili in your love letters," Frankie said to me. It was Andy's day off, and Frankie was the expediter. He had tasted the ragù with his finger after the dish was plated but allowed a runner to carry it into the dining room anyway, because it was going out with three other dishes and there was no time to prepare a new one without holding up the whole table. But he wasn't happy. "How could you fucking forget the chili—again?"

I turned to Mark. "How could I fucking forget the chili again?"

He looked at me flatly. "I've got no idea how you could fucking forget the chili again."

The station wasn't easy. The kitchen counts on its running smoothly, and there wasn't the luxury of having a journalist-tourist, infatuated with the mystique of what he kept referring to as *pasta fresca*, unless he was never going to make a mistake. It could be tense. "Did I just burn you?" Frankie asked one night when he was sautéing a pan of soft-shell crabs, which swell up in the heat until they explode, hurling water and hot oil in unpredictable directions. And before I could formulate a witty reply he said, "Good," and then emptied the leftover oil in his frying pan with such violence that it splattered on the floor and me, burning me again.

A FILLED PASTA is usually not served with a ragù because the pasta itself is a vehicle for ragù. (In the belly button dichotomy, it's an innie.) What you put on the outside to dress it was, therefore, very simple— usually a butter sauce. When Mario was in the kitchen, he called for small amounts of butter in the butter sauces and was always telling the guy at the pasta station to use less. When Mario was not in the kitchen, Andy called for immoderate quantities and was always telling the pasta guy to use more. (Once I protested until Mark shushed me. "Never challenge the person in charge, especially when he's wrong, or he'll make your life hell. He'll pile on more orders than you can handle. He'll find fault with everything. He'll make you redo dishes that were cooked perfectly the first time.")

A butter sauce is an emulsion. "Emulsion" was another term I incompletely understood, although I knew enough to know that I was creating one when I added butter to broth to make a meat sauce at home. In French cookbooks, this was a tricky moment, and great stress was put on everything being exactly right: the broth very hot, the butter very chilled and cut into very small bits, to be incorporated, one by one, into the broth with very steady whisking. The fear was that the emulsion might "break up" (whatever that meant). It's different in a restaurant: there you seem to be doing so many things, one after the other, that the thought never occurs to you that one might be trickier than another.

This is what happens. You're told to prepare an order of tortelloni ("Tort!"). You drop eight pieces into a basket bobbing in boiling water. Fresh pasta is less fussy than dried, and the cooking objective is different: none of this al dente business. You want a food that's soft and yielding rather than one that resists your bite. For the tortelloni, that's about three minutes, but you can leave them in for much longer. To prepare the sauce, you take a pan (from a shelf above your head), scoop out some butter (from a container against the wall), and plop it in. As at all stations, your hope is never to move your feet. You then tilt the pan over the pasta machine and scoop up some of the hot water. This was something of a finesse movement: dipping the trowel part of the tongs into the boiling water and flicking it so it landed in the pan and not on your forearm—which, of course, was where mine regularly arrived, causing it to swell with red welts, unless I missed altogether. I got Mark more than once, startling him every time.

Next, you add a flavor, an herb or citrus: orange zest for the tortelloni (or five sage leaves for the lune, or five scallions for the mezzelune— something strong but simple). You take the pan, which now looks pretty disgusting—a pool of cloudy pasta water, a lump of butter melting along the rim, some desiccated orangey twigs—and put it on the flattop and swirl. You check the basket in the pasta cooker: a few tortelloni have risen. You go back to the pan and swirl it. The contents have changed. With the heat and the pan movement, they are a yellow-orange soup (yellowish from the butter, orange-ish from the zest). You recheck your basket: the tortelloni are floating. You go back to the pan and swirl it again—almost ready, looking like a custard. But three more orders come in, you deal with them, and by the time you get back to the pan, just thirty seconds later, the liquid is mottled: still a sauce but a diseased one, very ugly, not something you want to eat. It is now broken. To fix it, you give the pan another tong flick of water (or perhaps a few tong flicks, until one lands) and return it to the flattop, and with one miraculous swirl the mottled texture melts away.

This is an emulsion: an agreement between two unlike elements (butter and water), achieved by heat and motion. If you get it slightly wrong—as when the sauce starts to dry out, destroying the balance between the fat and the liquid—the unlike elements pull apart and break up. Sometimes, during slow moments, I deliberately let my sauce get ugly, so I could witness its snapping back into condition with a small flick of water, like an animated chemistry lesson. Once, I was caught in mid-reverie.

I was making a mushroom sauce that illustrated two things that were characteristic of the station: how to use heat and how to stop it. Like most sauces, this one was prepared in two stages and used only a few ingredients: mushrooms (yellowfeet, although any wild mushroom works), some fresh thyme leaves, a finely chopped shallot, a little butter. To begin, you needed lots of heat. You put your pan on the flattop until it got really hot, until it darkened, until it seemed as though it might start melting, and then you splashed it with olive oil—the pan went smoky very quickly—followed by the mushrooms. Then: nothing. You didn't move the pan until you detected the sweet wood smoke smell of the mushrooms caramelizing. The mushrooms now had a crunchy, sugary crust, not burned but on the verge of burning. You sprinkled the pan with the shallots and thyme, held it until they reacted to the high heat, and then shoveled in enough pasta water to stop the cooking: the pan hissed, steamed, and went quiet. That was Stage One: from high heat to no heat. Stage Two was when the order was fired. You retrieved the pan and made an emulsion: the butter, the swirling-swirling routine, until the mushroom water became a sauce sticky enough to adhere to a pasta.

The reverie occurred at the end of Stage One, when I lifted the pan off the flattop and sprinkled it with the thyme. What can I say? I loved this moment. For a few seconds, nothing happened. The leaves were on the hot metal of the pan, taking in the heat. Then, one by one, they swelled, barely perceptibly, and exploded, a string of tiny explosions, like minuscule pieces of herby popcorn. And with each pop there was an aromatic eruption of thyme. I closed my eyes and put my face into the pan, breathing in the exploding herb leaves. I don't know how long I stood there.

"What the fuck are you doing?"

I opened my eyes. It was Frankie.

"What the fuck are you doing?" He was standing inches from my face. The others were staring at me.

"I like the smell of the popping thyme," I said weakly. I was expecting scorn or a string of profanities, mockery at the very least. Instead, Frankie seemed surprised and didn't know quite what to say. His face became soft and puppy-dog-like.

"Oh, well, then," he said, finally. "That's all right." I think he was embarrassed.

IN ALL THESE DISHES was an ingredient you can't get at home: the restaurant's pasta water. At the start of the evening, it was perfectly clear—you could see through it to the shiny bottom of the pasta cooker—and very salty. ("Like the sea," Mario always said, and then reminded you to keep dipping your finger into the boiling water, tasting it and adjusting it, until it evoked a childhood memory of your first trip to the beach, but I never mastered the quick dip or, for that matter, thought of my childhood—only that I'd just burned my finger again.) Midway through the service, the shiny bottom of the pasta cooker disappeared. This was the cloudy phase, about two hours before the muddy one, when the water ceased being normal water and became an increasingly thick vehicle for soluble starch: yucky-sounding (and yucky-looking) but in fact rather wonderful. By the time the water reached this condition it behaved like a sauce thickener, binding the elements and, in effect, flavoring the pasta with the flavor of itself. Even so, there was no escaping the fact that the water the pasta was cooked in at the end of the night was very different from what it had been at, say, six o'clock. ("I would never," Elisa confessed once, "order a pasta after ten.") Just how different was evident when you finally had to clean the "bitch," as the pasta cooker was called when you finally got to know her—my task, and an indication of my position in the hierarchy. Later, it slipped out that, when I wasn't there, I was known as the "kitchen bitch." Nice touch, I thought, as I mulled over the relationship between my status and my end-of-the-day responsibility: the kitchen bitch, cleaning the kitchen's bitch.

For all that, it was a straightforward contraption. After you removed the pasta baskets, it was just two sinks and a large, gas-fired heating element. The difficulty was in what you found at the bottom of the sinks— usually a layered expression of the restaurant's archaeology, composed of, say, goat cheese (because the tortelloni always leaked), butternut squash (because the lune lost a little as well), and tiny bits of everything else, including shellfish (where did they swim in from?). Also, the cooker was hot—furnace hot. Even when the heating element was turned off, it remained very hot, and the green abrasive "scrubby" that you used to clean it steamed on contact, softened slowly, and eventually started to cook, like a piece of plastic ravioli. It's not that you get hot, cleaning the bitch; you just don't cool down. You're already very hot and have been very hot for many hours. I have never been so hot. It would take hours before my body temperature started to drop. At four in the morning, when I finally went to bed, I continued to radiate heat, my insides a meaty something still cooking, my mind unable to stop the recurrent thought that this was my life: I'd become a sausage.

Why don't more people use pasta water at home? Sometimes I thought it should be bottled, because there is no way that your home water could ever achieve the starchy viscosity of a restaurant's. It would be cheap—being liquidy leftovers—and the jar should be very large, probably darkly tinted, like a wine bottle, because there would be no reward in looking too closely at what was floating inside.

The thought also made me curious about the moment in the history of American cooking when efficiency won out over taste and, instead of using a pair of tongs and pulling the spaghetti straight out of the pot, people started using a colander (an evil instrument) and letting all that dense, murky rich "water" rush down the drain. The practice is described in the original, 1931 edition of *The Joy of Cooking*, in its "Rules for Boiling Spaghetti, Macaroni, Creamettes and Noodles," along with the even more alarming one of taking your colander full of spaghetti (rather mushy, since you've boiled it for an hour) or macaroni (easy to chew, after being boiled for twenty minutes) or creamettes (no longer a supermarket item, alas, but once the essential ingredient in a baked creamette loaf) and rinsing it in cold water—oh, heresy of heresies—just to make sure nothing is clinging to it. I hold the author responsible for the many plates of sauce-heavy spaghetti that, as a feature of my own American childhood, were prepared by my mother, who was born two years after the cookbook was published. To be fair to both my mother and the author, a plate of spaghetti with meat sauce remains an eternal comfort food, even if the meal was not about the pasta. Still, the cultural disregard for the noodle contributed to my ignorance of it. It also contributed to my prejudice about dried pasta, a prejudice that I finally overcame in an epiphany of sorts.

The occasion was an impromptu late-night family meal—two family meals, actually. The first was a gigantic pan of linguine alle vongole (linguine with clams), which Mark was making for the runners and dishwashers (each one took a plate and put a bowl on top to keep it warm, and then hid it behind a pot or underneath a towel—too busy finishing up to eat the food now but too mistrustful of others to leave it out). The second meal was prepared by me, a bowl of steamed cockles for the restaurant manager and wine steward: the executives in charge and entitled, by virtue of their positions, to be served at a table out front.

I'd become curious about the difference between cockles and clams. Historically, cockles are the larger of the two shellfish and found around the Mediterranean. Clams, which proliferate along the New England coast, tend to be everything else. Generally, if you're perplexed by a shellfish, call it a clam. In practice, the two names are used interchangeably; at Babbo, they were interchangeable, because they were the same shellfish and came neither from the Mediterranean nor from New England but from New Zealand, every Monday and Thursday morning. These New Zealand "cockle-clams" were small, purple, and round, and prized for their uniformity: no variation in shape, no variation in cooking time, which, with your burner on at full blast, was exactly six minutes, a little less than the six minutes and thirty seconds it took to cook the linguine which, it turns out, wasn't actually linguine, which takes nine minutes, but linguine *fine* (a thin, faster-cooking cousin). Frankly, I hated both shellfish dishes. The preparations were so fussy: one ("Ling!") was started with garlic, red onions, and red pepper flakes; the other ("Cock!") with garlic, red onions, and slices of a fiery green pepper. Green pepper? Red pepper? Do you think you'd taste the difference? One took butter, the other didn't. One took white wine, the other tomato sauce. One finished with parsley, the other with Thai basil. Why Thai basil? Why does parsley work with New Zealand cockle-clams when they're called clams and served atop pasta but not when they're called cockles and served in a bowl without it? And, for that matter, why was I preparing cockles anyway? Where was the pasta? Why? Why? You know why.

By now, I had flash cards for all the restaurant's preparations and lost a morning memorizing the supposed and, to my mind, wholly contrived differences between Ling and Cock. It wasn't that I was having trouble remembering which was which—after all, it was the same shellfish in both dishes. I was having trouble doing that instantaneous, unreflected recall required by the pasta station. You got in trouble and fell behind if you switched your pan from your left hand to your right (it took too much time); you got in trouble if you had to look for your tongs (too much time); you got in trouble if you had to ask or wonder or remember, so you aspired to have everything memorized on such a deep level—like language or the alphabet or numbers—that you never found yourself thinking. Also, frankly, I didn't get the point of putting shellfish in pasta. You can't eat the shells, can you? And the eating was all so elaborate. You needed a bib, an extra plate, a finger bowl, an extra napkin, and an extra quantity of vigilance just to make sure that you didn't stick a shell in your mouth. It seemed a hygienic exercise, like bathing— in any case, not dinner.

I had another realization that night, which arose from my noticing that, when it gets late, the cooking that matters is for the staff and not for the diners who have just straggled in. Around midnight, the kitchen was something of a demilitarized zone, meant to be closed but still serving food, owing to the insistence of the maître d', John Mainieri, who sometimes accepted late seatings and was openly loathed by members of the kitchen staff as a result: they hissed at his appearance, whistled, and erupted in a braying chorus of posh-sounding "Hallo!"s (a distressing thing for me to witness, not least because I was fond of John). In general, it is possible to argue your way into a restaurant just as the kitchen is closing. But I urge you, the next time you find yourself trying to persuade a maître d' to accommodate you—bowing abjectly and apologizing, citing the traffic, the crowds, a fluent stream of obsequious servility, a crisp banknote in your palm—to recognize that the members of the kitchen know you're there. They are waiting for your order, huddled around the ticker-tape machine, counting the seconds, and heaping imprecations on your head because you cannot make up your mind. They are speculating—will it be something light, a single course, perhaps? ("That's what I'd order," someone says, and everyone else loudly agrees.) Will I be able to drain the pasta machine? Will the grill guy be able to turn off the burners? Or will the diners—and late ones are referred to simply as "those fuckers"—be so clueless as to order a five-course tasting menu? It happens, and the response of the kitchen—a bellowing roar of disgust—is so loud everyone in the restaurant must hear it. By now the kitchen is different. At eleven, beer is allowed, and for nearly an hour the cooks have been drinking. The senior figures have disappeared: Andy is downstairs doing something with a computer; Frankie is doing something in the walk-in. No one is in charge. The people remaining are tired and dirty. The floors are greasy and wet—this is when the walk-in door swings open and someone is suddenly airborne. The pasta machine is so thick and crud-filled that the water has turned purple and is starting to foam. Do you need more details? Let me rephrase the question: Do you think, if your meal is the last order received by the kitchen, that it has been cooked with love?

But then—in the rush to clean up, the washing, scrubbing, mopping; the search for one-quart containers (why are there never enough one-quart containers?); the crash of a tray; the speed with which you clear away the food at your station, wrapping up some, throwing away most, including the ingredients needed to cook that tardy, last remaining order (sorry, Jack, that's what you get for showing up so late); the trash talk about the maître d', who has returned to see if there's a family meal; the persistent hunger of the dishwashers (they have nothing at home); the late-night, slightly blurry, slightly drunken frenzy of a kitchen closing up, wanting to be done, wanting to get out—amid all this, I got the point of pasta with clams.

This is what happened: Mark, having cooked up a large quantity of linguine for its regulation six minutes and thirty seconds, emptied it into a pan of New Zealand cockle-clams, sloppily dripping lots of that starchy water on them in the process, a big wet heap of pasta on top of several dozen shellfish. He swirled the pan, gave it a little flip, swirled it again, and then left it alone so that it could cook, bubbling away, for another half minute. (This was curious, I thought, watching him—you don't normally leave a pan of pasta on the flattop.) Then he took a strand and tasted it. He gave me one. It was not what I expected. It was no longer linguine, exactly; it had changed color and texture and become something else. I tasted it again. This, I thought, is the equivalent of bread soaked in gravy. But what was the sauce? I looked at the pan: the cockle-clams had been all closed up a few minutes earlier, and as they cooked their shells had opened, and as they opened they released the juices inside. That's what I was tasting in this strand of linguine: an ocean pungency. "It's about the sauce, not the little snot of meat in the shell," Mario told me later. "No one is interested in the little snot of meat!"

Most pasta dishes are about the pasta, not the sauce (that *mere* condiment): that lesson had been drilled into me over and over. But here, in this strand of linguine, I had discovered a dish that wasn't about the pasta or the sauce; it was about both, about the interaction between them, the result—this new thing, this highly flavored noodle—evocative of a childhood trip to the sea.

IF YOU'RE TEMPTED to make linguine with clams according to the kitchen's preparation, you should understand that the only ingredient that's measured is the pasta. (A serving is four ounces.) Everything else is what you pick up with your fingertips, and it's either a small pinch or a large pinch or something in between: not helpful, but that, alas, is the way quantities are determined in a restaurant. (When a cookbook is prepared, a tester comes to the kitchen, picks up all the ingredients needed to make a dish, and takes them away to translate them into quantities that people at home might recognize. In the foodie publishing

world, these testers—who have very white kitchens with carefully cali-
brated ovens and computerized weighing devices—are the despots of
the written recipe. But I've never been persuaded by the reliability of
the translation: either the quantities in the restaurant original are so
large that they don't seem right when shrunk down—lamb shanks for
thirty-four doesn't look the same when it's done for two; the chemistry
is different, the sauce less rich—or the restaurant portions are so small
that they don't seem accurate when they're assigned a specific measure-
ment. For instance, do you really believe the Babbo cookbook when it
tells you that a linguine with eels takes four garlic cloves, that a lobster
spaghettini takes two, and that the chitarra take three? No. It's the same
for each: a small pinch. And what happened to the red onions, essential
to the lobster spag—a medium pinch, as it happens—but not mentioned? Were there no red onions the day the tester arrived?) The
downside of measuring by hand is what happens to the hands. At the
end of an evening your fingertips are irretrievably stained with some
very heady aromatics, and there's nothing you can do to eliminate
them. You wash your hands. You soak them. You shower, you scrub
them again. The next day, they still stink of onion, garlic, and pork fat,
and, convinced that everyone around you is picking up the smell, you
ram them into your pockets, maniacally rubbing your fingers against
each other like an obsessive-compulsive Lady Macbeth. At night, in bed,
my wife and I had some tough times when I was working at the pasta
station, ever since one of my hands flopped across her face and woke her
with a revolting start.

My advice: ignore the Babbo cookbook and begin by roasting small
pinches of garlic and chili flakes and medium pinches of the onion and
pancetta in a hot pan with olive oil. Hot oil accelerates the cooking
process, and the moment everything gets soft you pour it away (holding
back the contents with your tongs) and add a slap of butter and a splash
of white wine, which stops the cooking. This is Stage One—and you are
left with the familiar messy buttery mush—but already you've added
two things you'd never see in Italy: butter (seafood with butter—or any
other dairy ingredient—verges on culinary blasphemy) and pancetta,
because, according to Mario, pork and shellfish are an eternal combination found in many other places: in Portugal, in *amêijoas na cataplana*
(clams and ham); or in Spain, in a paella (chorizo and scallops); or in the

United States, in the Italian-American clams casino, even though none of those places happens to be in Italy. ("Italians," Mario says, "won't fuck with their fish. There are restaurants that won't use lemon because they think it's excessive.")

In Stage Two, you drop the pasta in boiling water and take your messy buttery pan and fill it with a big handful of clams and put it on the highest possible flame. The objective is to cook them fast—they'll start opening after three or four minutes, when you give the pan a swirl, mixing the shellfish juice with the buttery porky white wine emulsion. At six minutes and thirty seconds, you use your tongs to pull your noodles out and drop them into your pan—all that starchy pasta water slopping in with them is still a good thing; give the pan another swirl; flip it; swirl it again to ensure that the pasta is covered by the sauce. If it looks dry, add another splash of pasta water; if too wet, pour some out. You then let the thing cook away for another half minute or so, swirling, swirling, until the sauce streaks across the bottom of the pan, splash it with olive oil and sprinkle it with parsley: dinner.

I LEARNED many things at the pasta station, but I don't want to exaggerate my achievement. I never got through an evening without one profoundly humiliating experience. By now, I was in the kitchen five days a week, and each time the service commenced I had the same thought: maybe, tonight, I'll manage not to fuck up. The narrative I dreamed of involved my mastering the station, of proving Mario wrong, of showing that I could do a task that only twenty-somethings were able to do. I never made it. On the night I was finally on my own I didn't get through the first hour, although, for most of that first hour, I coped well enough. There were a lot of orders, and I was doing my Stage One prep, stacking my pans on the shelves surrounding the pasta cooker, filling them up, double-stacking them as I had been taught to do when it gets busy, and then triple-stacking them, an emergency efficiency. I was fast, assured, utterly ready, when I turned and heard the sounds of many pans crashing down behind my back and into the pasta cooker (Splash! Splash! Splash!), and the kitchen came to a frightful halt. The fear was that the water—now polluted by gobs of ragù, truffle butter, caramelized mushrooms, toasted guanciale, tomato sauce, shellfish, butter, plus all those aromatic pinches of onion, garlic, and pork fat—was no good. The cooker would have to be drained, refilled, and brought back to the boil. It would take an hour. There were twenty-eight orders pending. The kitchen would die. Tony Liu, in Andy's spot that night as expediter, walked over and inspected the water, boiling blackly, looked up at the shelf, observed that only many of the pans had fallen in, not all of them, and said it was okay. Was it? For the rest of the night, Mark retrieved random clams off plates at the last second "just as dishes were going out," and most of the pasta tasted, ineffably, the same. "The kitchen loves it when someone makes a mistake," Mark told me later. " 'Pssst: check it out! He dropped the pans!' They talked about you for a week."

In the event, Mark bolted, and I ran out of time. He decided it was time to move on. Having coached me at two stations and patiently endured the sort of trials a god would devise, he'd earned himself an Old Testament nickname. (What can I say? It had come to this: I was Kitchen Bitch, and he was Job.) And although he was next in line to be a sous-chef, he wanted a challenge. Mark would be thirty in the spring—Mario had been twenty-nine when he left his job in Santa Barbara—and, like Mario, he wasn't interested in the next senior position; he wanted to go to Italy. He asked Mario for help, and Mario, again flattered, found what he regarded as the perfect spot, a restaurant with a Michelin star and a reputation for the best handmade pasta in a region famous for its hand-made pasta: Il Sole, outside Bologna. Or at least that's where Mark thought he was going—"Mario talks so fast," he confessed, "I'm never sure what he's saying," which I thought showed a remarkable ease with his fate. Mark didn't know Italian yet; he'd learn it on the job, where— who knows?—he might remain for two years, maybe more. "I'll never have this chance again. I want to stay as long as I can."

Mark's going gave me pause. In emulating Mario's journey, he was going off to learn the real thing: handmade pasta fresca. Hadn't that been my mission? Instead, I came to understand something I'd once dismissed: that industrial product, pastasciutta. I was grateful for the instruction. But I was also a little jealous of Mark's adventure. Every-one was.

Meanwhile, a new person would take over the station and have to be trained, and as the training took weeks (even for grown-up cooks), I gave up my spot. There wasn't room for two students. With Mark's going, there was also another hiring: the structure was such that Mark, near the top, was replaced by someone who would start at the bottom, at the pantry station, preparing starters. (The invisible structure also meant that Abby was no longer the rookie.) The new guy was Alex Feldman. I was there the day he started: no small thing, as we'd be spending hours in his company and none of us knew what he was like. In fact, he was no small thing. He was six foot four, or at least that's what he said, but I didn't believe him. He seemed taller or, more frightening, might still be growing. (He had a growing boy's appetite. At the family meal, which featured hot dogs, he ate twelve.) He was twenty-two, excitable, gangly, clumsy, and oblivious. He called to mind a cartoon character— some floppy, long-limbed thing: Goofy with his puppy dog features. Alex's nose, for instance, was puppy-dog-like, big and not quite finished, as though still being formed. He had very big feet, like paws. He wore his long hair parted in the middle, like an overgrown schoolboy.

"Why would Mario hire someone so big?" Elisa asked under her breath. "He knows there's no room." But Mario had made up his mind before he'd met him, because, once again, Alex had Italian kitchen experience. He'd worked in Florence for a year at Cibreo, a restaurant known for its uncompromisingly Tuscan cooking. I hadn't heard of Cibreo. Actually, apart from Mario, no one had. But after a month or so, everyone knew a great deal: about the freshness of Cibreo's olive oil and how it arrived immediately after it was made—"not days or weeks but hours." (Alex tasted the Babbo oil and squished up his nose in a reflex of disapproval.) Or the importance of Cibreo's *soffritto*, the mystery of Tuscan soups, and how, at Cibreo, the preparation took all morning. (No one in the kitchen had heard of soffritto, but when Alex said the word his voice got whispery and reverential, and you understood that soffritto, whatever it was, was very important.) Alex shared his knowledge of the Italian language as well and corrected the pronunciation of anyone who got a word wrong. In fact, Alex tended to speak principally in Italian.

"Maybe," Abby said quietly, "what we have here is an acquired taste."

13

NEW YORK, 1995. On May 15th, an office assistant at a cable television start-up called the Food Network came across an article in *The New York Observer* that she felt might be of interest to the head of development, Jonathan Lynne. It was about a cabal of chefs hanging out at a downtown restaurant called Blue Ribbon. The restaurant was open late (last orders were between four and five in the morning) and took no reservations, except for a round table near the door which could accommodate between five and ten people. Batali had discovered Blue Ribbon shortly after Pó opened and often claimed the table for himself and several chef friends at the end of a Saturday-night service. "Just as the Algonquin Round Table of the 1920s and 30s gathered to commiserate about their literary careers and their love lives, and to zing wisecracks at each other," wrote Frank DiGiacomo, the author of the *Observer* piece, "so the Blue Ribbon round table gathers to share horror stories about customers from hell, culinary techniques, business gossip, and, of course, the trials of making a romantic relationship work on a chef's insane work schedule." In New York mythology, in which darkly creative things happen in wee morning hours, there are two archetypal settings: the round table that Dorothy Parker and her friends frequented at that famous Midtown hotel and the downtown artists' hangout, and people are always on the lookout for where one of the two archetypes will manifest itself again. Blue Ribbon, downtown and with a round table, had both.

Mario, then thirty-four, wearing clogs bought from a surgical supply company and dressed in "California jams," was described as the antic funnyman holding the group together (he may act like a clown, one chef told the reporter, but you'd be surprised—he's actually very smart), and his I-get-along-with-everyone attitude was illustrated by a story he told of being in San Francisco and having to charm a policeman who had wanted to arrest Batali's drinking buddy, the fortuitously met writer Hunter S. Thompson, who had pulled a gun on a cable car operator who refused to take Thompson to his front door: the evening ended with Batali's waking up in the Fairmont Hotel (he hadn't been a guest) wearing wet swimming trunks (the hotel doesn't have a pool). Other chefs at the round table—"a group of high-testosterone dudes," Batali said, to explain the enthusiasm with which the talent of the room was commented upon—included Tom Valenti and "the street-toughened, baby-faced" Bobby Flay. Flay had already published a book, won an award as "Rising Star Chef of the Year," and employed a publicist. "Where's Bobby tonight?" someone asked. "He couldn't make it today because the roof here wasn't able to support his helicopter."

I got a sense of what those evenings might have been like when, seven years later, I joined Mario at the same round table along with a few friends. The occasion was a visit to town by the novelist Jim Harrison, a self-described "food lunatic." Between Batali and Harrison, there was considerable admiration, and the exchanges between them constituted the table's entertainment. For Mario, Harrison was the Homer, the Michelangelo, the Lamborghini, the Willie Mays, the Secretariat, the Jimi Hendrix of food intellectuals: "an expert, a hunter, an eater, a stalker, a rabid mongrel and a drinker, not afraid to get excited about the kind of nuts a particular partridge must have eaten this morning to taste so damned good for lunch." Harrison, more modestly, described Batali as spiritual kin of some kind. "Probably from another life," he said, in his gruff, barely audible, I've-lived-through-so-much-I'm-surprised-I'm-alive voice. Mario clarified: "From the other life of pigs." They're both big men. Together, they occupied a lot of the round table—a semicircle, in fact, so much larger than normal people that they could have been walk-on parts in a medieval play about the deadly sins (all seven).

The first magnum of white wine arrived, and Mario reminded Harrison that they'd drunk twenty-eight bottles when they'd last met.

"There were other people," Harrison protested unconvincingly.

"They weren't drinking," Mario corrected.

He ordered starters off the top of his head, eighteen of them, including two dozen oysters, which Harrison couldn't touch, having just returned from Normandy, where he'd tested a view of the nineteenth-century food writer Jean-Anthelme Brillat-Savarin that grand meals had once begun by guests' eating a gross of oysters each (a gross is a hundred and forty-four oysters). Brillat-Savarin had confirmed the plausibility of the practice by weighing an oyster's meat, plus juices, which came out to less than ten grams. A gross, therefore, would be about a kilo and a half, or around three pounds. Three pounds of raw mollusks minus the shells seems like a lot, but Harrison was persuaded, and one evening he started dinner with a hundred and forty-four oysters.

He sighed. He could not recommend the practice.

A second magnum arrived, along with the first dishes. Fried oysters (to contrast with the raw ones); some salty sweetbreads, a Proustian trigger for Harrison involving a first girlfriend, aged fourteen; fried scampi; giant prawns grilled in their shells; barbecued spare ribs; and a sawed-up beef bone, roasted until the marrow was crispy and served with an oxtail marmalade.

A third magnum arrived. Harrison checked Mario's pulse ("Aah, you're still living") and made a toast. "Here's to us, Mario."

"And fuck the rest of the world," Mario answered.

Around midnight and our fifth magnum, the restaurant got busy, and because there was no other place to go, most of the crowd gathered round the bar, which was adjacent to our table. Soon strangers—but jolly friendly strangers—joined us (our sixth magnum), warmly, drunkenly welcomed, finding chairs to squeeze in with, including a Russian prostitute with very blond hair and an impenetrable accent. More magnums followed. Eventually, Mario led Harrison to a party celebrating the filming of something, the Russian prostitute inviting much of bleached Central Europe along with her, the evening coming to an early-morning close with a spot of improvised karaoke at the Half King bar, which had been recently opened by the writer Sebastian Junger. (I have the end of the evening on report. I had an office job then, still got up in the mornings, and went home early at one-thirty.)

When Jonathan Lynne read the *Observer* article, he thought: Wow! *This* is what the Food Network needs. "It was like bands hanging out late on a Saturday night in Seattle. Or artists in a bar downtown. A closely knit relationship of creative beings: that's what I wanted the

Food Network to foster, that's what I wanted to see on television." Lynne views chefs as "artists, like painters," and talks energetically about their "original vision," their "personal aesthetic." He is by no means the first non-chef to see chefs in this way, and ever since Apicius's *De re coquinaria* was translated as *L'arte culinaria*, both Italians and French have described what great chefs do with a metaphysical sense of hyperbole: no mean bunch of skills but a Da Vinci–like achievement.

Lynne phoned Batali, asked him if he wanted to be a TV star, and was invited to lunch: tortelloni with sage and butter, served with wilted endives, Lynne remembers precisely. (Batali remembers only the breathless enthusiasm of a stranger, interrupting his morning prep.) Six months later, on January 8, 1996, the Food Network launched *Molto Mario*, and three weeks after that the line of people waiting to get a table at Pó stretched to Bleecker Street, half a block away.

THE EARLY SHOWS, done on the cheap (face front to a camera, cooking on an electric oven because there was no gas), were crude but dominated by a remarkably familiar core repertoire, as though everything Mario subsequently did had been in place from the start: Swiss chard ravioli (grandmother's recipe again); cioppino, the cheap-o soup made with nothin'-o; orecchiette—Mario pretending to roll them out, when most had been made by a clueless prep kitchen, the orecchiette so large and deformed that they ballooned like bath toys when dropped into boiling water ("Oh, dear," Mario whispered, "this ear looks like it might have been Doctor Spock's"). But amid the predictable awkwardnesses, what is mainly conveyed is a passionate sense of mission. Mario, having just returned from Italy, has learned something few people knew: that traditional Italian cooking is different from what you think—simpler than you supposed—but its simplicity still has to be learned, and he is going to show you how.

I sat in on several "flights"—episode tapings—of a later version of the show. It was now presented in front of three friends on stools, being cooked for—a privilege, obviously, although a problematic one owing to a number of factors, including the hour. Guests were picked up before seven a.m. and had their first plate of food an hour later, while they were longing for another cup of coffee. One morning, it was gnocchi with braised cuttlefish. ("After making a little slit with our knife, the bone slides out like a guitar pick, and then you pull out the guts—oh, look," Mario says, his fingers enveloped in inky intestines, "this is exactly what the little guy had for lunch yesterday.") Two more meals follow, one after another, with a fourth just after lunch (who needs lunch?). When the shows air, you can tell where the guests are on the schedule, according to the expressions on their faces—zeal or a satiated glaze. "C'mon, guys, *buon appetito,*" Mario says, urging them at least to pretend to eat, strands of pasta coagulating on their plates, the gluten cooling to a waxy sheen, this being the twelfth helping one guest has had that morning.

The expectation is that the guests will put a question to their host when his fast-forward speech allows: this is the short, quick song they're expected to sing for their breakfast-supper. It isn't easy—each show is only twenty-five minutes long, organized around the three acts of an Italian meal, antipasto, pasta, and secondo—and both the explanatory patter and the cooking are done at sprint speed. It's really a theatrical kitchen monologue, delivered with such dispatch and such an unpredictable miscellany of references that few guests are confident enough to interrupt, not least because they're not always following what's being said in the first place. And besides, what are you going to ask that's *so* interesting?

For instance, in passing, Mario mentions that sardines, owing to their thin skin, should be covered with bread crumbs if cooked over a high heat (and you think, Hey, he's right, the skin is pretty thin); when, with no logic you've noticed, he tells you that celery is the unsung hero of Roman cooking (and you take that in, trying to recall the last time a stalk performed a heroic role); and then he hands everyone a ball of potato-and-flour dough and tells them to roll it out like a broomstick to make gnocchi, adding that, in preparing this at home, you'll want to use a starchy, not a waxy, potato ("Like an Idaho?" a guy on the last stool manages to get in). "Like an Idaho," Mario replies instantaneously, and continues, "And you'll want to mix it with just so much flour" ("How much flour?" the same guy asks, clearly on a roll), "Well, as much as it takes," Mario replies, citing his grandmother (being, in this, wholly genuine but wholly unhelpful), and sweeps up the lumpy examples of everyone's efforts, drops them into a pot of water that was boiling without your knowing it was there, and tells you that the lumpies will be fully cooked *not* when they float to the top, as most people incorrectly believe (have you held such a belief?), but only when "they're aggressively trying to get out of the pot" (whereupon everyone lifts up slightly from their stools, hoping to get a glimpse of what gnocchi look like when they're behaving like lobsters thrashing for their survival), when inexplicably Mario's voice goes all baritone and, like the master-of-ceremonies at a boxing match ("Ladies and Gentlemen!"), he introduces a piece of parmigiano as "the undisputed king of cheeses!" (And you think of that, too—can he possibly be right, that parmigiano deserves such a regal distinction?) In fact, it wouldn't hurt to ask him about the parmigiano because fourteen minutes have passed and you haven't said a word. When? What? Mario is plating the gnocchi, when he interrupts himself to assume yet another persona. (Go on, your brain is saying, this is your chance!) "In Italian cooking," he intones, inexplicably behaving like Socrates, "your dish should look as though it has fallen from the wings of a poet" (Whoa! Do you ask him about *that*—what food looks like when it's dropped from such a height?) "and not as though it had been made by nine French guys who were all beaten when they were children."

Finally, there's a break (Whew!), and you can relax, except that Mario, pent up by the effort to present a wholesome version of himself, lets loose with everything he's kept contained, an anarchic spilling out of naughtiness, involving whatever food item is to hand: like an artichoke ("Because it gives me so much wood") or cobra meat ("because it gives me *even more* wood than an artichoke, *big* wood, strong-like-a-tree wood," whereupon he embraces two female prep cooks bearishly and invites them to imagine they're in a post-cobra-eating circle, "*deeply* satisfied"). There's dancing, butt slapping, kissing, and extra meaning found in ponytails ("At least I know what to do with mine, baby") or Mario's shirt (which an assistant makes the mistake of observing is too stiff) or tomatoes, which a set manager refreshes with a water gun ("You, my lovely," Mario says, in his deep bedroom voice, "can spray my tomatoes anytime"). "Why am I not offended?" the set manager asks. "Why is that not a lawsuit?" retorts a guest. "Why can't we show *this* on television?" asks another—when the show's jaunty sing-songy theme song starts and, as though splashed with cold water,

Mario assumes his television persona, never deviating from it until the next break, by which time you still haven't said a word.

"I keep telling him to slow down," the director, Jerry Liddell, told me. "He's got plenty of time."

I was watching another flight of shows in Liddell's control room. He could have been producing a sporting event—no retakes, the camera choices made on the spot.

"Cooking is about transformation," Liddell said. "You take a number of ingredients, and they become something else. That's Mario's show. That's the narrative. For most of us, how a bunch of ingredients will behave together is completely unpredictable. Even here, in the control room, watching the show on the monitors, menus in hand, even *we* don't know what's going to happen next. That's the appeal of a live program like this—Mario's knowing the result and our trying to follow him." Even so, the effect of so many transformations, rendered at such speed, can be dizzying. "There is no question you learn something, but it's coming at you so fast it's almost too much: it's right on the verge."

BUT WHAT do you learn? To find out, I recorded nine months of shows and watched the videos, one after another (a visual diet analogous to eating a gross of oysters, and, like Jim Harrison, I wouldn't recommend it). There were recurrent lessons. "At home, you rarely get the depth of flavor that you find in a restaurant," Mario said on his first show, browning mushrooms in a ferociously hot pan, "because home cooks are not prepared to take the risks of professional chefs, who push their pans right to the edge. They want it *browner* than you'll ever do at home, *darker, hotter.*" He has been repeating the lesson ever since. It's why he lets his olive oil heat to the smoking point, which provokes the most frequently asked question—"Are you supposed to do that? Aren't you burning it?"—and one that, in ten years, he has never answered (the result is often a pan's bursting into flames, flamboyantly, just before a break). There is the pasta-water-in-your-sauce lesson, along with the your-sauce-is-only-a-condiment (heard on the first show and many times thereafter). There are pithy platitudes ("Squid—thirty seconds or thirty minutes: in between they're rubber bands"). There is an unsung cut of meat, the shoulder, invariably lamb, which, for all its historical neglect, has lyrical qualities that Mario has been singing for many years.

Then, midway through my stack, I remembered the first time I watched Mario on television, November 1st, 1996, when I made a preparation he'd demonstrated on the show, an *arancina*, a deep-fried risotto-rice ball stuffed with tomato sauce and smoke-dried fish. I went to the Food Network's Web site and printed out the recipe, because I happened to have a smoke-dried sablefish in my refrigerator (and had no idea why or what in the world I was going to do with it). I made two hefty arancine for a Sunday lunch, deep-frying them in two liters of my local deli's olive oil. Later, on a visit to Porretta Terme, I spotted crispy little arancine in the shop windows there and understood what the word meant. An *arancia* is an orange; *arancina*, a little orange, a fair description of Porretta's tangerine-sized rice balls. Mine had been neither tangerines nor oranges. Mine could have been carved out and put on the porch with a candle inside at the end of October.

The episode provides me with an occasion to account for how I found myself in this predicament, not just watching hours of *Molto Mario* but the whole package: hooked up with the guy, trying to survive as a line cook, wanting to learn about food in this sometimes punishing firsthand way. I am not a food professional—that's perfectly evident. Until now, I'd been a literary type. In fact, this Babbo business started while I was an editor at *The New Yorker* and, unable to get anyone to write a profile of Mario, I was allowed to take the commission myself and suspected, correctly, that I might be able to use the assignment to get into Mario's kitchen. I was there six months, a longish time to research a magazine article, and was sorry to leave. By then, I wondered if I was a magazine guy anymore. I had been on the verge of discovering something— about food, about myself. I also felt I had earned a new competence, maybe even enough competence to run a difficult station on the line without someone around to back me up, and this was something I wanted to do. (I was wrong—I wasn't close—but I didn't know that yet.)

The profile appeared, but I remained troubled by the thought that I was missing an opportunity, until two months later, when I quit my desk job and returned. There were other factors in my quitting— including my having been an editor for twenty-three years, which was plenty—but the result was the same: I went from a day spent sitting down to one spent standing up. Maybe it was a boyish longing—my wanting to be in a kitchen, like someone else's dreaming of flying an airplane or riding on the back of a fire truck—but it was also born out of a recognition that a chef has a knowledge about food that I wasn't going to get from books, and I wanted that knowledge. I was a flawed cook. My meals were chaotic, late, messy. But I was also a curious one (which was probably why I had a sablefish in my fridge).

The satisfactions of making a good plate of food are surprisingly varied, and only one, and the least important of them, involves eating what you've made. In addition to the endless riffing about cooking-with-love, chefs also talk about the happiness of making food: not preparing or cooking food but *making* it. This is such an elementary thing that it is seldom articulated. After my stint at the pasta station, Frankie urged me to go back to the grill and master it properly, because it would be more fulfilling: at the pasta station, he said, you're preparing other people's food. The ravioli, the ragù—they've been made beforehand. But at the grill, you start with raw ingredients, cook them, and assemble a dish with your hands. "You make the food," he said. The simple, good feeling he was describing might be akin to what you'd experience making a toy or a piece of furniture, or maybe even a work of art—except that this particular handmade thing was also made to be eaten. I found, cooking on the line, that I got a quiet buzz every time I made a plate of food that looked exactly and aesthetically correct and then handed it over the pass to Andy. If, on a busy night, I made, say, fifty good-looking plates, I had fifty little buzz moments, and by the end of service I felt pretty good. These are not profound experiences—the amount of reflection is exactly zero—but they were genuine enough, and I can't think of many other activities in a modern urban life that give as much simple pleasure.

THE FOOD NETWORK is a different enterprise from what it was a decade ago. During its first year, the network had six and a half million subscribers; now it has fifteen times that number and is a highly profitable member of a publicly traded company. With the bigger numbers, executives don't use words like "chefs," let alone "artists," but "talents" and "brands." *Molto Mario* is now openly talked about as "old-fashioned"—an example of the "how-to, stand-and-stir" format, according to Judy Girard, who was put in charge in 2000 and ran the network during its first financially successful years. "The format relies on the information being more interesting than the presentation, with a chef behind a stove, like a newscaster behind a desk."

Since Mario first appeared on television, there have been efforts to enlarge his "brand," but they have met with "mixed results," according to Girard. One was *Mediterranean Mario*—in effect, *Molto Mario* expanded to include North Africa, Spain, Portugal, Greece, and France. But the show was a stretch—Mario's preparing French Provincial dishes was not only wrong, it seemed immoral—and was abandoned after two seasons. More recently there was *Mario Eats Italy*, a foodie's road show, with a buddy and a script. But the script was somebody's hammered-up version of Mario (isn't the real one exaggerated enough?), and the role of the so-called travel buddy—a fat guy in a T-shirt, who was never introduced or explained—was to utter sentences that started with "Gee, Mario, I don't get it . . . " *Ciao America* was next, and for months Mario was somewhere else, a television crew in tow, seeking out Italian-American eateries and getting their proprietors to explain their specialties. But Mario had never been an Italian-American cook or a food journalist, and, after thirteen episodes, this, too, was discontinued.

Meanwhile, the network's programming was developing a house style, and it was difficult to see how Mario fit in. "Mario is high end," Girard said, "and you can't build a network around high end." The new shows put a premium on presentation rather than knowledge and tended to have intimate-seeming camera close-ups of foods, as though objects of sexual satisfaction. The skin-flick feel was reinforced by a range of heightened effects, especially amplified sounds of frying, snapping, crunching, chewing, swallowing. There seemed always to be a tongue, making small, wet, bubbly tongue sounds. The "talent" (also known as a "crossover" personality, usually a woman with a big smile and no apron) was directed to be easy with her tongue and use it conspicuously—to taste food on a spoon, say, or work it around a batter-coated beater, or clean the lips with it. The aim was spelled out for me by Eileen Opatut, a former programming executive. "We're looking for the kind of show that makes people want to crawl up to their television set and lick the screen." (I heard this and thought: Yuck.)

Jonathan Lynne is no longer with the Food Network. He quit for a number of reasons, including his colleagues' wish to buy a Japanese-produced show called *Iron Chef*, a competition that treats cooking like an evening of Sumo wrestling. ("I refused to be the American executive responsible for putting that show on air.") The show, acquired after Lynne left, became the network's most watched piece of television. When Mario appeared as a contestant on a spin-off, *Iron Chef America*—fast, spontaneous, dazzlingly improvisational, both large and larger than life—network executives realized that they'd *finally* found a venue for him: no script, just a stage. The brand, I've been assured, is intact. In the end, what did Lynne know? He was an old-fashioned sort of person. He didn't understand American television. But he did appreciate its power: those lines outside Babbo on a Saturday night, for instance, which number twenty-five or thirty people, even though the restaurant is fully booked. "That's because of the Food Network," Lynne told me. "Let's be frank, if it wasn't for the Food Network, Mario would be no one. He'd be an interesting but unknown downtown late-night chef running a popular local spot, but not a restaurant like Babbo, which visitors from Chicago or Los Angeles go out of their way to get into."

14

Is THERE A FOOD older than polenta? Not in Italy, at least from what I could discover, although until Columbus returned from the West Indies with a sack of corn what people understood polenta to be was gray mush, not yellow. For several thousand years, polenta usually meant barley: a stodgy cereal, easy to grow, indifferent to the excesses of the seasons, brown like mud, high in carbs, low in protein, and with the earthy flavor of a mature weed. In its barley incarnation, polenta predates rice and, for ten millennia, was what people put into a pot and stirred over a fire until suppertime. Some Italians claim the dish came from the Etruscans (not unlike insisting that fish and chips were served first at a round table by Merlin: maybe it's true, probably it's not, no one knows because no one knows much about the Etruscans except that, from their tomb paintings, they liked eating, drinking, dancing, and frolicky sex and are always pantheistically invoked as the forefathers of all qualities nationalists long to think of as Italian). The Romans, more persuasively, say they picked the dish up from the Greeks. Pliny, in the first century, describes Greek barley as "the oldest of foods" and the essential ingredient in a preparation that sounds a lot like—well, polenta. Where did the Greeks learn what to do with barley? No one knows, although the earliest evidence of it dates from 8000 B.C.

Barley doesn't have the gluten of wheat or the sweetness of corn, which is why you don't see it in many modern preparations except for barley water (a disgusting sugary brew, drunk mainly near the Scottish borders), hippie soups, livestock feed, and beer—brewers being the largest consumers of the world's harvest. But I'd become curious and set out to make a bowl of it according to a 1570 recipe written by

Bartolomeo Scappi, the private cook of Pope Pius V, which had been included in Scappi's six-volume *Works in the Art of Cooking*.

In time, I would become a Scappi admirer, but this was my first foray into a Renaissance text, and it wasn't easy for me to figure out what was being said. In the event, and after predictable struggles resulting in the obliteration of my useless Italian-English dictionary after it exploded on impact against the wall where I'd hurled it, I was able to locate and then follow a perfectly lucid set of instructions telling me how to wash the barley with three changes of water, soak it, cook it, and be vigilant to keep it from drying out before it is ready, a condition Scappi describes as a falling-apartness. I ladled out a hearty helping and poured myself a glass of malt whiskey, perhaps, in its long history, the cereal's most successful expression, my meal consisting then of barley in a liquid and a liquidy-solid form. But even the whiskey couldn't disguise that a bowl of barley polenta is a pretty drab business. You can add salt and pepper, of course, and a big splash of olive oil. Scappi suggests adding a spoon of capon broth, perhaps some cheese and butter, or sugar, even melon—anything to give the thing some flavor. It was a problem. I felt I was hunting for something tasty in a bowl of edible dirt. Traditionally, polenta is a winter dish—cereals can be stored when nothing else is growing—but after a bowl in its barley form I came away with a grim historical picture of what January and February must have been like for most of humanity, miserably sustained by foods that were colorless and sad, like the season's sky.

I was by now possibly a little fixated on what I'd come to regard as the polenta question (as well as its history, its various preparations, and its role in Western culture), and, from what I could tell, my fixation was shared by almost no one else in the world. We all have our limitations, and, in the matter of polenta, mine date from a specific meal, and, like a chemist unable to reproduce lab results of an experiment that had succeeded once, I hadn't eaten anything like it since, although I kept trying. Until then, I couldn't imagine what the appeal of polenta might be, because, until then, the only kind I'd known was the two-minute instant variety—pour into boiling water, stir once, serve—and the result tastes of nothing most of us are able to remember. I'd been utterly unprepared for the real thing, therefore, when I happened to have a bowl of it at an Italian restaurant. The chef had bought her cornmeal from an artisanal miller in Piemonte, and the polenta she made was a revelation—each grain swollen from the slow simmering and yet still rough, even gravelly, against the roof of my mouth. For a moment, it put me in mind of risotto. But risotto is cooked in broth and finished with butter and cheese, and tastes of the rice and everything else you've added. These crunchy stone-ground corn grains tasted only of themselves: an intense, sweet, highly extracted cornness. In an instant, I had a glimpse of the European diet at a juncture of radical change. For one generation, dinner had been gray, as it had been since the beginning of time; for the next generation, dinner was crunchy, sweet, and golden.

So far, I haven't been able to date precisely when this change occurred, although the first Italian allusion to corn as a food substance appears to be in a 1602 medical treatise published in Rome, more than a hundred years after Columbus's return. What interests me is how Italians then cooked it. For instance, no one imagined dropping a cob into boiling water, when, after two minutes, it can be eaten right away— smothered in butter, sprinkled with sea salt, and served with a barbecued hamburger on a summer evening. Instead, they thought, "Hey, what a funny thing! This looks like a barley ear but gigantic! We should shuck it, remove the kernels, dry them in the sun, grind them up into a meal, and cook them for hours." After 9,600 years of barley mush, Italians were obviously pretty set in their ways. They must also have been desperate, because they ate so much of it they gave themselves a disease, pellagra, which went undiagnosed for two centuries: no one understood the correlation between polenta gluttony and the subsequent appearance of the gluttoners, who tended to shrivel up in the winter with horrible disfigurements, unless they kept eating their polenta through the summer, in which case they shriveled up and died. (A diet of too much corn is deficient in niacin. Corn, originally a food of the Native Americans, was often planted with beans, a niacin nirvana.)

For all that, when Italians talk about polenta today, they still get a little soupy, not unlike the preparation itself, and are reminded of a blackened kettle and a long wooden spoon wielded by an aunt somewhere in the north (a northerner is called a "polenta eater," *mangiapolenta*, just as a Tuscan is a bean eater, and a Napoletano is a macaroni eater, the belief in Italy being not that you are what you eat but that you're the starch). Invariably they mention a passage in *I promessi sposi*—

"The Betrothed"—by Alessandro Manzoni, as proof that polenta is more than a food: it's the soul of their Italianness. *The Betrothed*—about the turbulent 1620s (invasions, bread riots, repressive land-owning oligarchs), written during the turbulent 1820s (invasions, bread riots, repressive land-owning oligarchs)—was Manzoni's only novel and is regarded as a great expression of national consciousness: every child reads it in school, and the first anniversary of the author's death, in 1873, was commemorated by Verdi's *Requiem*. The polenta passage is a *Little Dorrit*–like account of a peasant family at dinnertime, the father on his knees at the hearth, tending the meager supper, stirring until it can be ladled out (the family "staring at the communal dish with a grim look of rabid desire") onto a piece of beechwood. The appeal is in the ritual—the beechwood, the pot, the smooshy blobby way it's served—and the passage is cited in every polenta recipe you read, with one detail usually omitted: that Manzoni's polenta is made of buckwheat. (By the 1500s, just before corn arrived, Italians had got so sick of barley they pulverized every pulse-like thing they could get their hands on—green peas, yellow peas, black-eyed peas, chickpeas, and buckwheat—and called it polenta.) In fact, the buckwheat is an anachronism—the novel is set in the time and place where the polenta revolution had already occurred—but Manzoni had his reasons: that's how bad peasant life was, he's telling us, even the polenta was miserable. But it's curious that the buckwheat is so seldom mentioned. Is it because the detail undermines the ideology of the dish? After all, to acknowledge that the polenta in the famously nation-building passage is buckwheat is to concede that what is eaten now is a foreign ingredient and that at the heart of every-one's Italianness is a little piece of North America.

For my part, I didn't care if that restaurant bowl of polenta was American or Italian or Icelandic. Whatever it was, I ate it and was trans-ported. And like so many of those first polenta eaters, my world changed from an overcast sky to a sunny bright yellow one. No wonder those Italians went crazy. I'd go crazy. Actually, I did go a little crazy, and while I failed to track down that miller in Piemonte, I did manage to find some sole-proprietor, do-it-by-hand operation and ordered a twenty-pound quantity from a wholesaler. A parcel arrived, and I went to work, follow-ing the instructions—a cup of polenta to four cups of water, some salt, lots of stirring, in fact forty minutes of stirring, and *basta:* your polenta is ready. Except it wasn't, or I didn't think so, and, if it was, it was nothing like what I'd eaten. Also, after forty minutes of stirring, I was worn out and hadn't prepared the rest of my dinner, afraid that if I neglected the polenta it would stick to the bottom of the pot and be ruined. I had nineteen pounds twelve ounces left.

Maybe I could make corn bread, and the idea provoked an epiphany of resounding banality: corn bread is made from the same stuff as polenta. (Cornmeal: polenta. Cornmeal: corn bread. Why had this not occurred to me before?) The effect was miraculous: polenta was demystified. I get it! It's white-trash food! A southerner's devotion to cornmeal, I should explain, comes close to rivaling a northern Italian's (the American South is one of the only other places with a large-scale outbreak of pellagra, with this crucial difference: it occurred in the twentieth century, when people knew what caused the disease and *still* ate too much corn). I was born in Louisiana and grew up on this stuff. In a sentimental moment, I, too, can invoke a memory essential to my identity—of my grandmother, say, hunched over her blackened cast-iron skillet, the salty smells of hot pork fat and the sugary ones of grainy corn caramelizing in it, and a string of vaguely sultry, swampy associations to prove that corn bread is at the heart of the southern soul. Polenta, I finally understood, was corn bread without the baking powder. Even so, I wasn't getting it right. How difficult could it be?

Difficult enough that Batali wasn't telling home cooks to make it. On his show, he recommends the instant kind, even though he never serves it in the restaurant. (Why eat plastic if you don't have to?) In fact, from what I was reading, no one was telling people how to make it. The instruction on that twenty-pound bag I'd bought, for instance: a lie. I consulted other cookbooks: more lies. Their recipes were useless and misleading. It's not so much water and so much polenta and so much time, but water and polenta and time, in whatever quantities it takes, until the dish is ready, which is never forty minutes but as long as three hours.

I discovered this on a late January afternoon in the Babbo kitchen—nearly a year to the day of my first anniversary of working there—and the fact that I made the discovery then, after so long and during the hustle and bustle of getting ready for the evening service, was instructive. The kitchen, finally, was becoming comprehensible. What had originally been a blur of other people's busyness was now so many specific tasks, each with a beginning, an end, and a purpose related to what would appear on people's plates. It seems obvious. Then again, so was the discovery itself, which consisted of nothing more than my realizing that polenta, for most of its cooking, is left untended. That's it: a copper pot abandoned over a low fire. I peered inside: the polenta was bubbling away slowly, percolating more than simmering, making thick bubble-gum bubbles.

I understood the implications immediately. "So you don't have to stir it all the time?" I said aloud to nobody. I was very excited. If you don't have to stir it all the time, then you can leave it alone. If you don't have to stir it all the time, you can make other things. If you don't have to stir it all the time, you can cook it for hours—what does it matter, as long as you're nearby?

"Wow! I finally get it!" I turned to the sauté guy, Todd Koenigsberg. Making the polenta was the duty of the sauté guy, and since Dom had quit the station had been run by Todd, a man-child with dark curly hair, a dark curly beard, and flower-child looks. "Todd!" I exclaimed. "The polenta. Is it really the case you don't have to stir it all the time?"

Todd seemed confused by my animation. (Even now I can see the workings of his mind, visible in the baffled look on his tiny face, trying to answer not the question I put to him but the one he seemed to be asking himself, namely: What is wrong with this man?)

"Of course not," he said, finally, his tone conveying that although I might be happy being a kitchen imbecile, everyone else had to make a living.

Todd, it seems, did not suffer from an acute polenta affliction and was obviously in no position to share my enthusiasm. For him, polenta was a burden. To make it, you needed first to whip it vigorously with a whisk, as I had always done, but then, once it got going, it was largely left alone with the whisk in the pot, so when people walked by they could give it a stir, something that I, in my kitchen obliviousness, had never noticed. The burden was in the fact that the polenta was never made first thing. It was always the seventh or eighth thing. So if you got busy and forgot—if suddenly, at four-thirty, you found yourself saying, "Oh, shit, the polenta!"—you were in trouble. You can't crush three hours of slow cooking into sixty minutes. For emergencies, a box of the instant was hidden on the top shelf of the walk-in, but to use it was considered a failure of character. It also rendered Frankie apoplectic, who took these lapses as personal slights. "You're doing this to humiliate me," he'd say to whoever he'd just spotted, tiptoeing like a shoplifter, clandestinely slinking off with a box of the instant an hour before the service started. "You're doing this to make me look bad. You're doing this because you know we will fucking lose our fucking three stars if we start serving fucking instant, and if we lose our fucking three stars I lose my fucking job." Frankie took over the polenta, and there was cornmeal everywhere, and the best tactic was to be very quiet and, if possible, also invisible, because the atmosphere was going to be very bad for the rest of the night.

And then I had a chance to make the polenta myself—not the twenty servings you get from that copper pot, but two hundred.

THE OCCASION was a benefit dinner in Nashville, Tennessee, and one that, in the words of one guest, brought together the "local wine geeks and the country music geeks for an evening of uninhibited extravagance," drinking some of the world's most costly beverages and eating food prepared by a famous chef flown in for the purpose along with his accomplished kitchen crew, which, this year, included Andy, Elisa, Frankie—and me.

I'd never been in a kitchen where meals for hundreds of people were routine. The service area was very large, but the actual cooking space was small and consisted of only four devices—a neglected flattop (flames were leaping through a crack), an oven, and two giant contraptions: one looked like a steel coffin and the other like a cement mixer. Frankie, who had once worked in a hotel, told me that the coffin was a "tilted skillet" and capable of boiling tremendous quantities of water in seconds. It would cook the pasta. The cement mixer, he said, was a "kettle." He rubbed his hands across it. "We'll cook the polenta in this," he said quietly. The sight of both machines excited him—boy things with big engines.

I looked around. The rest of the space was taken up by long steel tables, more like a factory mailing room than a kitchen. The challenge of producing a meal for so many, I was starting to understand, was not in making the food (pasta for two hundred is pretty tricky but, theoretically, not that different from making it for two—you just need a bigger pot) but in putting it on plates. The plating was such an event that the organizers had put out a call for volunteers, and by midday there were thirty-two of them. They were all highly accomplished chefs, who (it was perfectly obvious) hadn't come to do the plating, although they were happily prepared to help out. A famous chef was in town, and they wanted to get in on some of the cooking.

To everyone's disappointment, most of it was already done. Short ribs were the entrée, and Elisa had been making them for a week. The famous chef didn't even need to be there. He appeared once, fleetingly, in and out, to drop off three crates of distressed-looking watercress and instructed the volunteers nearest him to pluck the leaves off the wispy stems. The leaf pluckers morosely gathered round a table. The task would take four hours, but at least they had something to do. At some point, two volunteers were dispatched to slice up some coppa—this would be the salumi antipasto—and they were delighted: that would take two hours. But there were still twenty-six volunteers. Andy, recognizing their distress, asked one of them, Margo, to slice up some horseradish (to be mixed with the watercress and mounted atop the short ribs), but she was uncomfortable with the slicer, a handheld guillotine called a *mandolino*, and awkwardly removed a quantity of her knuckles, blood everywhere, and now was in urgent need of bandaging, which involved eight Nashville volunteers (who, despite her distress, couldn't disguise their relief at having a duty).

In fact, the polenta was the only thing that needed cooking.

POLENTA, COOKED slowly for three hours, expands to about six times its original volume, so if you're making some for eight people, served with short ribs, perhaps (or any other darkly sauced entrée or juicy bird, polenta enjoying the same relationship to meat that linguine has to shellfish—yet another starchy vehicle to carry the flavors of something else), you want to start with about a cup. If you're making it for two hundred, start with ten pints. The amount of water doesn't matter, because you're going to add more than is worth measuring: you just want to make sure the water is hot so the cooking is steady. On this occasion, Frankie poured in enough to fill about a quarter of the kettle device, added the polenta, and I started stirring. The result looked like pumpkin soup, very runny, but within minutes it soaked up all the liquid and changed from being obviously too dilute to looking almost ready, as though you could eat it (not recommended, unless your idea of dinner is a mouthful of sandbox). I added more water; the grains soaked it up. I added more; they soaked it up, until slowly the polenta behaved as though it had quenched its thirst. I stirred, and it remained pretty wet. I stirred: still wet. It had reached an equilibrium of sorts, where the water content in the grains was close to the liquid it was cooking in: a condition of hot mush. At this stage, most polenta makers, in the cereal's long history, invoke a volcano crater. Personally, I've never seen a volcano crater, but it couldn't be too different from what I found myself looking into at the bottom of this hot, steamy basin: thick, heavy bubbles, like golf balls, until they burst and became thick, heavy bits of flying polenta splattering up my arm. So that's what lava feels like, I thought and then realized that the polenta was talking to me.

It asked: You wouldn't knowingly stick your hand in an active volcano, would you?

Of course not, I answered.

Go away, then, it said. Do something else. I am not temperamental like risotto. Go on: cook the rest of the dinner.

THE DAY WE LEFT for Nashville, Mario had told me to pack a jacket that I'd find in the coat-check closet. It was a grand article: double-breasted, with fabric buttons and square shoulders and the restaurant's logo sewn onto the chest. Frankie showed me his, which had his name on it, just under the logo, written out in a flourishing script. Mario had given it to him when he was promoted to sous-chef, and that's what the jacket told people who knew about these things: that "Frank Langello" was a chef.

Cooks and chefs aren't the same. By now I was a cook—I worked on the line—and answered to a chef. A chef was a boss. A cook's name never appeared on a jacket. During the kitchen's more demeaning moments, cooks lost their names entirely. "Hey, chickpea guy," Frankie had taken to calling Alex, not only when his chickpeas were done badly—for a while, Alex couldn't get his chickpeas right—but all the time, the implication being that Alex was such a contemptible person that his purpose in the kitchen amounted to nothing more elevated than making bad chickpeas. "Hey, white shirt guy!" Andy shouted once, in a fury, having caught a glimpse of a runner dawdling outside the swinging doors, in the space between the kitchen and the restaurant. (It was also where the restrooms were located, and the white shirt was worn not by a runner, alas, but by a customer.) Mario was addressed by rank. "Yes, Chef. Whatever you say, Chef. Right away, Chef." The construction works if you replace "Chef" with "General."

The Nashville volunteers had also dressed up. The head chef of Bound'ry—a small man with a goatee and rimless spectacles—presented himself as the sartorial equivalent of his menu (an East-West fusion thing) in a collarless black jacket and a black cap, very Chairman Mao. Margo, the one who had the knife fight with the mandolino, ran a first-name casual place called Margo. She was accompanied by her sous-chef, and they were both studiously folksinger friendly, with blue bandannas and matching baggy blue trousers. Nashville's kosher chef wore a baseball cap, a sweatshirt, and a Brooklyn accent. One man was wearing a giant toque, the hat associated with French kitchens. He stood perfectly erect, his arm crooked with a crisp white towel draped from it, in pin-striped trousers and a jacket made with a whiter-than-white fine cotton. The others seemed to be avoiding him, although it's possible he would have had no part of them anyway. He was very serious.

MY POLENTA, meanwhile, had changed: it was different to the touch (sticky) and to look at (almost shiny). Starch, which is the principal component of all grains, breaks down at high temperatures—for corn, between a hundred fifty and two hundred degrees—when the granules are then able to bond with water. This was why the water I'd added at the outset needed to be hot: to prevent the temperature from dropping and postponing this stage—the break-it-down-and-bond-it-back stage. The process is called "gelatinizing," when the cereal granules swell and become more wetly viscous. When I'd begun, I'd been stirring the polenta with a whisk with a long handle. But as granules bonded with the water, the polenta expanded and, creeping up the length of the whisk, was encroaching on the handle.

I added a splash more water—not much (after all, the polenta and water, in their happy new molecular relationship, were getting along just fine)—and resumed my stirring. The polenta crept up a little more.

When would it stop? I wondered.

Then a question occurred to me: Would it stop? Silly notion. Of course it would stop. But knowing when could be useful.

Another splash of water, some more stirring. It crept up further.

This was modestly alarming—not five-bell alarming, but a concern: to stir the polenta, I was beginning to feel I had to be *in* the polenta. Would I finish cooking it before I was enveloped by it and became the darkly sauced meaty thing it was served with? The sensible thing would be to remove the whisk and go for a walk. The polenta had already told me I didn't need to hang around. But with so much kitchen competition I was afraid to abandon my whisk, convinced that a thrusting Nashville volunteer would seize it and take over my task. That chef with the hat, for instance. He was now standing inches behind me. I'd been monitoring him in my peripheral vision. He had liberated himself from the others and crossed an invisible line that separated the Nashville volunteers from the cooking area. He'd done this one step at a time and after each step, seeing he hadn't been rebuked, he'd taken one more.

"Sooooo," he said.

I pretended not to hear.

"Sooooo," he repeated.

I knew what he wanted: my whisk. I was sure of it. I concentrated on my stirring.

He sighed. "Sooooo," he said again and added for emphasis: "Po-*len*-ta!" It was an alarmingly Italian pronunciation. I'd never heard the word said with such a forceful accent. I glanced at him sideways and noticed an Italian flag sewn into the neck of his pressed white jacket. This surprised me. I had thought that, dressed thus, he must be French. I looked again and saw on his jacket: Alfresco Pasta.

"Po-LEN-ta!" he said again, stretching out the middle syllable and flapping the roof of his mouth with his "t."

Yes, I agreed. Polenta.

"Permit me to introduce myself. I call myself Riccardo."

I moved the whisk from my right hand to my left, shook Riccardo's hand, rapidly transferred the whisk back, and resumed my stirring.

"I call myself Riccardo. From Bologna. I am here eight years."

So Riccardo was the real thing. Not only from Italy, but from northern Italy, from Emilia-Romagna, right up there in polenta land, adjacent to Lombardy, the homes of Maestro Martino and Alessandro Manzoni. Riccardo was probably a genuine mangiapolenta, with childhood memories of beechwood and a grandmother with a big spoon. But what was a chef from Bologna doing in Tennessee? You don't meet many people from Bologna. Life there is too good to leave it. I eyed him suspiciously. He was looking at my whisk (and there was no other word to describe his manner) covetously. I turned my back, slightly, thinking: thou shalt not covet my whisk.

He moved closer. I could hear his breathing. If he says "Po-LEN-ta" one more time, I'm going to smack him with my whisk.

Frankie appeared. He had to walk around Riccardo (who, having achieved his spot, wasn't about to give it up). Frankie squeezed in between us, avoided eye contact with this strange man wearing a soufflé for a hat, did that quick dip-the-finger trick, and tasted the polenta. He added more salt. "Nothing is simple," he said. "Everything needs to be made with love."

"Po-LEN-ta!" Riccardo said again, looking expectantly at Frankie, who walked away without pausing to reply. Riccardo then turned back to me. He stood, watching.

I stirred.

Riccardo didn't move.

I didn't stop stirring.

"Sooooo," he said finally. "Tell me a thing. Are you coming from New York?"

Yes, I said, I'm from New York. I looked at him. Why did he drape his towel on his forearm, anyway?

"Ah, New York," he said.

I stirred.

"How is New York?" he asked.

"New York is fine," I said.

"Ah, New York," he said.

The polenta had inched so far up my whisk that I was stirring with the last inch of the handle. I stopped and tasted my knuckles.

"You know," Riccardo said, "I do not know why I have come here to Nashville. I think but I cannot remember. There must have been a reason. I have wanted to go to New York. But when I have come here, I have met a girl. I did not come here to meet a girl. But I have met a girl. I have fell in love, I have got married, and now I am a chef at Alfresco Pasta," he said, adding, after a pause, "in Nashville." He sighed.

I stirred, but, despite myself, I was feeling something—I don't know what. Sympathy? Pity? How could I feel pity? I'd just met this stranger, wearing a piece of pastry as a headdress, confirming yet again that cooks are some of the weirdest people on the planet, and now he was wanting both my whisk and to tell me his life story.

"Nashville is very nice," I offered.

"I could have been a New York chef."

He said nothing for a long time, reflecting, staring at the round pot of polenta being stirred by me. "Instead I am a Nashville chef." He was very melancholy. "Love," he said. *"Amore."*

"Amore," I agreed.

MEANWHILE, the polenta was developing a new texture, its third meta-morphosis. In the beginning, it had been soupy but thirsty. Then, after an hour, it was shiny and cakey and coming off the sides: for many, an indication the polenta was ready. But by cooking it longer, an hour, even two hours more—stirring it every now and then, adding hot water when needed—you concentrated the flavors. In effect, the polenta was undergoing a modest caramelization by being baked in its own liquid lava—like a self-creating clay oven, drawing out the sweetness in the corn—and its actually being caramelized: along the bottom, a thin crust was forming from the granules browning against the kettle's hot sur-face. I scraped it up with my whisk and mixed it in. It was elastic, an elasticity I associate with dough. You also could smell the change. Pasta behaves in a similar way, and you can teach yourself to recognize how it smells when it is ready. Mario describes this as "giving up the gluten" and recalls how, in Italy, walking past open windows at midday, he could register the moment when a lunch was served by the sudden smell of something rich and gluteny, like a perfumed pastry cloud.

I licked some polenta off my knuckles: it tasted good. It was done.

Frankie and I poured the kettle's contents into metal canisters and put them in a warm bath—a "steam table"—and, just then, Mario appeared. It was six o'clock, and the volunteers, still crushed together on the other side of the invisible boundary, visibly relaxed, except for a now-very-morose Riccardo, who hadn't budged and managed to be both downcast and erect simultaneously.

There was an hour until service, and there were urgencies. Mario wrote out a schedule and taped it to a wall. ("Seven: Plate coppa. Seven-fifteen: Serve. Seven-thirty: Drop first pasta. Seven-forty: Plate and serve.") Frankie was concerned about the broken flattop: a canister of butter had been put on it but hadn't melted.

Mario looked: it was in the wrong place. "The flattop is hot," he insisted, and spat on it to prove it. (Whoa! Did he just spit on the flat-top? I looked: his spittle sizzled.) It was a theatrical gesture—his audi-ence gasped audibly—done, no doubt, because Mario, arriving in a rush, unprepared for the cooking class awaiting him, was suddenly conscious of being onstage. Later, when he dressed the watercress salad, he grabbed a bottle of olive oil and, holding it high above his head, made a flamboyantly streaming arc, like some Alpine guide pouring rotgut from a goatskin boda bag, and his rapt audience, not wanting to miss a thing—even volunteers who had been taking notes stopped their scribbling—held its breath. But spitting on the flattop? It's true, you don't normally cook food directly on it, although, at Babbo, the ramps, the pancetta—that's where they were cooked. It was a brassy thing to do. Maybe it was more difficult being a celebrity chef than any of us understood—the expectation that you felt constantly from the people around you, these strangers, your public, to be so much bigger than a normal human being. (I was put in mind of a story Mario had once told me, of the first time he'd been spotted on the street, stopped by two guys who recognized him from television, immediately falling into the "Hey, dude, wow, it's, like, that guy from the Food thing" routine, and Mario, flattered, had thanked them courteously, and they were so disappointed—"crushed"—that he now travels with a repertoire of quick jokes so as to be, always, in character.) In any case, the volunteers seemed happy: Mario Batali had arrived; he spat; he poured olive oil; he was larger than life.

The butter melted, and the service went smoothly, without histrion-ics or tantrums. Each course, rushed out at go-go-go speed, involved all the volunteers, now crowded around the longest plating table, assem-bling dishes in a fury. Mario had asked me to check them before they went out, wiping off the rims with a damp cloth, and I surprised myself. The volunteers were heaping too much on the plates, a natural temptation—too much parsley, too much orange zest, too much parmigiano. Flavorings are meant to serve the food, not compete with it. A Babbo platitude.

"Replate," I said with great force.

"No," I said. "Wrong! This is a mess. Redo!"

Another appeared. "Goddammit. Too much stuff. Again. Replate!"

And then another. "For fuck's sake, how many fucking times do I have to say the same fucking thing?" (Did I just say what I think I said? Was I a latent screamer?)

There were festivities afterwards—too much adrenaline for the evening to end—where much wine was drunk. I have a memory, blurry, like swimming with your eyes open, of Mario's making scrambled eggs in a rich man's kitchen. (How did we get here, how are we leaving, and how is anyone going to cook tomorrow night—er, well, tonight, actually?) For most of us, the evening ended at five in the morning—Mario in a Falstaffian snoring funk in the taxi that took us back to the hotel—except for Frankie, who, having befriended one of the folksy, informally blue volunteers, went off on his own and didn't get back until seven, fifteen minutes before we left for the airport. "Looking good," Mario said, already seated on the plane, as Frankie appeared, zigzagging down the aisle. Frankie was not looking good. In fact, he was looking very bad—perspiring, pale, unshaven, his skin damp and clammy, smelling of a long Nashville night, with all the charisma of a collapsed lung, wrapped in an assortment of dark things, a black shell jacket, sunglasses, a wet blue bandanna across his forehead. We landed in Newark and went straight to the kitchen and got through the service, Andy sometimes forgetting to call out an order, Frankie curling up during slow moments on the wet greasy Babbo floor for a nap.

The trip surprised me with its many lessons—over and above my polenta tutorial and another illustration of the body's ability to accommodate abusive excess ("Oh, c'mon, guys," Mario said as we neared Manhattan, trying to cheer up the slumping heaps in the seat, "the human organism is remarkably strong—it always bounces back"). I don't think I'd understood how rarely cooks get to cook and how much time they put in before they get the chance. Riccardo from Bologna put me in mind of Alex at Babbo—maybe because Riccardo, an Italian in

America, was a mirror of Alex, who had been an American in Italy.
Alex's year there had been life-changing, and he still talked about it.
What he never mentioned, until I asked, was this: he had never cooked.
For a year, he had chopped carrots, onions, and celery. "I was the
absolute bottom of the ladder the entire time. It was a humbling experience. I thought if I worked my ass off I'd be promoted. I never was."
Finely chopped carrots ("I really perfected my carrot-chopping technique"), onions, and celery are important: cooked slowly in olive oil,
they turned out to be the basis of soffritto, the foundation of Tuscan
soups. Alex never made soffritto or soup. Then, when he was hired at
Babbo, he was again told he wouldn't be cooking: he'd begin, as everyone did, with cold foods, making starters. After some months, if there
was a vacancy and Andy approved, he'd be allowed to cook on a trial
basis at the sauté station. At the time, I was in my obsessive pasta-
making phase and working mornings with Alejandro. That is, in Alex's
eyes, I was "one of the Latins"—low on the proverbial totem pole. After
a couple of weeks, I returned to the grill, as Frankie had recommended.

"Do you mind telling me why you're at the grill?" Alex had had
three years of cooking school, a year in Italy, and a job at a three-star
restaurant, and he still wasn't cooking. "Would you mind telling me
how you were able to jump ahead of me?"

"Alex," I whispered. "I'm not a cook. Sssssh. I'm a spy."

The Nashville trip had also showed me how much I knew, and I was
surprised by how much that was. I'd had no measure. Like everyone
else, I'd been locked inside a hot windowless kitchen, working alongside
the same people for more than a year. That weirdo life? It was my life,
too. Later in the spring, I joined Mario when he was a guest chef at a
James Beard House event. One of his chefs didn't show, and I ended up
cooking a number of things, including the pasta, enough for forty people. But I'd done this before, and the pressure wasn't more than what
you experienced at the height of service. The next day I got an e-mail
from Mario: "Thanks for the help yesterday. You are actually quite
helpful." I'd been working with him for nearly a year and a half. He'd
never thanked me. Implicit in my role, a pupil whose presence the
kitchen tolerated, was that I was to be the one expressing gratitude. To
be thanked—this, for me, was a big deal.

15

OTTO WAS NO LONGER One Fifth Avenue, but, even with a name change, the curse of the place seemed to persist. When the restaurant opened in January 2003, the curse resurfaced and had its way with the item at the heart of the whole enterprise: the pizza. The early experiments had mystified everyone in the Babbo kitchen; they then mystified diners at Otto. ("We don't have the Otto-speak sorted out on the pizzas," the headwaiter said, addressing the members of his staff during the second week. "If anyone asks you to explain them, call over a manager.") Mario continued to think of them as griddle pizzas, heated from underneath on a flattop rather than in a wood-burning oven. "No, they're not Italian, they're my take on Italian. They're what I cook for my boys"—Mario's two sons, Benno and Leo—"and they love them." The implication was that if Mario's children loved them, so would the world. The world wasn't so sure.

"I'm nervous," Joe said. "I find the pizzas inedible. My mother finds the pizzas inedible. They sit on my stomach like a rock."

There were complaints. They were too spongy. They were undercooked. They weren't crispy. You couldn't cut them with a knife. Joe wasn't sleeping: "Everyone is suddenly a fucking pizza expert."

"I got it!" Mario said one afternoon. "We shouldn't heat the plates they're served on. They should be cold." But the plates weren't the solution.

"I got it!" Mario said the following week. "I'm making too much gluten. The secret is twenty percent more yeast and only three minutes of kneading." But the result tasted of raw bread—Joe, eating one at the bar, made a face of unequivocal revulsion—and the complaints continued.

"I got it!" Mario said, two weeks later. "It's cake flour. Good old-fashioned all-purpose cake flour. Why didn't I think of that before?" But it wasn't cake flour. In fact, a few days later, Mario abandoned cake flour and was using "oo" instead, the refined pasta flour from Italy.

"At night, I'm studying my McGee," he said, alluding to Harold McGee's book on the science of cooking. Otto was in its second month. It seemed inconceivable that he could still be experimenting with the recipe. "I know everything there is to know about gluten. The solution is fifty pounds of flour—half all-purpose flour and half Italian oo—and only a tablespoon of olive oil, three tablespoons of sugar, and then you let it sit for three hours." I was impressed by the detail Mario was sharing with me—that the crucial ingredient was a single tablespoon of olive oil in fifty pounds of flour, for instance—and his belief that I would understand what he was talking about. I didn't, but it didn't matter, because this recipe wasn't the solution either.

"Finally, I really do have it," he said, when I found him one morning sitting at the bar. "It's flour plus sweat equals dough." He was exhausted. "Yesterday I swallowed thirty pounds of flour. I had a steam shower this morning and coughed up a loaf of bread. I've got to step away from this. I'm making five hundred pizzas a day. Are they good? Are they bad? How can I tell? I'm listening to too many people. I'm overthinking this. I can't start doubting myself now. I've got to go with my gut."

But even though the pizza recipe wasn't settled, the place was very popular. Tom Adamson, a Babbo bartender, got end-of-the-night reports from a colleague at the Otto bar, and he passed these on when he brought pitchers of beer to us in the kitchen at eleven: 800 covers one evening, 923 the next. "These are not restaurant numbers," he said. "These could be for a sporting event." Otto was getting almost four times the number of Babbo's customers. In the kitchen, these accounts were unsettling. Was it that Babbo was no longer the star? For Andy they were also demoralizing.

"Otto," Elisa observed, "is quietly driving Andy crazy."

"WHAT ARE WE going to do about Andy?" Joe asked Mario when I joined them for lunch one day in early March. By now no one had any idea what went into the pizzas, but it didn't matter. People were eating them, Otto was a success, and Mario and Joe could think about other things. Joe was at Babbo in the evenings; Mario hadn't been; he'd been filming Food Network episodes about stromboli. Joe knew they had a problem.

"Have you talked to him about being more proprietary?" Mario asked. Andy was openly angry and foul-tempered and had just fired a runner on a whim.

"How can I talk to him about being more proprietary when he's not a proprietor?" Joe was alluding to the elusive Spanish restaurant. The arrangement had always been that Joe, Mario, and Andy would be joint owners. But the reality was that no such arrangement existed because there was no restaurant. There was Otto.

"He's become *very* difficult," Joe continued.

"This surprises me. Frankie told me Andy was much better—that his moods were under control."

"Well, Frankie's wrong. Andy is not better. He's worse."

Andy was different from the others. He was well read and articulate. On his days off, he went to movies, gallery openings, plays. I thought of him as the only grown-up in the kitchen. He wasn't a screamer and didn't gossip. He had a quick mind. As an expediter, he had a picture in his head of every table, how long each one would take to finish its course, and the time the kitchen would need to prepare the next one so that it arrived the moment after the plates were cleared. He was responsible for tens of thousands of dollars of extra business, because he'd figured out how to squeeze it in. "I act like I'm an owner," Andy confessed. "What's wrong with me?"

But there was something you weren't seeing. Andy spoke fast, sometimes very fast, and his speedo speech could seem like crazy speech, a glimpse of a psyche running down a hill at full tilt. He could be shrill. "Oh, how I hated that voice," Elisa said, recalling when she worked service. "It was always on the verge of losing it, just like Andy."

"Andy's in a bad mood," Frankie whispered, going from person to person, just as we were about to start the service on New Year's Eve. How could Frankie tell? I looked at Andy. It was true. Something was wrong: a seethingness, a self-imploding stress. It then came out, but never directly and always on the job. For instance, you'd be very busy, and Andy would tell you to fire six more orders.

Hang on there, guy, you'd think. You can see I can't do more.

But as you took in the instruction, scurried to pick up the stuff, season it, get it going, Andy would tell you to fire another four orders. This time, you would say something (even if nothing more than a heavily intoned *"What?"*), whereupon Andy would add two more orders and ("Why not?") another two, and then ("What the hell?") four tasting menus. Why? Because he could. Because he was in a silent rage: at his plight, at what he had to do every night—no letups, no easy evenings, every day for five years—at Mario and the fact that he didn't have to be there because he had Andy. Then, as though obeying the dictates of some self-destructive impulse, he'd go home and stay up until three reading about Spanish cooking, devising menus for a restaurant that didn't exist.

There would never be a Spanish restaurant. I was convinced. At the end of my lunch—Joe's having agreed to have one more talk with Andy—Joe asked Mario if he wanted to go for a ride. There was a site, not far from the meatpacking district, that he wanted Mario to see.

Fifteen minutes later, we were standing outside it, a large, empty building, as Joe elaborated a highly detailed daydream. "What about a five-hundred-seater," he said, "with sweeping stairs and valet parking and a *tabac* shop off to the side."

"It's Joe's idea of elegance—valet parking," Mario explained.

Joe ignored him. "Let's go all out and show New York you can have a four-star Italian." Improvising, more ideas coming to him as he talked, Joe said, "No, on reflection, it shouldn't be Italian, but Italian American"—a return to his roots, a homage to the cooking of his mother, Lidia. I was witnessing a creative side of restaurant making—an exhilarating thing—and, within six months, Joe had got a lease, hired an architect, and begun constructing a version of the vision that had come to him in the street in front of me. The place would have an Italian name, Del Posto. *Posto* was Italian for "place." What it wasn't was Italian for "Andy's Spanish restaurant."

MARIO HAD assumed he had a clear picture of the Babbo kitchen, even when he hadn't been there, because he'd been counting on Frankie to be a reliable spy. Frankie was his Andy spy: that's why Mario had been surprised when Joe said there'd been problems. (There were actually many spies. "Don't tell Elisa," Gina told me one day, "but Mario asked me to keep an eye on her.") But Frankie would never say anything negative behind someone's back. Face to face was different; face to face, you'll never meet anyone blunter.

Frankie was the oldest young person I've known. He wasn't yet thirty but could have been fifty. Or maybe he was every bit his age but from a different era: a younger version of someone's grandfather. He was from Philadelphia—"South Philly" (also fifty years behind the rest of the world)—and was lithe and nimble, and a very fast cook, with speedy street-smart reflexes: very male in an old-fashioned way, except for those eyelashes and a pronounced birthmark on his cheek, which was like the beauty mark of a woman from a time when women had beauty marks. He was close to his family and often went home on his days off: his mother owned a building (the tenant was a hair salon); his father, now retired and in his seventies, used to drive a truck. I accompanied Frankie on one of his visits—Philly cheese steaks, stromboli, chicken cutlets, an Italian-American street market, all the buildings brick, most of them two-story, evocative of Edward Hopper paintings and the movie *Rocky*. We drove around, and I was shown the 'hood: the church where Frankie had had his first job, helping prepare supper for the parish priests; his mother's building, which he hopes to take over one day and make into an eatery ("Nothing fancy, just good food—I'll run it with my sister and her husband"), his street, where every September he'd wheel a tomato juicer from house to house. The juicer was a hand-cranked food mill, the kind that Italians still use to skin and seed tomatoes to make a sauce. In Frankie's neighborhood, it was called "gravy." In September, all the women bought tomatoes by the bushel.

Frankie pretended to go to a community college ("I dunno—accounting"), but he wasn't a good student, and one day he came home and found brochures for cooking schools on the kitchen table. His mother had sent away for them. Four years later, he got his first big job: at Le Cirque, then a four-star restaurant, when the head chef was the Cambodian-born, Paris-trained Sottha Khunn. At first, typically, Frankie wasn't allowed to cook. "For the first three months, I did starters, just like Alex is doing now. I did everything Sottha Khunn told me to do. It was always 'Yes, Chef. Whatever you say, Chef. Right away, Chef.' It was a French kitchen, so I was his bitch. Okay, if that's the way it's done, that's what I'll be. Three months later, Khunn told me to watch the guy on the grill. I wasn't supposed to cook, just watch. Then one day, he put me on the line—not on the grill, though, but at the fish station. The fish guy hadn't shown up. I wasn't trained. 'No time to train,' Khunn told me." It was a disaster. Frankie was nervous, and everything went wrong, and at the end of the night, disgraced, he was sent home: from now on, he'd be working mornings.

Sottha Khunn was a screamer. "If he asked for something, you gave it to him. If he wanted it in a different way, you did it. You never questioned, you never argued, because in the back of your head you knew that once he started screaming your evening was ruined. He didn't stop until you were sent home or fired." Khunn was also a perfectionist and, for Frankie, an inspiration. "I learned more in three months of Le Cirque than three years of the cooking school. I went to cooking school so I could get a job with someone like Khunn." Trained by a screamer, did Frankie then grow up to be one? Because as Frankie assumed more and more responsibility at Babbo, that's what he seemed to be becoming: the kitchen's screamer.

Alex got most of the screaming, although he admits he sometimes deserved it. He was still working the pantry station, but it wasn't any less busy than any other spot. There were thirteen appetizers, each with its own complex construction, and he wasn't, he conceded, always ready when the service started: a terrifying admission. It means you're doing your prep while orders are being called out, and the orders come fast.

If Alex wasn't ready, he fell behind. ("I wasn't used to being so busy—I made three or four hundred appetizers a night—and didn't have the time to reach up and get a glass of water.") A table might have ordered a pasta and a starter, and the pasta would be done, ready to go out, starting to cool, and Alex was messing around with his beans.

"Hey, Alex," Frankie shouted. "Do you know what *mise en place* means?"

Alex, characteristically, didn't get the point of the question—he was so caught up with what he was doing that he hadn't realized people were waiting for it—and he responded literally. He thought Frankie was asking for help with a French expression. He stopped and pondered the phrase, conjugating the verb, and was about to provide a translation, when Frankie stopped him. "No, you dickhead. It means having your shit in the right place in time!" Alex looked stunned. "Sometimes," he said to Frankie, "the way you give information is not entirely appropriate, and I think you could afford to be a little less coarse." It got worse. Frankie started timing Alex's dishes and counting off the seconds. He sent back others. The salads weren't high enough. *"Replate!"* They didn't have enough greens. *"Replate!"* He hadn't wiped off the dish first. *"Replate!"* The rosemary wasn't fine enough. The beans were overcooked. He'd forgotten the pancetta.

"He was busting my balls," Alex told me. "I'd become his bitch. He'd singled me out to kick my ass." In fact, Alex hadn't been singled out.

"I'm a dick, I'm a dick, I'm a dick!" Frankie announced routinely. "I've got to be a dick so we don't lose our three stars. I don't want friends." He turned on Mario Garland. Garland was the guy who'd replaced Mark Barrett at the pasta station. But his dishes were too wet. ("I made the mistake of being nice to him," Frankie told me. "He thought of me as a buddy rather than management.") He turned on Holly because she kept "talking back." "She wasn't getting enough color on her duck"—meaning her pan wasn't hot enough and she wasn't browning the bird sufficiently—"and I told her, 'You need more color,' but she wants to explain. We're in the middle of service. I don't want an explanation. I want to hear 'Yes, Frank, right away, Frank, whatever you say, Frank.'" Every place Frankie looked, he saw something he didn't like. "There are a hundred ways to cook an ingredient. I'm here to make sure that it's done Mario's way." The trouble was that Mario wasn't in the kitchen. "I've told him to show his face. I need people to see that what I say is coming from him. They're not listening to me."

Frankie wasn't naturally a manager; he was naturally sociable and capable of being one thing one moment (a friend, a confidant, a prankster—whipping up a bowl of egg whites and pretending to sneeze them down the neck of the dishwasher) and a frightening, abusive person the next. When he showed up at midday, I'd scrutinize his face to see which Frankie we were going to get. It made for a peculiar work environment, although one that was never dull. I may have been entertained more easily than the others, because I had so little at stake. I didn't mind being criticized—I was there to learn—and accepted my servile status. "Yes, Frankie," I would always say.

"Am I right, Bill?" he'd shout so the whole kitchen heard.

"Yes, Frankie."

"Am I always right?"

"Yes, Frankie."

"Is it possible that I could ever be wrong?"

"No, Frankie."

Then he'd smile.

But my turn was bound to come.

The occasion was a staff shortfall. Abby had taken six days off. For some time, she'd been entertaining the notion of having cosmetic surgery. This had become a peculiar subject—should she? shouldn't she?—but not much more peculiar than any other kitchen confidence: Holly's sex life, say (a vivid chronicle), or Garland's efforts to impregnate his wife (an ongoing one, with daily updates). When you spent so much time together, you had no secrets. And then, decisively, Abby resolved to have it done.

She was expected back on the following Monday. I had been working with her at the grill, splitting the job into a two-person station, as I had done with Mark. In the beginning, I cooked the meat and she prepared the contorni, and in time I was also preparing the contorni and plating the dishes, although Abby was nearby in case something went wrong. On the Sunday, she phoned. There were complications. She needed one more day. Who could cover for her?

I'd been hoping for such a moment. It was March 17th—fifteen months after my first day in the kitchen. Was I ready? Yes and no. Yes, because I almost knew everything I had to do. No, because I only almost knew everything.

The prep alone was so complicated that you never mastered it until you had no choice. (Or rather, I should say, it was so complicated that I'd never mastered it until I'd had no choice.) I had a map of the station and had just about committed it to memory. The meat and fish were under the counter in the lowboy. That was under control. The problem was what was on top: the little trays of contorni and various embellishments. There were thirty-three different ingredients, and most had to be prepared before the service started, including red onions (cooked in beet juice and red wine vinegar), salsify (braised in sambuca), and *farotta* (cooked in a beet purée). There were six different squirter bottles, two balsamic vinegars, two olive oils, plus *vin santo*, *vin cotto*, and

saba, not to mention the Brussels sprouts and braised fennel and rabbit
pâté—and damn! Today, I look at the map and am astonished I had any
of it in my head.

I was nervous and started off in characteristic fashion by slicing
myself. I was preparing Jerusalem artichokes, the knotty, remarkably
ugly bulbs that look like dirt clods. But sliced thin and fried very hot,
they have an earthy flavor that someone must like. Mario, I suppose.
(Sometimes I'd put these dishes together and wonder: how in the world
did he think this combination was a good idea?) Once the chokes started
to brown, you added shiitake mushrooms and a splash of vinegar and
finished them with a handful of parsley: it was a vegetable bed for the
lamb chops. But it was edible only if the Jerusalem artichokes were cut
very thin—a thinness you get only by using a meat slicer, that round
spinning blade that you see at the deli. The slicer is big; the chokes are
small and slippery. There was a grinding sound. I did my customary
leap. Everyone froze. Tony Liu bent over to see if he'd find my finger
jammed in the blade.

"No, no," I said. "Just the nail and fingertip."

I did my routine: disinfectant, bandages, and a rubber guard, which I
slipped over a now foreshortened forefinger.

It wasn't a good start, and I was now behind on my prep. Actually
everyone was behind, and there was a feeling of pressure—a nasty, pissy
kind of pressure. Elisa stayed later than normal and in her rush dropped a
container of cockles, which scattered across the floor like marbles. Frankie
said something. "Fuck off, Frankie," she said. He mumbled something
else. Elisa repeated herself loudly. "Frankie, fuck off." She was irritable.
Frankie was irritable. Was I the irritant? I was taking too long slicing my
rosemary, Frankie said. I was taking too long preparing the thyme.

Tony Liu joined him. "You have to move faster. There's a lot of prep.
You're too slow."

The service started, and for the first two hours every piece of meat I
cooked was inspected.

Okay. I'm being tested. Don't panic. You know how to do this.

There was an order for lamb chops, medium rare. I cooked them,
assembled the plate, was about to put it up on the pass, when Frankie
stopped me, took the dish apart, and squeezed each piece of meat. He

said nothing: no eye contact, nothing. A rib eye, medium rare, and four people immediately crowded round the meat after I cooked it, prodding it with a skewer, and then touching the lips with it to judge the meat's doneness. A pork tenderloin; the same routine: the dish was taken apart. The meat was fine. I could see Frankie's disappointment. "Put it back together," he said.

Tony Liu saw my hand. "Get rid of the plastic."

"I sliced my fingertip," I reminded him.

"Get rid of it. You can't cook meat wearing plastic. You won't have the touch."

I peeled off the plastic and threw out the bandages. For a while, I tried to use my other fingers, but they were ineffective. I couldn't do the quick touch. I had to use too much of my middle finger to get a reading and burnt it and then couldn't interpret what it was telling me—and so I gave in. I pressed my forefinger against a lamb chop on the grill, pressing the wound into meat. The wound spread and opened. The meat was salty and glistened with hot fat. I felt the salt (burning) and the fat (another kind of burning). Well, that was the drill. I turned to rinse my hand in the sudsy plastic container, but it was black, except for the surface, which was shiny. I paused and then dipped in my hand.

Frankie was inches from my face. "You don't have Abby to protect you. Tonight you've got me. It's just me and you."

He picked up two slices of pancetta, which I was cooking on the flattop. They had the string around them. "We don't serve string," he said.

I knew that. This particular pancetta had been badly rolled and was coming loose, which Tony had observed when he'd delivered it to me from the walk-in: he'd told me to cook it with the string on and remove it when I plated the pancetta. I started to explain, but my explanation was provoking.

"Yes, Frankie," I said.

He peeled off the string and threw it in my face.

"You're with the big boys now. You're on your own."

I filled a sauté pan with orange juice, reduced it, added some butter, and dropped in the fennel. The fennel goes with the branzino.

Frankie picked up the pan.

"Do you think this fennel is good enough?" he asked. I thought he was going to throw the pan at me. I braced myself. He didn't move. I looked at the fennel. There were two pieces, each one a third of a bulb. I didn't know what to say.

"Would you be happy if you had so little fennel on your plate?"

I looked again. Okay, maybe this bulb was a little small.

"It's not fucking good enough," Frankie said. "Do it again." He picked up the hot fennel pieces with his fingers and threw them at my face. He missed. They landed on the tray where my meat was resting, spraying it with buttery orange juice. I picked up the bulbs, tossed them, wiped off the meat, and started another pan.

"Tonight you're with the big boys. Tonight you've got to carry your own weight."

Andy fired a rabbit.

It was a favorite dish, because it was the most complex. The rabbit is cooked three ways—sautéed, grilled, and confit—and served on dandelion greens. It's done in stages, requiring several people to work together. During the day, a prep cook roasts the foreleg and back leg. Just before service, I brown them in a hot pan, add thin slices of parsnips (which caramelize quickly), a splash of vin santo (which explodes in a flame), pancetta, and rabbit stock (a radical French addition, and I'm still not sure why it was tolerated). I then put the pan away until it is needed. The grilled bit is the rabbit loin. And the confit is a pâté, which is spread on a piece of toasted bread like a *crostino* and placed on the top of the dish, very architectural.

It takes two people to finish the dish, me and Frankie.

I'd prepared a shelf of sauté pans before the service. I took one out and put it on the flattop. I placed a loin on the grill and got another pan for the dandelion greens. When the loin was almost done, I put a slice of bread on the counter, which Frankie was meant to toast. While it was toasting, I got out the pâté. That was the routine, anyway.

I put out a piece of bread.

Frankie smashed it.

That was confusing. Was there something wrong with the bread? I looked up at Frankie. He was full of rage.

"Get me another."

I cleaned up the smashed bread, wiped away the crumbs, and got another piece.

Frankie smashed it.

This piece had been identical to the last one. I didn't know what was wrong.

"Get me another."

I cleaned up the smashed bread and got another piece. Frankie smashed it. I looked at him. What the fuck are you doing? He was profoundly, irretrievably irrational, as though some scary chemical thing was going on in his head. I looked for Andy, but he had turned away. This, too, was peculiar. Wasn't he waiting for the very dish that we were failing to complete because Frankie was smashing the bread that needed to be toasted?

"Get me another."

I got another piece, no different from the previous three pieces. Frankie took it, and we assembled the dish and put it up on the pass.

It was a long night. There were other mishaps. At one point, Andy fired a branzino, but I hadn't heard the order (could I have not heard it?) and hadn't cooked one. Later it was an order of lamb chops. Had I missed that too? I stared at Andy. His face said nothing.

Maybe there were more things. The night was a blur. When John Mainieri came into the kitchen and said "All in," I was overcome with relief. It was early, only eleven o'clock. I'd been there since one. I was drenched. My cook's coat was stuck to my back; it had melted. When I got the chance to pee, it was bright yellow. I was dehydrated. The night had begun with such high expectations. I got home, I put a chair in front of a window and stared out and didn't move until dawn.

I WENT TO WORK the next day—with, perhaps, a noticeable lack of bounce in my step. I was the embodiment of slowness. Everything about me was slow. My thoughts were arrested in some kind of brain molasses. I could have been running in water. I had a career idea: I could be the mascot for the slow-food movement.

Abby had returned but shouldn't have. She was pale and fragile and couldn't lift her arms. You can't cook if you can't move your arms. The kitchen had a real problem. The day before, Tony Liu had come in on his day off, just in case something went wrong. Today there was no backup. Abby knew she shouldn't have come in; she also knew that she was expected. The kitchen motto: no one gets ill. (Until I worked there, I'd always wondered why so many people in New York suddenly got ill in

the winter. Was it the subway and the exposure to so many germy people pressed together? Or simply that most people in New York don't
cook at home and get their meals from a professional kitchen?)

Once again the same challenge. Was I ready?

Yes. And yes.

I set up the station. I saw what was missing. I cooked and browned
my fennel. I cut my rosemary—fast: bam, bam, bam. I sorted out the
thyme. I prepared six sauté pans of rabbit. And the more I did, the looser
I got, like an athlete warming up. The thickness in my head melted
away. My movements became more fluid. I completed a task and knew
what I had to do next and what I needed to do after that one was done.
The service started. I was ready. I fell into a rhythm. I was seeing the
kitchen in a way I'd never seen it. I seemed to be seeing everything. Was
this adrenaline? Was it a clarity that comes from exhaustion? I couldn't
explain why I was feeling so good, especially after feeling so bad. I knew
where everyone was at every point in their preparations. I understood
all the tickets and all the items on them. I was working with Frankie, but
again somehow, I don't know how, I knew what he was going to do
before he did it, when he wanted something before he asked for it. "Bill,
I need the—" but whatever it was (red onions, sprouts, a piece of bread)
I already had it. I was cooking: fast, hard, effectively. It was the most satisfying evening of labor I'd ever experienced.

When the evening was over, I sat at the bar. I had to cool down. I
asked Tom for a beer. Frankie appeared and sat on the stool next to me.
He wanted to thank me. "You did good. Don't let no one tell you no different. You saved our ass."

I finished my beer. Okay. I did good. I liked that.

Pasta-Maker

〜〜〜〜〜〜〜〜〜〜〜〜〜〜〜〜〜

My experience of Neapolitan gastronomy was expanded by an invitation to a dinner, the main feature of which was a spaghetti-eating competition. Such contests have been a normal feature of social life, latterly revived and raised almost to the level of a cult as a result of the reappearance on the black market of the necessary raw materials.

Present: men of gravity and substance, including an ex–Vice Questore, a director of the Banca di Roma, and several leading lawyers— but no women. The portions of spaghetti were weighed out on a pair of scales before transfer to each plate. The method of attack was the classic one, said to have been introduced by Fernando IV, and demonstrated by him for the benefit of an ecstatic audience in his box at the Naples Opera. The forkful of spaghetti is lifted high into the air, and allowed to dangle and then drop into the open mouth, the head being held well back. I noticed that the most likely-looking contestants did not attempt to chew the spaghetti, but appeared to hold it in the throat which, when crammed, they emptied with a violent convulsion of the Adam's apple— sometimes going red in the face as they did so. Winner: a sixty-five-year old doctor who consumed four heaped platefuls weighing 1.4 kilograms, and was acclaimed by hand-clapping and cheers. These he cheerfully acknowledged and then left the room to vomit.

—Norman Lewis, *Naples '44*

16

I WAS NOW PREOCCUPIED by the question of when, in the long history of food on the Italian peninsula, cooks started putting eggs in their pasta dough. Was this a reasonable concern? Of course not. But the question wouldn't go away. It also raised other issues that got me thinking as well, including the possibility that the word "pasta" was misleading, if not outright wrong. Conventionally, there are two versions, dried and wet—right? The dried, like linguine, is called pastasciutta, and the wet, like Miriam's tortellini, is called pasta fresca. But now I believe that they are much more different than most people realize and that it is only an accident of language that makes them seem as if they're the same. They're made with different kinds of wheat (durum, the protein-heavy kind, goes into the dried; ordinary bread flour, from a starchier grain, goes into the soft), in different preparations (one is dressed with olive oil, from a tree; the other with butter, from a cow), and from wholly different cultures: dried pasta appeared in Sicily in the early twelfth century (nearly two hundred years before Marco Polo returned from visiting the Chinese, possibly bearing *their* version), and had been introduced by Arab traders, who would have known nothing about the fresh kind, even though it had already been around for a thousand years in a form known to us as lasagna, to the Romans as *laganum,* and to the Greeks as *laganon.*

The confusion arises from the fact that, until the second half of the twentieth century, "pasta" wasn't really a kitchen word (you almost never see it in the old cookbooks) but an inventory word, meaning a food, any food, savory or sweet, made with dough. (It appears as a book-keeping item in Cagliari in 1351, used by Sardinian shipping agents to distinguish crates of dried noodles from the other cargo on their docks:

salted fish, wheels of cheese, wine, sheep, canisters of saffron, and that stuff stacked up against the wall—that's right, that dough stuff, the pasta thing, that goes over there.)

Instead of dried pasta, you had macaroni. *That* had been the generic word people used for five centuries or so, meaning not just the tubular kind but all kinds, originating in Sicily and then spreading to Sardinia and Naples and shipped through Genoa to the principal ports of Europe. Thomas Jefferson ate it in France and was so taken with it that he dispatched trunkloads home, becoming the first person to introduce dried pasta to the United States. (Twenty-six years later, his annual order was fifty pounds, enough for two hundred and fifty meals. He doubled it in 1817, plus an extra fifty pounds for his grandson, and doubled it again the following year: having acquired the taste, he, like so many of us, couldn't get enough.)

Macaroni has always been big business; fresh pasta never could be. Fresh pasta was made in the North, usually by women in homes or small kitchens, not in factories, and by its perishable nature was impossible to export. It was sold, therefore, by the people who had just prepared it—since the 1300s, by *lasagnari*, lasagna makers, because "lasagna" was the generic term for what we now think of as a fresh pasta: a dough rolled out into a sheet *(una sfoglia)* from which you then cut, square, twist, stuff, and make the many possible toys that, among Italians, go by the name of dinner. Since Greek and Roman times, lasagna was flour and water, kneaded to stretch out the unique proteins of wheat and unite them with water molecules to produce the elastically accommodating combination known as gluten—the enduring mystery of the European meal. And since Greek and Roman times, there was no egg in the dough until—when?

There is no egg in a recipe in the *Liber de coquina*, written by an anonymous author at the end of the 1200s, which calls for a sheet of fermented pasta (a quasi-leavened dough mixed with an uncooked bit from the last meal). The sheet is rolled out as thin as possible, *più sottile che puoi*, and cut up into squares, no wider than the length of your finger, which are boiled and served with cheese and spices, probably nutmeg and cinnamon—a simple pasta, and one that reminded me of the trip Joe Bastianich and I took to Porretta Terme, where Betta made a similar preparation called quadrini, "little squares," dressed with butter and parmigiano.

There are no eggs in the Tuscan version of *Liber de coquina*, written in the late 1300s. The anonymous author *(anonimo Toscano)* calls for a good white flour *(farina bona, bianca)*—the fluffy, starchy kind—and recommends dressing it with cheese or lardo. There are no eggs in the later Venetian version (written by another suspiciously anonymous author, *anonimo Veneziano*).

By the fifteenth century, there are still no eggs: none, it seems, in the pasta made by Maestro Martino, although he does call for egg whites, a breakthrough of sorts. He uses them in his Sicilian macaroni, to make the noodles stiffer, but says nothing about what to do with the leftover yolks. The lack of instruction is perplexing because the Maestro loved his eggs (poached in sweet wine, grilled, coddled, roasted, made into shapes, cooked in milk or oil or on red-hot coals) and recommends using one as a binding agent to hold together the ingredients inside the ravioli. What he doesn't say is to put another in the dough that you make the ravioli from.

THE QUESTION was pressing because, at the last minute, I'd impulsively got on an airplane and gone to Italy. The reason, of course, was pasta, *once again*. I don't want to diminish the importance of my time at the Babbo pasta station—I will remember it for the rest of my life, if only for what I now know about linguine and shellfish—but, in essential ways, I was very far removed from the real thing. After all, I was learning how to make a rustic, age-old, highly local Italian preparation in a fast, busy, metropolitan kitchen in New York City. I wasn't even being taught by an Italian but by cooks who had been taught by other cooks who had been taught by Mario who (finally!) had been taught by an Italian. And the pasta itself was produced on a machine, whereas I was always hearing that the best kind is rolled out by hand on a wooden board with a *matterello*—the long Italian rolling pin, round at one end to shape a sheet of dough into a square—and the result, made *with* wood *on* wood, was supposed to have that cat's-tongue texture that Mario was always going on about, like his grandmother's ravioli or Miriam's tortelli. That was what I still longed to make, and, after all this time, I didn't know how. So why not ask Miriam herself?

I called. Miriam, I said, I want to work with you.

"*Certo,*" she said. "Phone me when you are next in Italy and come by one afternoon."

This was difficult. I wasn't thinking of an afternoon when I happened to be in the *zona,* but, you know, a couple of weeks. A month. Or longer: something planned for, with lodgings and all the trappings of an apprenticeship.

She panicked. "What are you talking about? A month? I never let anyone into my kitchen—*ever.*" (She made a funny sound. Was she having trouble breathing?) "I don't know what to say. Are you crazy?" She was very angry.

That plan didn't work out, but I had another opportunity the very next week. The occasion was a visit to New York by Valeria Piccini, the chef of Da Caino, widely regarded as the best restaurant in Italy, located in Montemerano, a hill town in the Maremma, the southern part of Tuscany by the sea. Alain Ducasse—the most renowned French chef at the time—had invited Valeria over to be guest chef at his New York restaurant. I wanted to meet her and managed to attend the event.

For Valeria, the evening was an unmitigated disaster. The kitchen was wrong. There were too many people—they were heartless and *too* efficient—and she was compelled to make food she hadn't touched ("I need to touch every dish") and on plates so impersonal she couldn't bear to look at them ("I had to close my eyes"). The pasta was a catastrophe, she declared, appearing at the end of the meal, on the verge of tears. She apologized to the Italians (who nodded, knowingly; with no idea that anything was wrong, I had devoured my plate in a condition of brainless contentment) and collapsed into a chair next to me. She didn't understand how it had gone so badly. She had made the dough in the normal way, she explained (to me, to the ceiling, to no one): so much egg, so much flour, but the result was wrong. She threw it out. Maybe she'd forgotten something. She made it again—so much egg, so much flour— but it still wasn't right. "I was confused. How can this be?" By now orders were coming in. "I want to go to bed. I want to go back to my hotel and hide. I'm so embarrassed." She paused, distressed. Physically, she resembled Miriam—the hooked, masculine nose; the broad face; the white chef's cap; but younger (forty-five to Miriam's sixty-two). Like Miriam, she'd worked in only one kitchen (her own), in the same restaurant (her own), and in her own town. I remember thinking: you don't meet people like this in New York.

"Was it the flour?" she was saying softly. "People told me to bring my own. I said, 'What are you talking about? This is the best restaurant in New York.' The eggs? People told me to bring eggs. 'Trust me,' I said. 'They have chickens in America.' "

I listened to this sad monologue, utterly captivated. (Actually, that's not quite true: in one ear, I listened to it, uncomprehendingly; in the other, I listened to my wife, Jessica, a fluent Italian speaker, translating it for me.) The monologue confirmed everything I had thought about pasta. It was so simple and yet so difficult. Simple ingredients (flour, egg) and a simple process (making a dough), and yet, even in the hands of a great chef, it didn't work, and she had no idea why.

"Let me work for you!" I blurted out in English.

She looked at me blankly.

"Let me work for you!" I repeated. I'd got very excited. "I can leave tomorrow!"

She was puzzled, and I could see my message was taking a long time to get through. Maybe my enthusiastic American thrustingness wasn't the strategic approach. In fact, once my message had finally been understood, I could see that my enthusiasm was not, by any means, reciprocated. She straightened up, seemed to remember where she was (when I saw myself as I must have appeared to her—as a stranger with an inexplicable capacity to enthuse about plates of failed food) "Oh," she said guardedly, in English, "you want to be an intern?"

"Yes!" I said. "Yes! Yes!"

"I'm afraid that would be very difficult to arrange."

So that plan didn't work out either. Why? I didn't know why. Because she doesn't like Americans? Because she didn't like me? Because she's a xenophobic, grumpy Italian mountain person, suspicious of strangers? Or was it because she didn't want to share her pasta secrets? *That* was obviously why, although, now, after the event, I recognize that there might have been another element.

The clue is the word "intern." Italy is in an intern crisis, and chefs of any stature have lists of people wanting to be their slaves. You'd think such a state of affairs would be a happy phenomenon—why waste money on labor when you can get yours free?—but it's a problem. Most of the slaves are Japanese, but there are also virtually every nationality except the French. Slavery is so much the rage that you now need permission to be one: there are slave regulations, slave visas, a protocol, and a slave stamp in your passport that you get only by applying to the Italian immigration authorities, supported by a written "contract" with a restaurant that includes its pledge not to pay you for the work it has already agreed to make you do. (It is a curious moment in the history of kitchen labor relations.) In fact, unknown to me, Mark Barrett—in many ways, my intrepid role model in this matter—had found himself outside the law. His not having one of those I'm-your-slave-don't-pay-me visas meant that the restaurant he'd indentured himself to couldn't exploit him. Mark had managed to work without pay for about four weeks before finally being told he had to go home. His New York friends weren't ready to welcome him back. In the words of one, they were "still recovering from all the festivities" of his leave-taking. ("Oops," Mario said. "I guess things have changed since I last worked there.")

One day, I found myself sitting with Mario and Mark. Mark was miserable, still trying to figure out how to get around a law he didn't understand and return to Italy and work for people for no pay, when an obvious idea occurred to Mario.

"Why not work for Gianni and Betta?" he declared. "Gianni knows everyone, he'll figure out the visa. You only have to work for him for a few months, and, in exchange, he'll fix you up so you can stay for years."

Mark mulled this over. Maybe Gianni could sort out the visa. But when Mario had worked for Gianni and Betta, they'd been running La Volta, a serious restaurant with serious ambitions. Now they had a pizzeria. Why should Mark go to Italy to work at a pizzeria?

"Why?" Mario replied, with exaggerated astonishment. "Because it's a pizzeria that serves pizza *and* pasta, and because Betta makes the pasta."

Which was why I was in Porretta. It was also why I'd got so interested in the egg, because, on my first morning, watching Betta prepare the dough, I saw that an egg was a modern pasta's most important ingredient, provided it was a *very* good egg, which was evident (or not) the moment you cracked it open. If the white was runny, you knew the egg had come from a battery-farmed animal, cooped up in a cage, and the pasta you made from it would be sticky and difficult to work with, exactly like the unhappy batch Betta produced one evening after Gianni fell asleep, having had too much wine at lunch, and failed to buy eggs from the good shop before it closed and had to drive to the next town to the *cattivo alimentarii,* the nasty store, and pick up a dozen of its mass-produced product. The yolk was also illuminating. The nasty store's were pale yellow, like those most of us have been scrambling for our urban lives. But a proper yolk is a different color and, in Italian, is still called *il rosso,* the red bit, arising from a time when you ate eggs in spring and summer, the egg season, and they came from grain-fed, half-wild, not just free-ranging but virtually proprietorial chickens that produced a yolk more red than yellow, a bright primary intensity that you can see today if you're lucky enough to get your eggs not from a super-market but a local *mercato* or a small farm.

Betta's pasta recipe was one egg for every *etto* of all-purpose flour. An etto is a hundred grams, one of those universal Italian measurements that might be translated as "medium-to-large-ish." You don't add water because there should be enough liquid in the egg (*if* you found a good one). You don't need a flavor intensifier like salt or olive oil because all the flavor you need is, again, already in the egg (*if* you found a good one). At Babbo, Mario compensated for his being unable to find a reliable supply of half-wild, genuinely small-farm eggs by tripling up on the yolks he could get: for every pound of flour (call it four *etti*), he'd use three eggs, plus *eight* yolks, not to mention salt, a dribble of olive oil, and a little bit of water. (This recipe is not the one you'll find in the Babbo cookbook and was, until this moment, a kitchen secret.) Was Mario's yolk-tripled pasta better than Betta's? No, it was different, and both are good. But Betta's is the one I remember: one egg, one etto. I also liked the simplicity of a recipe that depends wholly on the goodness of one ingredient: one *good* egg, one etto.

I'D BEEN in such a rush to get to Porretta because I wanted to get there before the classroom got too crowded. I'm not sure why I was in such a hurry. Betta wasn't. By the time Mark arrived, about ten days after me, Betta had finally consented to my touching the dough: I was permitted to knead it. Until then, I had watched.

"Watching is good," she said. "That was how I learned as a child: hours and hours, watching my aunts." This was a familiar lesson, but how much watching did I need to do? "When Mario was here, he wasn't interested in watching. He wanted to make pasta immediately. Every morning, he'd ask, 'Can I make the pasta now? Can I? Can I? Can I?' " She snorted with indignation, as if to say how could he possibly make pasta without memorizing the hands of women who have been doing this for decades?

I snorted, too, just to be agreeable, until I remembered why I was there. (The exchange confirmed my suspicions of a conspiracy: they really don't want us to know how to do this.)

Even so, the kneading by hand was not without interest. It wasn't done at Babbo, because there the dough was bashed around by a machine, "for forty-five minutes," Mario boasted to me one day, much longer than anywhere else, "in order to draw out more of the glutens" (a metaphor that seemed to regard gluten proteins as garden snails that appeared when you weren't looking). In fact, unknown to Mario, the dough was bashed for only ten minutes, which I'm sure was perfectly sufficient, and Alejandro looked at me as though I were an insane man when I asked if maybe it needed another half hour.

For me, the hand kneading alone may have justified the journey to Italy: crushing the dough under my weight, folding it in half, crushing it again, warming it slightly with the heat of my skin, stretching it with each repetition. Bread makers know these moments and get all lyrical about their tactile sensuality. Slowly the dough becomes shiny and more pliable, stretchy, just as the wheat proteins themselves are being stretched, and after a few minutes you can actually smell the glutens coming together, an evocatively fragrant perfume. In a poetic spasm, I thought of it as an oven at the far end of my memory. For the longest time, bread and pasta were also both made with water. Now pasta makers use an egg instead. And for me, naggingly, the question was: When?

I WAS CONVINCED I'd discover the first recipe in Bartolomeo Scappi. I had first consulted Scappi's *Opera* for precorn polenta preparations and, having then acquired a two-volume facsimile edition of the 1570 text, I couldn't stop myself from peeking at it, a page here, a page there, struggling with the ornate sixteenth-century script until eventually I was enjoying what seemed like an unmediated glimpse into a disciplined Renaissance kitchen. Scappi, proud and a little vain—his portrait on the cover looks like Plato with an appetite—includes meticulous accounts of his grander meals, and I lost hours in the menus, like the one for a lunch on October 28th: no indication of the year or occasion, the tongue-in-cheek implication being that it was like any autumnal *pranzo*, this year's, last year's, ho-hum, the sort of thing whipped up every October 28th. According to Scappi, the meal was a bit of everything, *di grasso e di magro*, fatty and lean, non-fasting and fasting, and consisted of eight courses, 1,347 dishes in all. Some were quite rustic—hams boiled in wine, for instance, or clams cooked on the grill. Most were pretty elaborate, like the meatballs made from capon breasts served in a veal-foot jelly; or the pigeons, boned and filled with rooster crests and pork jowls; or something called *sommata dissalata*, a bittersweet tummy delicacy, a mishmash of meaty bits, conserved in brine, stuffed into a stomach like a beach ball, cooked on a spit, and served with lemon and sugar. There were a hundred and sixty tiny grilled birds (*ortolani* in Italian; *ortolans* in French—the item prepared by Marco Pierre White in the early pub days), two hundred fried frogs, eight peacocks, plus unspecified numbers of turkeys, guinea hens, wild ducks, pheasants, geese, doves, thrushes, woodcocks, larks, and just about everything else that flies. Only a few people, the deadpan Scappi concedes, worried about dinner.

Soon I was reading Scappi for instruction, especially for lessons in what goes with what: familiar themes like game birds with fruit (pheasant stuffed with prunes, crab apples, bone marrow, and nuts), or the raw with the cooked, or the raw with the cured, as in a pork terrine that Scappi wraps with slices of prosciutto. His tortellini were made with a veal and capon filling—bovine and fowl, an unmodern pairing, and one I associate with the meats you find in a Bolognese ragù. One ravioli stuffing combined beets and spinach, another blended peas with three cheeses, and *that* was the kind of thing I liked learning, that you could add ricotta, parmigiano, and pecorino to summer peas and fill a pasta with the mix. But when I found Scappi's instructions for the dough that encased these fillings, I was disappointed. Apart from a splash of rose-water, butter, and some sugar, it was the familiar two-thousand-year-old eggless preparation.

Elsewhere the egg makes an appearance. A yolk shows up in Scappi's gnocchi. It reappears in his Roman macaroni (a thick hand-rolled noodle that takes half an hour to cook). But the important moment is in a tagliatelle soup. The recipe is simple: two pounds of flour, the ubiquitous warm water *(acqua tepida)*, and—hark!—three eggs. The amount of water isn't specified, but you can figure it out. Scappi is using medieval measurements, and two *French* pounds of flour—the pound then was twelve ounces—was about 700 grams. Scappi then adds three eggs: three eggs for 700 grams of flour? I tried the mix at home. To get the requisite wetness, you need enough water to match the volume of the eggs and probably a little more. The liquid used to make the dough, therefore, wasn't wholly water or wholly egg, but a mix of roughly equal portions of each. Eggs had not replaced water, but, for the first time in pasta history, they had an equal billing. I closed my book. I hadn't discovered the egg moment, but I had to be close. As they say in blindman's bluff, I was getting warm.

Then I had a thought: I should write the secretary of the pasta museum in Rome, Amelia Giarmoleo. She would know. We'd been in touch before, and I cursed myself for not having written earlier.

"Gentile Signora Amelia Giarmoleo," I began, in an e-mail entitled *"Domanda urgente"*—urgent question. When did the egg replace water in pasta dough? I summarized my findings: nothing in the fourteenth century, a little egg white in the fifteenth, and then, toward the end of the sixteenth, this almost eggy moment in Scappi. When did pasta go all-egg? Who was the first?

A reply arrived three days later. Signora Giarmoleo didn't know. She put the question to her colleagues. They didn't know. She did not know who had first used the egg.

She didn't know? She runs the pasta museum. How can she not know? And why didn't she say, "I don't know but I'm going to keep looking"? Could she receive a question of this magnitude and abandon it because she didn't have the answer to hand? I didn't understand: How can you run a pasta museum and not be interested in the first eggy pasta?

WHEN I WAS finally permitted to roll out the dough, I tore it.

"Ha!" Betta cackled. "You did a Mario!" *(Hai fatto un Mario!)* Doing a Mario was tearing the *sfoglia*, the rectangular sheet you make the dough into. "When Mario was here," Betta explained, "he was in such a rush to learn how to make pasta he always tore it." Betta took over, pressing my torn pasta back together with her thumb and forefinger, and rapidly rolling over the injured dough with her matterello. "Mario," Betta added with undisguised pride, "was not very good at pasta."

"Mario," Mark whispered to me, "would almost certainly disagree." Mark was now with me in the kitchen, having secured his slave visa. As Mario had predicted, Gianni knew somebody who knew somebody who owed someone a favor. Because Mark was going to be in Italy for a long time, he let me do the first pasta lessons on my own. I had given myself three weeks. I had a week left.

The second time I was permitted near the pasta, I was left alone with it for several minutes, rolling a sheet around the matterello like a jelly roll and unrolling it, back and forth, over and over again, something I'd always regarded as a pastry-chef trick and one I never believed I'd live long enough to do. In my limited experience with dough, I hadn't succeeded in doing any tricks. The dough usually stuck to my hands, to the board, to the rolling pin, to itself. But here I was, rolling up dough on a matterello and unrolling it. I don't think I ever felt so cool. I was so caught up in my revelry—already making an imaginary video of myself, rolling and unrolling, determined not to tear the sfoglia, not wanting to do a Mario—that I failed to notice that Betta had folded her arms across her chest in disapproval.

"You look like an old woman," she said. She hit me, smacking a shoulder. "Why are you behaving like an old woman? You don't have old woman's arms. You will never learn how to make pasta if you roll it out like an old woman." She sighed, took the matterello, and attacked the pasta with vigor, until it was so thin you could see the board underneath. She stepped back and pointed to the sheet.

"See?"

"I see," I said and made a promise: I will not be an old woman.

By now I knew what to do—I had watched Betta enough to understand the principle—but I kept having trouble with the implementation. The principle was that the dough needed to be stretched as thin as you could make it, and, once it had reached that condition of thinness, you made it thinner. In fact, the principle was that you would *never* be able to make it thin enough, a daunting prospect, like a mathematical problem involving infinity, and you stopped rolling it only when you couldn't do any more. The whole enterprise, once I'd ceased being an old woman, turned out to be surprisingly physical, and I was in a sweat by the end. There were additional anxieties—like doing a Mario at the last second and ruining everything. After so much huffing and puffing, the dough, even mine, got pretty thin (which you want), but it was also very easy to tear (which you don't want), and if it tears when it's so thin it's impossible to repair, and you have to throw the torn bit away, unless it's a big tear, and then you throw away the whole thing.

"I will never make it thin enough," I confessed to Betta. I was trying to be witty. "Air!" I declaimed. "Why go to all this trouble to make air?" The conceit was Betta's wanting a pasta so thin it consisted of only air, but the sentence I intended wasn't the one I uttered. I don't know what I said. By now, I'd completed all the language classes offered at the Scuola Italiana in Greenwich Village, but my Italian was a pretty fragile achievement, and this exchange was one of my first conversations without my wife nearby to rescue me. Why did I think my Italian was so good I could make jokes?

Betta looked at me blankly. Then she cackled uproariously and turned to Mark. "*Che pazzo dialogo!*" she said. What crazy speech! "Who knows what will come out of his mouth?"

But Mark had no idea what she was saying, which was, of course, that she had no idea what *I* was saying. "*Che?*" he said. "*Cosa?*" "Sometimes," he whispered to me, "I have no idea what Betta is saying."

We were a curious threesome. By now we were spending every day gathered round Betta's pasta board. It was large—square, almost four feet across—and a crafted object, made of pieces of inlaid wood, designed, I assumed, to produce that grainy-in-the-mouth feel. Underneath was a strip of wood. This was like an anchor—it fit against the edge of a table—and kept the board from sliding. It was also covertly used to keep the dough from moving as well. This was a pasta maker's secret and the most important lesson I learned from Betta. The trick was in the strategic use of your belly: by positioning a flap of dough over the edge of the board—just a couple of inches—you ended up pressing against it when you rolled it out, squishing it and holding it in place. This made it easier to stretch your pasta. That was the theory, anyway. In practice, it was one of those finesse maneuvers that wasn't so easy for me to master. The problem was my belly, which was otherwise being subjected to an ambitious culinary education—many pedagogical plates of pasta had been deposited inside in it, what I regarded as a program of tummy tutorials—and it had grown a little unwieldy. Or else I just wasn't accustomed to using it to cook with. Initially, much pasta was maimed. Actually, most of it just dropped to the floor, having been cleaved against the edge of the cutting board from the slam-bam force of my body as I tried to roll the whole thing out to its impossible thinness.

You don't have to have a board with a stopper. Scappi didn't use one. He made his pasta on a long table but the operation involved two people. One person rolled it out, leaving a bit of the sheet over the table edge, Betta's trick, and the other held on to it from the other side, stretching it further. You also don't need a matterello, although I'm pleased I own one, big enough to be used by two people at once, like playing piano with four hands. I purchased it at a Saturday market in Porretta, when I returned later in the summer (pasta, according to Betta, could be learned only in installments), on a memorably damp morning of oppressive humidity. By evening it had gathered itself into a ferocious five-hour thunderstorm and canceled a *festa* Gianni had planned to inaugurate the pizzeria's summer season, with live music, outdoor grilling, and hundreds of paying diners. Days of preparation went for nought, which confirmed for Betta the fickleness of life there and her belief that, in this part of Italy, nothing is ultimately in your control. (Its history, I would learn, was a punishing roller coaster of good and bad fortunes. Even the modern prosperity of Porretta—building airplane parts in a rugged, inhospitable terrain, an unexpected bounty—had been a dictator's whim and had arrived as fortuitously as it had then unexpectedly disappeared, as though a debt collected by the Devil.) The Appennines, Betta said, teach you a "mountain fatalism."

Sometimes I was struck by a sense of many people having learned all this before me—not an unpleasant feeling, akin to making a turn in an unknown landscape and discovering a horizon-filling view of natural beauty. The sensation was of being made wonderfully small. When Betta taught me how to make tagliatelle, the easiest of fresh pastas— you let the sheet dry for a few minutes, then roll it up like a paper towel and cut across with it a knife (*tagliatelle* means "little cut things"), shaking the noodles out afterwards, like so many strands of golden hair in a magic trick—I noticed that her phrasing was almost identical to words used by Scappi. "You let the sheet dry out, but not too dry," she said—*si asciuga ma non troppo*. ("The sheet will be dry, but not too much," Scappi writes—*sarà asciutto però non troppo*.) Have people been passing on the instructions, word for word, for five hundred years? Sometimes this sense expressed itself as so many ghosts looking over Betta's shoulders. One day, she said she'd like to show me how to make tortellini—the region's most famous pasta—but stopped herself. "You will tell Mario. Mario did not learn how to make tortellini when he was here."

"No, no, no," I said, with a hearty butter-couldn't-possibly-melt-in-my-mouth irony. "Of course I won't tell Mario. Why would I do that?"

"You will tell him. I know you will."

I didn't know what to say. I looked hard at Betta. She wasn't joking.

The next day, Betta still had tortellini on her mind. They speak to her of Christmas, she said. That's when you make them, and they are then cooked in a clear chicken broth, not in boiling water like a normal pasta. She will always associate tortellini with childhood. They were the first pasta she remembers being prepared.

Betta comes from Vergato—a hill town twenty miles away, about halfway to Bologna—and grew up in an extended family of five women: Betta's mother and her four aunts. Every December they gathered round a kitchen table and made the pasta, a warm, noisy convocation: banter, gossip, high hilarity, storytelling, the smells of food, a fire burning, everyone's fingers busy. Making the tortellini, Betta said, was always social (she had been unprepared for the loneliness of a restaurant kitchen), and, as a child, she felt privileged when these older, cultivated women asked her to join their circle. She was twelve years old, and the tortellini she made were her first handmade pasta—no small feat. They are complex, tightly layered pieces of food sculpture, an achievement associated in Betta's mind with bigger things: the city (Bologna), the region (her *zona*, the food like a flag of statehood), and becoming an adult. "My learning how to make pasta was learning how to be a grown-up and a woman." Now, when she makes tortellini, her aunts come to mind: sometimes in the pasta-making lessons they taught her (one aunt prided herself on a pasta so thin you couldn't eat it with a fork because it slipped through the tines) or in their preparations (another made tagliatelle so exquisitely delicate that they cooked the moment they hit hot water—"You drop them, you pull them out, they are ready"), but usually in fleeting images. The Christmas table, the sound of giggly laughter, their faces. They are now gone.

"I don't think Mario understands how much we gave him. You can only learn these things here—from people who have been making these foods their whole lives. Do you understand? That's what we gave Mario. Something he can get nowhere else."

Betta was contemplative. "Maybe tomorrow I will teach you how to make tortellini."

PORRETTA WASN'T the obvious place for lessons in making the region's most complicated pasta. The town has never been known for its food, and there are only a few historical references to it. There is an obscure mention in Casanova's autobiography, dating from the 1790s, when, accompanied by a Florentine beauty and in flight from her mother, he stopped nearby, rousing an innkeeper after midnight with demands for food and drink, and then found himself so sated by macaroni he was unable to perform an act of love. The side effect was not addressed in a collection of food narratives written around the same time by Doctor Luca Zeneroli. His 1771 *Selection of Medical Stories pertaining to the Porretta Baths*—the food stories are the appendix—appears to be the only surviving culinary text in the millennium-long history of the town. Goethe may have passed through, crossing the Appennines via the Porrettana, but seems to have made the journey on an empty stomach. George Eliot, traveling in the other direction to Bologna (Porretta has always been on the way to somewhere else), also didn't stop to eat.

The difficulty is the extreme winter. Some livestock survives it, if there's an adequate shelter. I was taken to an example of one, a hut of hand-hewn stones with a thatched roof and a solid wood door, where I was then introduced to a remarkably ugly pig of gigantic proportions. (People could only guess at its weight—two thousand pounds? three?) The pig was a boar—although he didn't seem like one boar, but several, linked together like cars of a freight train—and, for several years, had been personally, even if indirectly, responsible for most of the region's prosciutto. Even so, I had no idea the species could be so ugly or so large. Apart from the pigs, there wasn't much else. The land was dense forest, too cold for grapes or olives, with only one local crop, hay, which you saw growing in the few cleared areas.

But there were butchers, a proud clan. One night I found myself at a table, under a balmy starry sky, with a half dozen of them. The occasion was Gianni's postponed *festa*. The good weather had finally arrived, and five hundred people had shown up—the first warm night of what would turn out to be the hottest summer in five centuries. (With the uninterrupted warm evenings, Gianni's pizzeria would finally turn a profit, although the unexpected treasure raised questions about a business that relied so absolutely on the mountain's fickle climate.) The butchers had grilled the meat; Gianni and Betta prepared pizzas; Mark and I cooked the pasta; and now it was midnight, and we were exhausted—the happy exhaustion of feeding lots of people—and were having an impromptu family meal of steak and red wine, gathered round a table by a still-burning barbecue fire.

I was curious about the invisible culinary history of the region. I wondered what distinguished the food here from what you might eat anywhere else in Italy, and the people around me agreed that it was in theirs having to be foraged: it came from the woods.

People hate to buy vegetables, a butcher confessed, because vegetables are expensive and not from here.

And it was true. A white truffle, which elsewhere might sell for hundreds of dollars, seemed easier to come by than something fresh and green. What could be got from the woods was free and amounted to a diurnal dining diary that everyone kept in their heads. May was wild asparagus, arugula, and artichokes. June was wild lettuce and stinging nettles. July was cherries and wild strawberries. August was forest berries. September was porcini.

"But too many porcini," a woman declared. "Every day—porcini, porcini, porcini." In September, her son goes out in the afternoon and returns with fifty pounds of porcini. "What am I to do with so many porcini?" She cooks them, she dries them, she freezes them, until *"Basta!"* she throws them out.

October was wild boar. "There are thousands of them in these woods."

"Not thousands?" I protested.

"Yes," people answered in unison. "Thousands. And pigeons and deer and even wolves," and at the mention of wolves I looked out into the night and studied the zigzaggy mountain crests above us, unpatterned like the broken teeth of an old comb, and the forests, black against the dark blue summer's starry light, and felt a primitive Grimm awe for what was out there and an equally primitive comfort in being here, by a fire, surrounded by people.

They continued through their calendar, reaching chestnuts (November), whereupon everyone sighed. Chestnuts were such a problem. No one could eat them.

"This is a poor community," a butcher explained, "and we grew up eating many dishes with chestnuts. For us, they mean poverty. We now can't eat chestnuts. There are recipes that will disappear unless they are passed on soon, but for now, no one can touch them."

By the end of the calendar (the cruelest month was March, when there was nothing), I understood something new about Betta's pasta—its importance. Its value was different from pasta in the life of Miriam, say, or of Valeria. For them, pasta was a culinary tradition that they'd grown up in, a feature of their culture, their identity. For Betta, it was a tradition she wanted to belong to. She lived in the mountains, where you were always reminded of how little you controlled. This year, even the reliably over-abundant porcini, which I had finally concluded was the taste of Porretta, never appeared. The ground was too dry. Dadi, the man who ran a food shop—catering to day-trip Italians expecting to return home with bags of wild mushrooms—was importing them from Sweden. For Betta, pasta was crucial to how she thought about herself. "Mario," she said, "is now a great success, and I am not. Mario is now rich, and I am not. But he was never very good at making pasta. He was never as good as me. I am very, very good."

THE NEXT DAY Betta was in the kitchen when Mark and I arrived. She was resolved: today she would tell us how to make tortellini, although, before she began, she renewed her conditions.

I understood them. I will not tell Mario.

"Do you promise?"

Mark and I looked at each other. (We said nothing, but what was communicated between us was unmistakable: this, we agreed, is very weird.)

I promised.

"Okay," Betta said. She was solemn. "This is what goes inside. There are four meats: pork, chicken, prosciutto, and mortadella." The measurements were in etti. "You start with two etti of pork, ground up."

"Any cut?" I asked.

"The shoulder or butt," she said, indicating her own shoulder and butt, that cook's thing of pointing to the cut in question as though it had been butchered from your own body. "A lean piece."

I repeated the quantity and wrote it in a notebook. Two etti is about eight ounces.

"About half as much chicken. The breast. Also ground up. You cook both meats together in a pan with butter."

I wrote a formula: Maiale + pollo = padella con burro. Pork + chicken = pan + butter.

"Next. The cured meats. Half an etto, or fifty grams, of the prosciutto and mortadella. You grind these up, too." Fifty grams is about two ounces. Prosciutto is found all over Italy but is at its most refined in the Po River Valley, the heart of Emilia-Romagna. Mortadella—a fatty pork mousse in a casing—is another specialty associated with Bologna (thus "baloney," the bastardized name of a bastardized version). These were the tastes of the zona; you won't find them in a Tuscan preparation, even though Tuscany was so close I could see it from the kitchen window.

"You add your ground-up prosciutto and mortadella to your pan. Cook them slowly. You want the flavors to mingle." In all, there was about a pound of meat. "Let it cool, and add two eggs, some parmigiano . . ."

"How much?"

"Enough to thicken it. And some grated nutmeg . . ."

"How much?"

"A little." She bunched her fingers together. "You mix it with your hands. That's the filling."

The result—like grainy sand before the eggs, cheese, and nutmeg are added; like a gray mushy toothpaste afterwards—wasn't much to look at, but, since it was about to be tucked inside a piece of dough, what it looked like was irrelevant. The smell, however, was powerful. What was it? The Bolognese meats? The combination of the raw and the cured? I stuck my head in a bowl and my mind said: pizza toppings and eggnog and a barbecue on the Fourth of July. It was all my holidays in one. My mind also said: This is not a smell you know. It wasn't of the mountains, which I'd now come to think of as damp and mushroomy brown. It was different. Appetizing, certainly, and wintry, and, somehow, highly specific. This was a taste I knew I would encounter nowhere else in the world. An urban medieval perfume, I concluded. This, I wanted to believe, was the fragrance of a Bologna kitchen, learned by someone in Betta's family, preserved and passed on until it had reached the aunts in Vergato.

Betta wouldn't show me the next step—preparing the complex pasta engineering that encased her filling—until I met a new condition. I would have to return later in the summer, my third trip. It was, I concluded, a test of my promise that I wouldn't reveal the recipe to Mario: if enough time had elapsed and she got no reports of her tortellini on the Babbo menu, she could assume the coast was clear.

If you're a boy, your principal difficulty in making tortellini, I discovered (because of course I returned), is your fingers, which, alas, really need to be a girl's, and not just any girl's, but an elfin girl's.

Your fingers need to be small because all the action occurs on the top of the smallest one, the pinky—in Betta's case, the tiny top of her very petite pinky—where you place the puniest square of pasta. You then pack the puny square with largest amount of filling possible and fold it, corner to corner, to form a miniature but bulging triangle. You next tip the top part of the triangle forward, as though it were bowing in an expression of gratitude, and then (the crucial step) pull the other two corners forward, as though securing the bowing head in a headlock. You then press it all together to form a ring. When you turn the pasta over, you'll be astonished by what you created: a belly button. (What can I say? It's wildly erotic.)

Each infinitesimal tortellino takes a *long* time to make, and during the whole delicate process I found myself always on edge, hoping against hope that I wouldn't crush the fuckers. (I crushed many fuckers.) And, given how *little* time it takes to eat the peanut-sized little bastards, you come away with an understanding of what they are: munchkin food made by people with a lot of time on their *tiny* hands. And yet, for all that, it is an angelically yummy munchkin food. You simmer it in a clear broth, turn off the flame, and let it sit for a while in the pot, doing that back-and-forth thing that a good pasta does, taking in the broth's flavors, releasing its own starchiness, until it is tender and floppy and bloated with taste and can then be served, smelling fragrantly of Christmas.

The truth is, Betta was right. You learn pasta by standing next to people who have been making it their whole lives and watching them. It seems simple, and that's because it is simple, but, characteristic of all Italian cooking, it's a simplicity you have to learn. My advice: Go there. Make Betta a star. Isn't it about time? You'll have to put up with Porretta—very authentic because very ignored, and characterized by the temperamental irritability of a place that feels it has been abandoned (don't even think about getting change for a parking meter) and stay at an overpriced hotel with no bathroom, occasional water (sometimes hot), plastic walls (although wood-colored), no windows (you think there's a view?), and a dysfunctional telephone that works from noon on Sunday to early on Monday morning. And then, once you've settled in (hah!), wander down to the bottom of the valley, listening for the River Reno, and, near the old aqueduct (now housing a sewer—you'll smell it), watch out for a sign, painted by hand, virtually illegible and probably fallen down. It says "Capannina." There will be an arrow. Follow it, and after half a mile, where the river bends around itself, a peninsula of Emilia-Romagna surrounded by Tuscany, you'll find the pizzeria. Betta gets in at about four. Good luck.

AFTER LEAVING PORRETTA, I became a tortellini student. I was curious to see if I'd find Betta's recipe elsewhere. I didn't. But I can't say there's a lot of difference between hers and, say, the twenty-five other recipes I came upon. Since the sixteenth century, the filling of this tiny folded pasta has almost always involved a bird (capon, chicken, or turkey), a cut of pork, a cured meat (or bone marrow and cured meat), cheese (almost always parmigiano), and occasionally herbs. And, since forever, it has been cooked either in broth or with cream *(panna)*. But the quantities of these ingredients vary from recipe to recipe, even if only minutely, and these variations are what one generation passes to the next, always as guarded secrets, each family convinced that its recipe is the definitive one. The arguments about what constitutes a genuine tortellino were so passionate that, in 1971, a convention was held, La Dotta Confraternita del Tortellino, the Learned Confederation of the Tortellino, to determine once and for all the correct preparation. With considerable ceremony, the preparation was published three years later, on December 7, 1974, and then locked away in a vault in the Camera di Commercio di Bologna, the city's chamber of commerce. Today you can find it on the websites of various agricultural and official-sounding institutions, introduced by appropriately solemn injunctions about the dangers of not following the instructions precisely, but the effort is to miss the point. The Learned Confederation cannot tell you the one recipe because it doesn't exist, and to go looking for it or to experiment with the many variations until you persuade yourself that you've arrived at the definitive one is to miss the intimate ideology of the dish. There is not one recipe; there is only the one you've been entrusted with. "You are not to tell Mario this recipe," Betta instructed me again. "This is my gift to you."

I honored the terms of the gift and didn't pass it on to Mario, while knowing that he had no use for it anyway and that the injunction would have baffled him and made him sad. Would he have understood the resentment implicit in it? Gianni and Betta have long been accustomed to not getting their due. They're mountain people. There is a hardship in their cooking. In their eyes, they took in a man they genuinely believed couldn't cook (probably because they themselves understood only one way of cooking) and taught him what they knew. When he returned to America, he became rich and famous, telling the story that he'd learned everything from his "second family" in the mountains. But Mario hadn't come here to learn a region's cooking in order to reproduce it faithfully, as though from a textbook. I find myself thinking of the Mississippi Delta and the visits made by students keen to learn the mournful lyricism in the music that you can still hear in the juke joints there. Mario is forever making food his own way, not just griddle pizza or a porky linguine alle vongole or carbonara with raw eggs on top, but his whole approach, that nightmare display of contorni that I worked with at the grill, the secret sauces, the ingredients never revealed on the menu, the squirter bottles of syrups and acids and juices, the performance: like a musician.

For my part, I'd come for the textbook and was glad to have it. Betta's tortellini are now in my head and my hands. I follow her formula for the dough—an egg for every etto of flour, sneaking in an extra yolk if the mix doesn't look wet enough. I've learned to roll out a sheet until I see the grain of the wood underneath. I let it dry if I'm making tagliatelle; I keep it damp if I'm making tortellini. I make a small batch, roll out a sheet, then another, the rhythm of pasta, each movement like the last one. My mind empties. I think only of the task. Is the dough too sticky? Will it tear? Does the sheet, held between my fingers, feel right? But often I wonder what Betta would think, and, like that, I'm back in that valley with its broken-combed mountain tops and the wolves at night and the ever-present feeling that the world is so much bigger than you, and my mind becomes a jumble of associations, of aunts and a round table and laughter you can't hear anymore, and I am overcome by a feeling of loss. It is, I concluded, a side effect of this kind of food, one that's handed down from one generation to another, often in conditions of adversity, that you end up thinking of the dead, that the very stuff that sustains you tastes somehow of mortality.

AND THE EGG?

I hadn't given up, although it now seemed obvious that the pivotal recipe that had changed the nature of pasta probably didn't exist. After all, writing has a better chance of survival than a piece of food (can you imagine the misfortune of coming across a five-hundred-year-old tagliatelle with ragù?), and chefs are rarely writers, and if the Eureka event occurred when no scribbler was in the kitchen the discovery would have gone unrecorded.

But I pressed on, even after my discouraging exchange with the pasta museum. After Scappi's *Opera* in 1570, the next known food book was *Il Trinciante*, in 1581, by Vincenzo Cervio. A *trinciante* was a "carver," an important person at a Renaissance banquet, and Cervio's book—in effect, the first autobiography of a butcher—deals with meats, including useful advice about castration, addressing a range of questions such as which animals need it and which ones don't (you'd hate to do the wrong one). But Cervio, a dedicated meat guy, is silent on the issue of eggs.

I proceeded chronologically. In 1638, there was *Pratica e scalcaria* by Antonio Frugoli. *Scalcaria* means being a *scalco*, the head guy in the kitchen of a grand house. Since there were no restaurants, a scalco was the equivalent of our celebrity chef, and the 1500s and 1600s are full of scalco memoirs, often, like Frugoli's, self-aggrandizing accounts of how my banquets are better than yours. Other books followed: *The Three Theses* of Mattia Giegher, including lessons in napkin-folding (1639); Bartolomeo Stefani (1662), the head chef at the Spanish Court in Venice. I thought of myself as a food detective, gathering up suspects so I could eliminate them. You there, what are you doing with that egg?

I wrote academics. Massimo Montanari, a professor at the University of Bologna and an authority on the medieval kitchen, understood my question and its urgency. Yes, he agreed, the egg moment was important in the history of pasta—he even introduced me to a term to describe its function, which was to hydrate the flour *(idratare la farina)*, the process in which the egg's liquid content takes the place of water—but he didn't know when it had first occurred. In his judgment, there had probably been not one moment but several, a gradually increasing use, begun in the Middle Ages, when eggs were added for taste, until, in the modern era, they were also used for their liquid.

But when?

He couldn't hazard a guess. He consulted a colleague, a pasta specialist: nothing.

Then I found it: a first eggy recipe. It was late in the chronology, the end of the seventeenth century, in *Lo scalco alla moderna* by Antonio Latini—another scalco fellow. The recipe was headed "How to make macaroni, lasagna, and gnocchetti exquisitely" and credited to a chef named Meluzza Comasca (a typical concession—in Italy, there are no original recipes, only discoveries). Comasca, it has been suggested by one commentator, was a rhetorical creation, and, I admit, it's troubling that the man's name appears nowhere else in the history of food. Everything we know is in Latini's introductory homage: that, after leaving us with his new pasta recipe, Comasca died prematurely of an insect bite— a malarial mosquito, I suspect, although the phrase *(morì di pontura*, in its seventeenth-century spelling) calls up an image of a fat man in an apron scratching himself to death—and that his doughy inventions were so famous they were described in an epitaph on his tomb. There is no mention of where Comasca was buried, but the insect allusion suggests the Maremma, the stretch on the Tuscan coast known for fatal bugs, and not far from Da Caino, the restaurant run by Valeria Piccini (unlike Comasca, a chef who will go stubbornly to her grave before she shares her pasta preparations with me).

The recipe is mainly about the process—the taxing effort of making the dough *(un poco di fatica)*, how you roll it into a sheet about six fingers in length (everything according to the hands) and roll it some more, until it reaches its requisite thinness. The pasta recipe itself was simple: four eggs mixed with about six etti of flour (not quite Betta's proportions but not far off), plus a sprinkle of salt, and, it's true, a little water, but only a splash. The principal hydrating role is performed by the eggs, and, until now, this role had never been recognized in Italian cooking.

Why did I find this when others hadn't? I considered what I'd done wrong, including the possibility that my egg question was so dumb no one else was asking it. But the explanation may be that my discovery is overshadowed by a more radical one: not what to put *in* your pasta but what to put *on* it. *Lo scalco alla moderna* includes the first recipe for tomato sauce. Until this moment, no Italian had eaten tomatoes. This very recipe—a half-dozen tomatoes, peeled by blistering them on a grill and removing the charred outside (which brings out the sugar in the fruit), plus red onions, red chilies, and red wine vinegar, an early expression of the now very familiar sweet-sour-spicy approach—is what persuaded the wary people of the Italian peninsula that the suspiciously shiny American fruit that acts like a vegetable wouldn't kill them. Could there have been anything more important? Taken together, these two recipes, the eggy noodle and the sauce that goes on top, have been at the heart of pasta preparations from their publication until today. In the history of cooking, I cannot think of two other instructions that, though seemingly modest, have had such enduring consequences.

Latini's *Lo scalco alla moderna* is the most elegantly written book about food since an arty humanist on a summer holiday wandered back into a cardinal's kitchen and wrote about what he found there. Even I, with my elementary Italian, appreciate that Latini is a stylist, with a strong voice and a flair for narrative. Until 1992, when a manuscript of a Latini memoir was discovered, nothing was known about the author, a great but virtually anonymous chef of the late Italian Renaissance, a culinary humanist with an extraordinary sway, determining how Italians ate for the next four centuries.

What the memoir reveals is that the author wasn't Latini. Latini could scarcely write. In fact, his spelling is so bad it has been wondered if he was dyslexic. The stylist must have been a friend. Latini was illiterate, a street urchin who invented himself in the kitchen. The story calls to mind Marco Pierre White or any number of people who entered a kitchen as one thing and exited as something entirely different. Latini lost his family at age five (Marco lost his mother at seven). He moved to Rome to make a living (Marco arrived in Harrogate at the same age) and, knocking on doors, found work in a cardinal's household, where he learned to be a trinciante (a butcher, Marco's achievement, at the same age) and then a cook, moving up a hierarchy of household stations, until, at twenty-eight, he became a scalco, a kitchen's highest honor (Marco earned his three stars at roughly the same age). Latini is regarded as the last author of the Italian food renaissance (the *gloriosa tradizione gastronomica italiana*), and it's tempting to see a relationship between the way the era ends with the way it began, nearly three centuries before, with Platina's copying out the recipes of Maestro Martino. In the beginning, there was a writer; the ghost was the chef. In the end, there was the chef; the ghost was the writer. In the beginning, a humanist borrows from the artisan, anxious that the subject may not be sufficiently serious. In the end, the self-invented artisan invents himself as a humanist, robust in his confidence that his subject is fully dignified.

After Latini, the glorious age of gastronomy ends, as if there were nothing left to do: Italy now had its dishes, its cuisine, its philosophy. Two decades later, Latini's book went out of print. Scappi's works, in print for nearly a century, were no longer available. Platina's account of Maestro Martino was being read in France but in Italy had disappeared. For the next two centuries, there were no notable cookbooks. The Renaissance was over, as was its spirit of adventure: that spirit, it seemed, had been packed away, like some evanescent genie, and disappeared into saddlebags on a train of horses crossing the Alps. I now understood why Italians believe that Caterina de' Medici took the secrets of Italian cooking with her. How else to explain such a definitive demise?

. . .

ONE DAY I phoned Miriam. I was unhappy with our last exchange, and maybe, too, I wanted some recognition for what I'd learned. At the very least, I felt I should take up the offer she had made—that she was prepared to let me into her kitchen for a day or two. I would like a day or two to refine the technique.

She was happy to hear from me. I told her my news and asked if it might still be possible to pop by.

"*Certo,*" she said. "Phone me when you are next in Italy."

I now understood the informal never-make-a-commitment approach. I would phone when I was next there. But Miriam was curious. "What do you think I can teach you?" she asked, repeating her motto: "I am not an original cook."

I went through my refrain: the mysteries of pasta fresca, the labors of wood on wood, the elusive know-how of getting the texture.

"What in the world are you talking about?" she said. "I have old arms. My old arms cannot do this kind of thing anymore." Besides, she added, she can't get a *pastina* anymore.

This was not a term I knew.

A pastina, she explained, is a local woman who makes pasta. That was her job: every day, to roll out the sheets. "I always used to be able to get a pastina. No one does that sort of thing anymore. They're too busy. Modern life. I use a machine. I make the dough and cut it by hand. But I use the machine to roll out the sheets."

A machine? Miriam, my romantic defender of the traditional kitchen, a disciple of Maestro Martino, a descendant of Scappi, a student of Latini—*this* Miriam uses a machine? I could scarcely speak.

"*Certo,*" she said. "The pasta is fine. What's important is the eggs. My eggs are the best in the region. They are very, very good eggs."

Yes, I agreed. The egg is very important.

17

By now, the symptoms of the "What-are-we-going-to-do-about-Andy? problem" had grown so impossible to ignore I was convinced he was going to be fired. He wasn't making it easy. For Andy, there continued to be only one solution, and it involved an investment of someone else's money in his own restaurant, the elusive Iberian eatery, a venture he stubbornly believed was going to happen. Even I wondered: Why should Joe and Mario back this? Their heritage was Italian. But Andy persisted, never explicitly saying anything was owed to him, but manifestly thinking it was. Maybe, it occurred to me, his hope was born out of the burnout nature of the labor—that you can cook someone else's food, under this kind of pressure, for only so long: the regimentation, the stress, the voice, not yours, saying, "What about a little citrus or a little salty to get the saliva glands working?"

Sometimes I wondered if Mario wasn't a great burden in Andy's life, that the most consequential day of his life might have also been the most damning, that evening all those years ago when Andy had wandered into someone's kitchen and discovered a man performing an act of stove-top wizardry involving fruit candy and foie gras, and decided he was going to be a chef. For much of the next seventeen years, that stove-top wizard had been Andy's boss, starting at Pó, where Andy had been Mario's deputy and the two of them ran the kitchen—thirty-six covers, a line outside the door, a hundred and fifty people a night. Three years later, when Mario teamed up with Joe Bastianich and opened Babbo, Andy had followed and for the next five years had been the executive running the kitchen. By now Mario had a second life. "He's a chip in my brain," Andy said. "I couldn't remove it if I wanted to." For five years, Andy had never cooked, which had been Memo's justification for quitting, believing that because Andy didn't cook, he couldn't cook, and how could Memo take orders from someone who couldn't cook—a perfectly pitched piece of slander, since no one knew a thing about Andy's cooking as few had ever witnessed it. "For five years," Andy told me, "I put pasta on plates and screamed for runners. By the fifth year, I thought of myself as a self-basting turkey and my red Butterball button had long popped. I was dry and overcooked."

I accompanied Mario and Joe (now flushly swaggering from the undeniable success of Otto) on a visit to a possible Iberian venue, viewed by them as the potential "next big thing," an empty monstrosity in the West Village, two floors, a courtyard, and a roof garden, large enough to seat hundreds (since a giant pizzeria worked, why not a giant Spanish place?). The two novice entrepreneurs then crunched their numbers unpersuasively; the exercise in itself—amounting to more than two million dollars before the first ingredient was ordered—illustrated the price assigned to Andy's loyalty. Later, in the Babbo kitchen, I told him about the excursion. He hadn't been invited along. He was curious but reluctant to reveal his curiosity, because it would betray the helplessness of his position. His face conveyed distress. "The size is wrong," he muttered finally. "That would be a crash-and-burn paella beer hall."

Then Andy himself found what he wanted—small, recently deserted, cheap by New York standards (the rent was eight thousand dollars a month instead of twenty), near the Union Square green market, on a corner of Irving Place, a street only six blocks long, where the author Washington Irving had once lived. Peering through a window and noting a miraculously apposite Spanish-themed ceramic floor, Andy realized he had known the place he wanted without ever being able to describe it.

Andy discovered food in Spain: it was there that he first saw how a culture (its history, its habits of mind, its way of being) can manifest itself not just in paintings or music or architecture but also in what it eats. I knew Andy had lived there as a teenager; until now, I hadn't realized that he had been there at the same time as Mario. Armandino, as a Boeing executive, had lived in an expatriate's apartment in Madrid; Andy's parents had lived in an artist colony on the Costa Brava. (His mother was a tap dancer; his father, a painter of cowboys and western sunsets.) Barcelona was Andy's Porretta, and year after year he has returned to it, especially to its "dirty, low-rent" food places, reinvigorated by each visit, liking their simplicity, their lack of pretension, reminders of why he was a cook. On one such trip—during his honeymoon—he discovered Cal Pep. (Andy's wife, Patty Collins, a former Babbo cook, was pregnant with their first child; a hopeful, happy couple, but it makes you wonder at the social lives of chefs—*of course* Andy would have met his wife on the line, and *of course* their honeymoon had been an excursion of food research.) On another trip, he discovered Bar Pinotxo.

Bar Pinotxo is Andy's model restaurant. It is in the Boquería, the Barcelona food market, Andy's teenage discovery as the Spanish speaker in the family, doing the shopping for his mother. The restaurant could be called a "market eatery," run according to an ideology of freshness: ingredients only from the stands just outside, an open kitchen, counter service, crowded, no menu, and, when you finally got the attention of a chef, you pointed to an item, he prepared it, you ate it. "The appeal," Andy said, "is its honesty. No magic, no tricks, no secrets. Good ingredients, barely touched. Even today, I get goose bumps when I talk about it." Unlike most restaurants, the cooking at both Cal Pep and Bar Pinotxo is not done beforehand, but, always on view, is by one of three methods: *a la plancha* (on a flattop), deep-fried, or in a pan. The razor clams are pried open on being ordered, drizzled with olive oil, sprinkled with salt and pepper, cooked facedown on the flattop for thirty seconds, and finished with raw garlic. The *croquetas*, balls of salted cod, are deep-fried. The baby squid are thrown onto a very hot sauté pan and swell on contact, inflate like balloons, and release a puddle of oceanness, which you swirl, reduce, and swirl some more; at the very end, you drop in a handful of baby rice beans to soak up the liquid: another sea juice–starch composition, a fundamental food of the globe. This, Andy said, would be the basis of his menu.

"Dude," Mario said, having accompanied Andy to Barcelona, "you've got a home run."

But did he?

Back in New York, Joe inspected Andy's venue: "This is one fucking small place." He didn't know how Andy could make money; there wasn't the room to seat enough people to run a business; and Andy, panicking, drew a map on a napkin proving you could seat forty-two people—"Seven more than Pó!"—provided you enforced a rule of no

standing, made everyone wait somewhere else (perhaps in the abandoned coffee shop next door—maybe it, too, could be rented), allowed
no one near the bar (otherwise dinner would come to a trafficky rush-
hour stop), and ordered tables with a drawer underneath to stash the
water glasses (to keep them from getting knocked over). Andy did the
calculation: if he could make nine thousand dollars a day (two thousand
more than Pó), he'd probably break even. That is, if he filled up every
night, he'd be fine. Realistic?

Which raised the next concern: Could Andy cook?

I was invited along as a member of a team of tasters informally
assigned the task of finding out. Eight people (Mario, Joe, some friends)
showed up to eat from the first menu Andy had done in his life.

Andy was a wreck. "I have big-day jitters." For years, he had been
preparing Mario's menu. Now he was cooking his own. "What if it
sucks? What if I make all this food, and no one shows up to eat it?" The
restaurant was budgeted to cost two hundred thousand dollars, and
Andy, to secure a twenty percent stake, had borrowed from his Aunt
Doris and Uncle Floyd. He hadn't been sleeping. He'd lost weight—
forty pounds so far. He had a limp—he'd been on all fours using an acid
to clean his floor and hadn't noticed he'd incinerated the muscle tissue
of his knees. Plus, his wife was days away from giving birth. Nearly two
decades had passed since that night in Santa Barbara, and all the subsequent effort—the four years at the CIA, the apprenticing, the training,
the long stint of doing his time—had come down to one moment.

Andy later showed me Mario's report card of the day, an item-by-
item response to every dish, graded on a scale of one to ten, a glimpse of
two chefs' talking to each other in code. The cockscombs (my first
rooster's crest—the texture is vividly squishy) were ten out of ten, but
Mario suggested a drizzle of olive oil and serving them on a room-
temperature plate. (I read that note and thought—cockscombs! A
room-temperature plate! Why didn't I think of that?) The *bacalao*
croquetas—"Perfect." The orange aioli that Andy devised to accompany
it—"Perfect." The quail—"Perfect, perfect!!" (a "10" underlined twice).
The oxtail—almost perfect, but "make sure you degrease the pan before
you reheat the oxtails." (And Andy looked at the note and said, "Silly
me, I knew to degrease the pan—what's wrong with me?" and I nodded
sagely and thought: What's he talking about?) The calamari—"Almost

perfect, but better if topped with lemon zest and parsley. The lamb chops—perfect, but followed by a one-word note, "underneath?" which I knew to be Mario's shorthand for splashing the plate first with a secret sauce (at Babbo, the disguised, never-mentioned-on-the-menu red-hot-chili-red-pepper yogurt) to mix with the juices of the meat: a trick, and not in the spirit of the "look-Ma-no-hands" Andy approach and probably some spicy, salty, sweety thing to get the saliva glands all worked up and full of spit. Andy would ignore the suggestion; he was not going to put anything underneath *his* lamb chops: it was not in the style of *his* restaurant, he was now *his* own chef, and if he wished not to mess with your saliva glands then that was *his* entitlement.

Joe's report was more concise. "The cooking is through the fucking roof."

We were at the bar, the flattop, sauté pans, and fryer in front of us, every ingredient on view. The kitchen was cramped and smoky, and the restaurant felt crowded with fewer than a dozen people. We ate all the dishes on the menu, thirty items, and because the food was so good we ate many of them again. Eventually we got off our stools and sat in a corner of a restaurant on a corner, surrounded by big glass windows, Washington Irving's eighteenth-century brownstone just across the street, the sidewalks busy with people, the city at night. Someone opened a magnum. At that moment, there was nowhere else I wanted to be. Andy would call his restaurant Casa Mono, the Monkey House. He was now a chef.

18

WHAT WOULD BABBO be like without Andy? At the very least, what happened next would test the widespread practice of the omnipotent chef: that a success like Mario (or a Marco Pierre White or an Alain Ducasse) can create a restaurant so perfectly in his own image that he doesn't need to be there. The practice had been possible when Andy was in the kitchen, but Andy believed he had a Mario-like sci-fi operating system in his brain. Would his successor have the same implant?

Memo, once the heir apparent, was no longer a contender: by leaving, he'd removed himself from consideration. But he wasn't happy. "When you see Mario next," Memo urged me, "tell him that I was asking after him. Will you do that for me?" Memo's time at Naples 45 hadn't got easier. To enhance the mood in the evening and persuade people to linger longer than the time it took to knock back a beer, eat a slice of pizza, and bolt for the train home, he wanted to put out votive candles (permission denied). He tried to prepare seasonal specials (permission denied) or make changes to the menu (permission denied). He was told that the restaurant was losing money, so he proposed reducing the over-head (proposals denied). "Someone in receivables"—and this was new, that Memo would have used a phrase like "someone in receivables"—had got a deal on a pasta, and Memo was instructed to cook with the new brand. ("It was, you know, okaaaay.") Someone in receivables had got a good price on twelve-ounce steaks from Kansas, and Memo was told that this was the meat he would now serve. "This was not okay," he said (and added, without explanation, "kickbacks"). Someone in receivables had got a supply of lobsters; a European beer. One day Memo was visited by Peter Wyss, a vice president of Restaurant Associates.

"Is this working for you?" he asked.

As Memo, a big guy, recalled the exchange, he puffed up, inflating himself with indignation, as I'm sure he did at the time, repeating the question in a fury of ironies, inflections in all the wrong places. Or else in all the right places if the objective was to convey to Mr. Wyss that he was a little man who knew diddly shit about cooking—which may or may not have been the case but, conventionally, is not a message you send to your boss. "Is THIS working for ME?" Memo boomed and went on to itemize the ways in which THIS was NOT working, not only for him but also for the restaurant. Mr. Wyss thought the restaurant had been perfectly fine the way it was, and Memo was out of a job. Maybe, he thought, it was time to return to a four-star restaurant run by one of those "French pricks"—Thomas Keller, the chef of The French Laundry in California, was opening up a place—and Memo phoned Mario for advice, wondering if he would recommend the career move, but the call was never returned. "He was probably away," Memo said.

Memo was thirty. "I've got time," he said—a chef's career takes years. "What I'd really like is a small place, thirty to forty covers, preparing the food of my childhood—a Mexican Pó."

In this, Memo was like just about every other chef at Babbo, falling irretrievably for the idealized-hole-in-the-wall-neighborhood-restaurant myth of Pó, which punishingly entered their heads as a tantalizing vision they then spent years hoping to realize—one day, when they had the money, when they had a partner. Memo already had a Pó-rhyming name. It had occurred to him years before, just after he'd finished the service at Le Cirque. "*Ajo,*" he said. Spanish for garlic. "It came to me at three in the morning, when I was on the bus to Harlem, going home. *Ajo.* Very small. Very intimate."

Tony Liu was not a contender for Andy's job. He and Frankie were the two sous-chefs, but Frankie had seniority. But in Tony's view, neither he nor Frankie was qualified, and the position should go to someone from outside. "Frankie," he told me, "is good with food but bad with people. I am completely against his being appointed, which I told Mario." Tony was the least volatile person in the kitchen—even-mannered, understated, no tantrums. His objection to Frankie seemed out of character. Besides, what would happen if Mario ignored the advice—would Tony resign? But Tony had also become the informal representative of the kitchen and felt a responsibility to express the kitchen's position. He was seen as the only levelheaded senior person, and, at some point, everyone had summoned him to the walk-in for an out-of-earshot, out-of-sight impromptu meeting to deal with the most recent display of Frankie's increasingly high-handed behavior.

"It was called the 'F Factor,'" Tony explained. "And I was always in the middle. Frankie would have one of his tirades. They were always very personal. And the victim would appeal to me for help. For a while, I tried to talk to Frankie, but you can only have that kind of conversation so many times. Frankie didn't like to talk."

Holly was the most affected. Since I'd witnessed her hiring, she had worked every station and was now an accomplished cook, but she had regular run-ins with Frankie. "He was always on Holly," Tony said. "I don't know why. Maybe it was just a case of Frankie's having a bad day, but Frankie was having a lot of bad days. He was abusive, and Holly could take only so much, and then she'd want to talk it out. Frankie refused: not during service, or after, or ever." One feature of the F Factor, evidently, was the silent treatment. "This was a five-year-old's behavior. 'No! I'm not talking to you. Na, na, na, na, na.'" In Tony's eyes, the kitchen was degenerating dangerously. "You had Gina in one corner and Elisa in the other, and in between you were going to put Frankie in charge? How was that a good idea? The place was already so moody—so up and down, so many tantrums. I wanted to shout at all of them, Gina, Elisa, Frankie. 'Hey, guys, don't you know how to act like adults?'"

Did Mario know what the kitchen was like without him? According to Tony, "Mario knows exactly what he doesn't want to know."

What he did know was that Frankie was an exceptional, dazzling cook. No one else was so fast or so instinctual. I found him exhilarating to watch. He was not cerebral, like Andy. There was no chatter about a computer chip. Frankie didn't think or talk—language was a burden, an impediment to speed. For Frankie, cooking was a physical feat: he had Mario's food, and how to prepare it, memorized. It was in his muscles. What more did Mario need to know? Besides, he never saw the Frankie experienced by the kitchen because Frankie was never that person in Mario's company. When Mario was around, Frankie changed. He drooped, sloping his shoulders, or else bowed his head, his chin somewhere south of his collarbone, avoiding eye contact, deferential, his posture reinforcing the status of who was in charge.

"Frankie's the man," Joe had taken to saying, and Frankie was duly made executive chef.

Garland was the first to go. I ran into him one afternoon around four o'clock, the kitchen twilight hour. This was when all the city's restaurants stop, all at the same time. Once I'd been educated in the moment, I started seeing New York in a new way, a restaurant city shutting down, one shift handing over to the next, the relay between prep and service, both crews relaxing together, gathered unceremoniously in their soiled coats and sweaty bandannas for a family meal around the best table in the house, or by the service door, or on a stoop, smoking a cigarette or catching the day's last light before returning to the hot boxy space where they would spend the next ten hours. Garland was leaning against a wall of a new Mexican restaurant off Union Square, owned by a former boss: the job offer, running the place, had come up just when Frankie took over. "I didn't leave only because of Frankie— this is a good job—but I would have left anyway." Garland was happy and, according to the Gina edict, had, like everyone else who leaves Babbo, promptly lost twenty pounds. "There's not a lot of butter in Mexican food."

Holly was next. She packed up and went to Italy. She had saved some money and wanted to make food with Italians and be reminded of why she was a cook.

Then Alex. He had lasted eleven months. But by leaving before a full year was out, he deprived himself of a job reference from Mario. Alex knew the rule, although he openly wondered what possible reference Mario would have written: according to Alex, Mario hadn't been in the kitchen when Alex was there. (In fact Mario had been in the kitchen, but Alex had been too panicked to notice.) But Alex, a congenital optimist, had identified positive things in his Babbo experience, including his relationship with Frankie. "For instance, Frankie taught me a method that was new to me for making spaghetti alla carbonara," Alex said happily. "You render your guanciale, and make a sauce with it and the egg whites, and then, *after* you've plated it, you add your yolks, uncooked. That's just one example of how Frank turned out to be such a great guy—that he took time out of his busy day to show me how to make this carbonara, even if it was in the form of his yelling at me."

The yelling, too, was not without its life lessons. "When Frankie was abusing me, he was always doing it for a reason. He was trying to make me a better cook. I also found the abuse was good for me, because I learned what kind of person I don't want to be. When I become a sous-chef, I now know I'm not going to conduct myself in this way. I have Frankie to thank for that insight." He paused, taking in the enormity of the influence. "We've had our differences, but Frankie is now my best buddy."

Tony quit. "I didn't want to be a member of Frankie's kitchen." He was hired to run a new restaurant in the West Village, a fifty-seater ("not much larger than Pó," in Tony's predictable description), called August (no one knew why), dedicated to European food—an elusive idea, but the perfect next place for Tony. In his mind, he'd done French, Spanish, and Italian. Now he could learn Belgian dishes, the occasional German one. The menu, when I ate there later, was like a concoction of a European Union bureaucrat—a little something for everyone (a sauerkraut dish alongside one made with chorizo)—but the food was good because Tony was a good cook. When Holly returned, Tony asked her to be the sous-chef. "I prefer working with women. There is so much less testosterone bravura."

By the time Abby quit (there would be no women left working service), the evacuation was complete: a cook from every station had left. In the five-year history of the restaurant, such a wholesale emptying had never occurred. The situation was urgent, and a sous-chef was hired from outside—quickly, without Frankie's being consulted: a mistake because Frankie refused to work with him.

"I worry about Frank," Memo told me. "He's so unhappy. He's so angry. Something's going to happen."

What? I wondered. I didn't find out until much later, because I had my own demons and had to leave New York to deal with them.

APPRENTICE

~~~~~~~~~~~~~~~~~~~~~~~~~~~~~~~~

About the time of Tiberius, there lived a man named Apicius—very rich and luxurious—for whom several cheesecakes called "Apician" are named. He lived chiefly in Minturae, a city of Campania, and spent many drachmas on his belly, especially on very expensive crawfish, a local speciality that was bigger than those of Smyrna and even than those of Alexandria. On hearing that the crawfish in Africa were also very good, he sailed there without delay, leaving that very day. The voyage was difficult and he suffered exceedingly. Before he reached the shore, he was greeted by the local fishermen who approached him in their boats, offering him some of their very fine crawfish (the news of his visit had created a great stir among the Africans). But when Apicius saw the crawfish, he asked if there were any finer, and when he was told that these were the finest available, he recalled the crawfish of Minturnae, turned his ship round without disembarking, and returned to Italy.

—ATHENAEUS, third century A.D.

19

I'D CONCLUDED I needed to return to Italy and be there properly: for a long time. Actually, I had no idea how long—a stint, or two stints, or more (how long is a stint, anyway?), long enough to stop a feeling that continued to haunt me, that I would never have this opportunity again. Mark Barrett knew the feeling: it was why, having completed his time with Gianni and Betta (his *first* stint), he was now zigzagging across the peninsula in Mario's footsteps, from restaurant to restaurant (Bologna, Florence, Calabria), hoping to learn as much as he could. Mark was hoping to be away for years. I couldn't go away for years (or could I?), but I knew I had to get back to Italy for a length of time, whatever it might be, or else I'd end up regretting it for the rest of my life. I was in a state. I'd experienced this kind of haunting a year earlier, before I had quit my job and taken up a spot on the line in the Babbo kitchen. Now, feeling it again, I found myself trying to persuade my wife that what she really wanted to do was quit her job as well (Jessica was a highly paid Manhattan magazine editor) and accompany me to an Italian hill town where we would know nobody and where I'd work really long hours for no money—*if* I was lucky and someone took me on, and *if* I then managed to be put in a position where I'd actually learn something. (I did not want to go to Italy to perfect my carrot-chopping technique.)

Jessica considered the proposal. "Haven't we just been to Italy?" she asked.

"Well, yes, it's true, a good point. We have just been to Italy."

"And didn't you learn how to make tortellini?"

"Well, yes, that's true, too." But tortellini was only one dish, and I'd become convinced that there were culinary secrets—an attitude, a touch, the thing that Mario was always saying that you can learn only "over there"—that I needed to discover. That was why we had to go back.

Jessica took this in. (It was a testing moment in the marriage.) "And who exactly is going to tell you these secrets?"

So I told her about Dario Cecchini: he, I'd become convinced, was the person I should work for. He didn't know me, and I had no idea if he'd take me on. But there were already so many connections between us: he had to take me on! When Mario's father, Armandino Batali, quit his job at Boeing and decided to learn how Italians prepared meat, he went first to Dario's butcher shop for instruction. I phoned Armandino and asked him why. Because Dario was the most highly regarded butcher in Italy, he said, and because his shop wasn't simply a butcher shop but a museum of Tuscan cooking: raw and cooked meat, cuts of Chianti beef along with ragùs and sauces and cured porks—a university of the zona.

I also knew about Dario from Elisa. In the summers she conducted a weeklong cooking class nearby and visited Dario's for inspiration. (She kept a picture of him by her station in the Babbo kitchen.)

And the food writer Faith Willinger had discovered fennel pollen at Dario's, the stuff she secreted into her luggage and smuggled across the Atlantic, which was then sprinkled atop Mario's tortelloni. On one of Willinger's trips to the United States—the twenty-fifth anniversary party of Chez Panisse—she'd also brought the butcher with her, a visit that had been reported in the *International Herald Tribune*, which, coincidentally, I had torn out and saved: it described Cecchini as the most famous butcher in the world.

I phoned. Signore Cecchini, I said, I am a friend of Mario Batali.

"*Accidenti!*" he declared (which seems to mean something like "Well, I'll be damned!" but what did I know?).

Mario, as you know, is the son of Armandino, I said, reading from a piece of prepared text. (Italian telephones scared the jeebers out of me— I'd been rehearsing my questions all morning long.)

"*Accidenti!*"

He is also a friend of Faith Willinger.

"*Accidenti!*"

And I would like to learn how to be a Tuscan butcher.

"*Accidenti! Vieni! Pronto! Ora!*"—Come! Quickly! Now!

Then Dario passed the phone to a woman who introduced herself as his wife, Ann Marie, and who, thankfully, was an American and able to confirm my understanding of the exchange I'd just had. One week later, there I was, on a Sunday, crossing the busy Chiantigiana, the hill highway that runs the length of Chianti, from Florence to Siena, and cuts through the middle of Panzano, and experiencing a feeling I'd had when I walked into the Babbo kitchen for the first time: that I would be a different person when my stay here was completed, but I had no idea how.

DARIO'S BUTCHER shop, the *macelleria,* was on a steep street next to the post office. Actually, it was two shops joined together. The lower one was like a family sitting room (or, more precisely, the sitting room of a family that lives with its animals). There were a dining table with chairs, a bookcase, a bust of Dante, and a ceramic fountain (the kind cows drink water from). There were also a menacing set of black spikes (entitled "Welcome to Tuscany") and a papier-mâché depiction of something—of people, I'd discover, life-size, disappearing into the flames of Hell. The upper shop, where the wares were displayed, was impossible to get into. There was a crush of people: inside, in the doorway, on the sidewalk, spilling into the street. How many? A hundred? More? They were sweaty and excited. I stood on my tiptoes. Someone had a television camera on his shoulder. There were flashing bulbs. I could hear loud choral music of what I thought might be Mozart's "Requiem." (Why a requiem? Then again, it's a butcher's shop: why not a requiem?)

I pushed my way in. Everyone seemed to be holding a glass of red wine in one hand and feeding themselves gobs of a frothy white cream with the other.

"*Lardo,*" a man said, offering me some. *Lardo crudo.* Raw, not cured. It was spread across his cheeks like toothpaste.

I pressed forward. A man in a suit was swinging a *fiasco* of red wine—straw-covered, like one of those bottles you see in really bad restaurants and learn never to drink. He tried to pour me a glass but missed, and the wine landed on my shoes. It wasn't eleven o'clock in the morning, but an energetic raucous tipsiness was everywhere: you smelled it, it elbowed you, it laughed harshly in your face. Behind a glass display of meats, salumi, and sausages was the butcher, standing on a platform, towering above the room, oblivious to the people below him, who were clamoring and giving him things: orders, money, paper for an autograph. He ignored them. He, too, was drinking wine—quite a lot, it seemed. He had a happy half grin. The music was very loud— *"Dies irae, dies illa!"* ("Days of wrath, days of doom!")—and people were shouting to be heard. In one hand, the butcher held a shiny serrated knife, more military saber than butcher's tool. He was tall, over six feet. At the time I thought he must be six and a half feet, but that was the effect of the platform, which made him seem comic-book tall, like a cartoon caveman. (*"Solvet saeclum in favilla!"* "The world in ashes!") His hands were gigantic. They might have been the largest hands I'd seen in my life. They were way out of proportion with the rest of his body. They looked as if they might be half the length of his arms. The fingers were comparably long, like limbs. He was wearing pink clogs and socks, a pink bandanna round his throat, and a pink cotton shirt—taut, almost ill fitting over the shoulders, which were large and overdeveloped, giving him a hunchbacked appearance. His hair was cropped, closely cut to the side of the head, crew-cut style, and he had big eyebrows, a big nose, big lips. A face of big features. He was in his late forties, my age.

I thought: So this is Dario Cecchini, and he spotted me spotting him. He turned off the music and commanded silence. The place went quiet. *"Nel mezzo del cammin di nostra vita,"* he boomed, *"mi ritrovai per una selva oscura, ché la diritta via era smarrita."* Even I recognized that this was the beginning of Dante's *Inferno.* "Midway through the road of life, I found myself in a dark wood, on a lost road." Midway through my life, indeed. Is that where I was? Lost, on the road to Hell?

It started to rain, and more people crushed inside, pushing hard, to get out of the wet. Dario continued. Or maybe he'd embarked on something new. Whatever it was, it was being said with great gusto. His eyes were veined and red, and his pupils were dilated. I could observe them because he'd jumped off the platform, seized me by the shoulders, and, inches from my face, was spraying me with a saliva-foamy verse. He seemed to be declaiming rhyming couplets, very singsongy. One was shouted; the next was whispered. He crouched low, as though trying to take his audience by surprise. Then he thrust himself upright, as though making an announcement. He made his eyes big; he made them small.

He wagged his finger; he brought his hands together in prayer. I've never seen such a melodramatic reading. (Someone was now playing a fiddle.) It called for gaslights and Victorian top hats: this was what Dickens must have sounded like. Frankly, it seemed ridiculous. But the room loved it, and when Dario stopped and bounced back to his platform, the audience, in a high metabolic euphoria (the drink, the raw fat, the hot, closed space, the privilege of being in it) erupted in uproarious vaudeville applause, which Dario acknowledged, waving a hand in the air. He jettisoned the Mozart CD, turned up the volume, and popped in a salsa-sounding Italian number.

"*Festa!*" he shouted, gyrating to the end of the podium. "*Festa! Festa! Festa!*" He spun and came back in the other direction. "*Festa! Festa! Festa! Festa!*"

I was to report to work the next morning at eight.

20

O N A MONDAY MORNING, Panzano was different. On Sunday, the place had the energy of its visitors and probably some of the romance they'd wanted to find there. On Monday, it was an out-of-the-way village, quiet and rather ugly.

There were nine hundred people. They were served, I would learn, by two butchers, two cafés, two bars, four family-run food stores or *alimentari*, two restaurants, two hotels, and (uncharacteristically) three bakers. I would also discover that, with the town's offerings so precisely divided, the task of buying, say, a loaf of bread or a coffee was believed to reveal things about your character, probably your politics, and—who knows?—maybe your attitude to the afterlife. Wine was an entirely different category, because there were not two winemakers but eighteen, and ordering a glass at a bar could be a delicate social feat. There were also, fittingly, two towns: ancient and new.

The ancient town was a maze of old and imitation old: remnants of a castle (the archways), a medieval wall, a twelfth-century church rebuilt in the twentieth century (both it and the castle had been destroyed just about every hundred years since the 1100s), bad sewage, noisy neighbors, and no privacy. It was a characteristic feudal fortification constructed on the top of a hill during the long wars between the Sienese and the Florentines, both defense and shelter for the people who worked the land. You could see that land, looking more or less as it has at any other time in Panzano's history, spreading out in a series of basin-like valleys: more giant bathtubs than conventional river-carved ravines. The view was pretty and tranquil-making. I was surprised by how much was still wooded and wild. What was cultivated was mainly grapevines: their proliferation represented the only significant change in the landscape in the last five hundred years. It was the beginning of April, and the vineyards were long lines of plowed dark earth, a mathematical map of gnarly black stumps with tight fists of tiny green leaves that would open any day now, like a hand.

The new part of town was made of stucco walls with few adornments: a postwar efficiency. Like many hill towns, Panzano had been occupied by the Nazis, who had set the buildings near the main road alight when they retreated. The conflagration destroyed structures that had been standing for centuries, including the Antica Macelleria Cecchini, which had been in the same spot, run by the firstborn male of the Cecchini family, for eight generations. Upstairs, in an abandoned floor above the macelleria, I got a sense of what the old building had been like: the stone walls and floors are still intact, the very place where Dario's grandfather, the man Dario was named after, housed twenty-two members of his family, protecting them in adversity. During the war, he sold meat to the partisans, who crept up the hill before dawn; two hours later, promptly at eight, the Fascists appeared. In Chianti, I would discover soon enough, no one goes without meat.

This morning, the macelleria was in a frenzy. It was a "production day." I would learn this later; at the time, I understood only that I was always having to get out of the way of people moving very quickly. In the back, there was a small kitchen— an oven, a marble counter, and a butcher's block, where an older man worked. He was referred to as Il Maestro, "the master," and treated with unrelenting respect. All exchanges ended with this title. It was: How are you today, Maestro?

Would you like a coffee, Maestro?

May I remove these scraps, Maestro?

Around eleven, the Maestro had something to eat, which was bread (the "Maestro's loaf," cooked in a wood-burning oven and purchased by someone on their way to work) with olive oil and sprinkled with salt.

May I prepare it for you, Maestro?

Are you finished, Maestro?

May I remove the plate, Maestro?

Only two people were allowed to use a knife: Dario and the Maestro. Dario wielded his in the front, in view of visitors. The Maestro, in the back, kept his in a drawer underneath the butcher's block. The Maestro was sixty-two, dressed in his own white smock (everyone else was in

the butcher uniform—a medieval floor-length "Antica Macelleria Cecchini" apron). He lived in the next valley, near his son Enrico, who
owned a thousand olive trees and made a fragrant, intense oil, very hard
to come by, mainly because Dario bought most of it. The Maestro had
silver hair, a thin, expressively lined face, black eyebrows, big ears, and a
large masculine nose. "Look at that face," a friend of the Maestro's
instructed me some time later, when I'd become comfortable enough in
Italian to follow some of the back-and-forth banter of the place. "Isn't
that the face of an Etruscan? Don't you recognize it from the tomb
paintings? It's as old as these hills." The Maestro was deliberate (in
that ancient masculine way) and understated (in that ancient masculine way), and spoke with what sometimes seemed like an exaggerated
gravitas, gathering his long fingers together like a piece of punctuation.
The fingers were enormous. Astonishingly, the Maestro's hands were
bigger than Dario's. His hands were so big they made me uneasy. (Why
were mine so small? I often asked myself at the end of a long day, staring at them on my walk home. I now realize that they aren't that small.
In the normal world, they might be called large. The last time I needed a
pair of gloves, that's what I bought: large ones. Even so, the whole time I
was at the butcher shop, I would re-examine my hands from time to
time: they were so pudgy, the fingers so runty, the whole package so
inadequate. Maybe that's what you need to do this job: gigantic hands. If
you don't have forest animals growing at the end of your forearms, take
up pastry.)

Ann Marie used to work at the butcher shop but now came in only
on Sundays. Sundays were so busy that anybody with a connection to
Dario (even my wife, eventually, when she popped in to say hello) was
ordered to put on an apron, pour wine, spread lardo on bread, and serve
whatever meaty thing Dario had made for his visitors to sample. On one
such Sunday, Dario had proposed to Ann Marie, climbing down from
his podium, pulling out a big ring, and getting down on his knees in
front of everyone there to ask the question, amid applause and hooting
and picture-taking. This was several years ago, and even though the
two hadn't actually married—"He gave me the movie instead"—she
referred to herself as the butcher's wife. Ann Marie was five foot seven,
but, next to Dario, seemed dinky and waif-like. She had bright, untam-
able copper hair, willful like a broom, a pale freckly complexion, a Phyl-

lis Diller cackle, and an attitude of irrepressible irony. She wore red cowboy boots, turquoise jewelry, and a piece of bright green—somewhere: a redheaded study in color conflict. Her background was in fashion, her first job had been preparing costumes for the movie *Flashdance,* and she had come to Italy on behalf of the Banana Republic and never left. She had devised Dario's antilogo logo, his labels, and his business card (a fold-over piece of peek-and-see design, with a vivid picture of a piece of raw meat inside, held in his giant hands).

In most ways, the shop was run by Carlo and Teresa, a husband and wife. They had been Florentine factory owners, making men's dress shirts until men had started wearing T-shirts instead and their business had gone bust, and were now, by their own description, living in "reduced circumstances." They still had an apartment in Florence but in Panzano looked after a widow in exchange for room and board in her farmhouse. Carlo tended the butcher shop's accounts and deliveries. He was fifty-five, with a dark moustache and a dark manner—a man still owed his dues: a hard man with a soft, bruised heart. For the first year after the bankruptcy, Dario told me, Carlo had never spoken, not a word. Now he speaks—in fact, every three days or so, he also smiles—but the difficulty for me was his accent. Florentine speech is exaggerated. The "c"s are soft rather than hard: *casa* is "hasa." But in the Tuscan hills, that "casa" is not a quiet "hasa" but a spit-spraying fricative "HA-HA-HA-HAAAAsa," more animal than human. Even today, I don't easily ask Carlo anything, because I fear I won't understand the reply.

His wife, Teresa, looked after the kitchen: all the items that were cooked or prepared, which represented more than half of the shop's activity. I didn't understand what they were yet—jellies, sauces, terrines, beans, some sold in packages, some by the ladle from a bowl. None of it was what you'd expect in a conventional butcher shop. I would learn that most of it was so unusual it wasn't found in any other butcher shop anywhere.

Teresa was short, with round hips, very feminine, permanently on a diet (she made the salads at the two o'clock family meal, the only time you saw fresh vegetables), always changing her hair color, and effervescently happy. She hummed, broke out into song, laughed at the slightest absurdity, and because she found the world delightfully absurd she laughed all the time, unless she laughed too hard, and then she cried.

She was the daytime to her husband's darkness. Like her husband, she had no experience in a professional kitchen, even though she was now running one. In this, she was like everyone else. Many people had some kind of job at Dario's (previous experience not only not required but not wanted), even if it was nothing more than coming in at ten to read the newspapers and highlight articles about Tuscanness, or at eleven to make the coffee (two jobs, two different people). To be hired, you needed a misfortune and a capacity to sprint. The misfortune could be bankruptcy (like Teresa and Carlo), a sick husband (like Lucia, who came in to wash the aprons), visa problems (like Rashid, who appeared one morning from Morocco without a passport), a bit of trouble with the law, a dying mother, a father with cancer, an abusive parent, a spot of incest, mental dysfunction, a speech impediment, a walking disability, a collapsed spine, or simply some tic of socially inappropriate eccentric behavior. "Tuscans," Dario told me later, "have an affection for crazy people—I can't explain it." The capacity to sprint was needed because, whatever your task, that's what you did: you sprinted flat out to Dario's beck and call.

"Ri-ccaaar-DO!" Dario shouted all day long. He had a way of saying a name so that the middle syllable was stretched out long and impatiently, with a last irritated stress on the final one. "Ri-ccaaar-DO!" and Riccardo would appear, panting, looking exactly like the butcher's apprentice I expected to find: round and fleshy with rosy cheeks and floppy black hair and seeming fourteen. (He was twenty-one.) "Fi-nal-meeen-TE!" Dario would say, stretching out that middle syllable again and spitting out the last one. (Fi-naaaa-LY!)

Often, Dario simply invoked ingredients. "Pe-PE" he shouted, and, back in the kitchen, everyone scrambled to find the pepper and grind it by hand. In the macelleria, there were only three machines, and you got the sense that they'd been purchased reluctantly and after much internal debate. "A-GLIO!" Dario said to no one, but boomingly because he was also playing a loud Puccini opera, and someone grabbed garlic from a straw basket, peeled it, and rushed it to Dario. *"Boh!"* he said, a Tuscan grunt conveying his wonder that you hadn't known he needed it without his having to ask for it, and then minced it in a hand-cranked mill stuck to the counter with a suction cup.

I tried to be helpful—advice I'd got from people at Babbo about what to do when you're in a new kitchen: be invisible, be useful, and eventually you'll be given a chance to do more. I swept floors, washed pans, pulled thousands of rosemary leaves off stems. After a day or two, I knew enough to grind the pepper when Dario called out for it. On my third day, I prepared red peppers for a fiery sweet jelly called a *mostarda*. The peppers were boiled with sugar, chili peppers, and gelatin, and, after seeing my writing down the recipe, Carlo grew concerned that I would walk off with the shop's most lucrative secret. Then he took me aside, a businessman trying to get back into the game, and suggested, in his heavy Tuscan accent, that maybe when I got back to New York the two of us might set up an enterprise together: "America is a very big country." By then I'd prepared 2,500 peppers (each box contained 50, which I know because I was desperately keeping count), quartering each bell-shaped vegetable, meticulously slicing away the white part, and brushing away the seeds. I wasn't about to steal a recipe. I haven't eaten a pepper since.

I went home that night with stained red hands, wondering: What is this place? It was famous for its *bistecca fiorentina*, the legendary Florentine steak. Poems were written about it, poems which Dario sometimes recited. Each *bistecca* weighed about five pounds, was five to six inches thick, and cost around a hundred and twenty-five dollars. But they were scarcely sold. I had been at the butcher shop four days before anyone actually scored one. On my first morning, three requests had been refused for no reason that I could understand, except, in Dario's eyes, the customers hadn't been worthy. Then, instead of selling meat, the place virtually closed down to make gallons of pepper jelly.

The experience was akin to my being back in Elisa's prep kitchen, but a weirder, more single-mindedly purposeful version. Each day, we made another new thing. After the pepper jelly, we prepared a terrine called a *pasticcio rustico*. In fact, it was very, very rustico. I couldn't imagine people actually wanting to eat it (neither the Maestro nor Teresa could bring themselves to taste it) unless they were very poor *and* without a refrigerator *and* hallucinating from starvation. The principal ingredient was very old pork that had been aging in its own blood, sealed in a plastic bag. When you opened one, the smell hit you like a stinging slap of stinky molecules. The smell was so bad ("*Mal' odore!*" Teresa shrieked) that Dario rushed back to turn on the extractor fan: customers in the shop were uncomfortable. We started our stinky terrines in the morning, cooked them in the afternoon, and chilled them overnight. The next day we prepared salt. We took bags of it, mixed it with dried herbs, and put it through a grinder to make a herbal concoction called *Profumo del Chianti*. The result was indeed aromatic and evocative of summer camp when I was eight, and, having been finely pulverized, was fluffy and snow-like. But for the next six hours, five of us poured fluffy salt into tiny one-and-a-half-ounce jars. Hadn't machines been invented to do this sort of thing?

What I really wanted was to learn meat. I didn't yet understand the culture surrounding Tuscan butchery. I hadn't come here to learn about it because I hadn't known anything about it. The truth is I came here because I wanted to make food in an Italian way, and, frankly, any place would have sufficed, because every place would be different from anything I'd known. But I was here and, fortuitously enough, I was interested in how you prepare an animal as food.

There is a reasonably extensive literature for non–meat eaters. But there is no such literature for those who eat meat, probably because they rarely believe they need to justify what they do. My suspicion is that, at some point, most meat eaters have asked themselves why they eat meat but have been able to answer the question without getting too philosophical. I eat meat because I like it and have never wanted to talk myself into giving it up: end of self-scrutiny. I've been happy as a carnivore—for me, eating meat is natural (to my mind, either side of the what-is-natural? debate can be defended pretty persuasively)— although, like the rest of the thinking world, I recognize that much of the meat I've eaten probably wasn't produced naturally but treated instead like something that's not meat (the hormones, the antibiotics, the brutal results of confinement rearing), a unit of production, a reproducible item in a mass-market business. But I was frustrated that my picture of the business wasn't much more informed than that. The meat world was so unknowable that I could never get what seemed like an honest view about how an animal was made into food, short of buying one and bringing it home and having my way with it. There was an elementary knowledge I didn't have, and, now that I was in a butcher shop, I was hoping I'd get it.

I wanted to be tutored in butchering. But I was also haunted by Alex's story of a year in a Florentine kitchen, cutting vegetables. Was my prospect any better, when only two people were allowed to wield a knife? And there was the overwhelming daily routine, making pepper jelly and pouring salt into tiny jars.

THERE WERE mishaps. I bashed myself. I cut myself. I fell: I had been myopically focused on a task, peeling garlic, and hadn't noticed a heavy bin of beef at my feet until I walked straight into it and became airborne. Teresa looked up, dumbfounded by what she saw: this large American, inexplicably perpendicular to the floor. When I landed (in the meat, garlic peels now everywhere), she rammed a fist into her mouth to stop from laughing hysterically, at least until she confirmed I hadn't been injured, and then that's what she did: laughed hysterically. Then she started crying.

I split my head open. I was cleaning a machine used to pound meat. It was like an instrument of punishment, the height of a man, all metal angles, gunged up with muscly goo. I must have assumed an unnatural position, wanting to remain at arm's length while needing to get close enough to scrape out the red fluff, when I slammed my forehead into something and split open the skin. It was so unexpected I didn't know what I'd hit. I felt the edges of the wound: deep. A minute later, I did it again. I slammed the *same* part of my forehead into the *same* sharp something, whatever it was, splitting open the earlier wound. I had to sit down; blood was all over my face.

I missed Babbo: its rules and knowing how to work in them, the adrenaline of the service, the recognition I'd earned for myself. I was starting over. Then I caught on fire.

I was making a pot of what was called *ragù alla Medici,* named after the famous Renaissance Florentine family whose kitchens, according to Dario, represented the high point of Italian cooking.

The meat was beef that had been sitting around unsold, having reached its sell-by date or exceeded it: raw, marinated, even cooked, whatever was to hand. These were all put through a meat grinder and plopped into a four-foot-high pot. The vegetables, the usual suspects—red onions, carrots, celery, garlic—were put through the grinder as well, a long column of brightly colored mush. I was given a paddle, five feet long, like a shovel, with a flat burnt edge for scraping the bottom. A big burner was put on the floor so that I could stand above the pot. I was to stir for eight hours.

Actually, it was only six hours, because there was a two-hour break for lunch, a family meal, a pasta served with an impromptu condiment made with olive oil, garlic, and the season's first cherry tomatoes, during which Dario suddenly started reciting the end of the *Divine Comedy*. I have no idea why. Something about the food. The tomatoes, maybe. The tomatoes, being red, reminded him of Hell, and he was off. Everyone stopped and were respectfully silent, until it became apparent that Dario was going to continue for some time. Carlo made his I-can't-believe-he's-doing-this-at-lunch-again face and the people at the table then resumed their conversations, finished their food, picked up the plates, washed them—Dario still going on—and got back to their tasks. I didn't have this liberty because I didn't know better. I hadn't yet realized that this was akin to a plumbing problem. "Damn, there goes the toilet again!" "Damn, there goes Dario on that last canto!" I also felt I had no escape, because the recitation—Dario sweating, his face a fevery sheen—was being projected at me. When he finished, invoking a love that moves the sun and the other stars, he got up and went to the cupboard for a bottle of whiskey, knocked it back, and assumed his position on his platform, visibly shaking, his hands on the counter, only his back on view to me. He turned. He was crying. "Every passion, every feeling of fury or anguish, every thought, is compressed into those lines."

I nodded. I'm sure he was right. But I had things to do. I was making my first ragù. Wasn't this why I'd come to Italy—to be told by an Italian how to make a ragù? I returned to my pot joyfully, relit the burner, and resumed stirring. The meat, long cooked, looked like gravelly dirt. Eventually, Dario appeared. He'd recovered from his Dante recitation and had come to inspect my work. He added some tomato—not much, more tomato water than tomato sauce, deepening the color from dirt brown to dark dirt brown. I kept rolling the meat round, each time pushing some to one side, exposing the hot bottom of the pot, then rolling it back again. With each pass, the meat hissed, and steam enveloped my face. I was hot: the wet-shirt, sweat-pouring-down-my-face-neck-arms routine. Marco Pierre White came to mind ("All big boys season their food with their sweat—you can taste it"), and I wondered if sweat really is a kitchen's secret seasoning, because there was no doubt where mine was falling, even though it converted to steam on impact.

I had concerns. One was that, in paddling the meat from side to side, I might accidentally push the pot too far—each time it bumped against my knee—and it would tip over, spilling hours of good work. (That'd be the kind of thing I'd do, wouldn't it? I hugged the pot a little closer.) The other was that my apron, which was floor-length, would catch on fire. I rehearsed in my mind the possible scenario. The apron is secured around the waist with a string belt. To get it off, you had to untie the string. So that was the first thing—untie it. If I didn't, it could be ugly. I pictured myself in flames, being unable to remove the apron, and Dario's rushing over, all heroic and decisive, picking me up with his giant hands, hurling me to the floor, and stomping out the fire. (I did not want to be stomped.)

Around five o'clock Teresa looked into the pot. "Dario, *è pronto*"— it's ready. Dario came over, scooped up some ragù onto the paddle, and shook it, like a tin-pan gold prospector.

"It's meant to be like sand," he explained. He tasted it. "*Boh!*" He passed the paddle to Teresa.

She tasted it—"*Boh*,"—and passed the paddle to Carlo.

Carlo tasted it. "*Boh.*"

Riccardo tasted it. "*Boh.*"

The Maestro tasted it. "*Boh.*"

Oh, what the hell, I thought, and I tasted some, too. Everyone looked at me. "*Boh*," I said finally. (What else could I say?)

Dario tasted it again. "*Perfetto*," he declared. I stared at it, the hours of my stirring, this dirty sticky sand.

"*Pepe!*" Dario called out to the ceiling. Pepper appeared.

"*Sale!*" Salt appeared.

"*Limone!*" And there was a bowl of lemon zest. Cinnamon, coriander, nutmeg, cloves. It interested me that the seasonings were added after the cooking. The seasonings themselves, this Medici compilation, also interested me. You'd never find these in a conventional ragù. It was nothing like a Bolognese, even if it had the same consistency. (Are all of Dario's preparations simply polemics dressed up as food? "We have no idea where these things come from," Teresa told me once. "Dario goes home, he reads an old book, he has another dish.") I leaned over and took in the new aromatics, which were like Christmas and Easter and mushroomy autumn in one complex smell. Then Dario called out for vin santo—two whole bottles.

My mouth dropped. Oh, no! After all the effort to get rid of the liquid. Am I now going to have to steam this away as well? He poured them in, and I looked inside, disbelieving. It was now soupy. And, just as I feared, I was told to resume stirring. I was tired. Then I was on fire.

The flames started at the hem and, like that—two seconds—the whole apron was burning. Wow! Just like the movies. (It's animal fat, it occurred to me—of course! I'm a grease fire!) The fire was well under way before I noticed it, even though I'd been expecting it, and had already raced around the apron. It was, fittingly enough, a circle of flames: very *Inferno*-like. But I knew what to do. Evidently, so did Dario. Where did he come from? I went straight for the belt, *fast*, and located the end of the strings so I could undo the knot—a simple bow, one tug. But Dario, with heroic urgency, also went straight for the belt. I was much more relaxed, probably because I'd been rehearsing the fire drill all afternoon. Dario, however, was so focused on undoing my apron knot that he failed to notice that I was already there and grabbed the strings I was already holding. (How do you say, "Hey, Dario, kindly remove your gigantic fucking paws"?) We struggled. My hands went one way, his another, until I found I was once again holding the strings, which was good. But Dario was now clenching the knot itself. How can I undo the knot if his hands are all over it? But between his efforts and mine, the knot somehow came undone. The apron was then ripped off and hurled violently to floor: whereupon Dario stomped it.

Later that night, in something of a metaphysical mood, I was visited by Mr. Commonsense, whom I hadn't heard from in some time. He addressed me: Why did you want to be a butcher? Doesn't Benny, in the West Village, give you good service? And this language thing—what's wrong with English? And why did you ever want to learn to cook? Really—at your age?

THE BREAKTHROUGH MOMENT was *soppressata*. Teresa asked me to help. It was the next day's project.

From what I could tell, soppressata is pig meat and pig fat in an intestinal casing—like salami, but meatier, fatter, bigger—and each region seems to have its own version. Dario's is a *sopressata de' Medici,* a sixteenth-century spelling, because the by-now-familiar Medicean ingredients—cloves, cinnamon, nutmeg, citrus zest, and sweet wine— were added to a very gelatinous pork filling. The fascination with the Medicis was a daily theme. I knew elements of the story: that after Caterina de' Medici left Italy in 1533 to become the future queen of France, she not only jump-started the culinary revolution there but also gave away all of Italy's kitchen secrets. Her pack train, it was said, had been loaded with lettuces, parsley, and artichokes (familiar in Italy, foreign in France), and her kitchen help included banquet stewards, butchers, and pastry chefs, so that, when she finally settled in, she was able to introduce pastries, custards, profiteroles, vegetables, and herbs to a population that had never had such things, plus the best of Renaissance cooking, along with an attitude of seriousness about food, as well as that enduring utensil, the fork (an Italian invention—how else could you eat pasta?). In educated food circles, much fun is had at the expense of Italians who still think the story is true: there are the Tooth Fairy, and flying carpets, and . . . Dario, of course, had no such doubts. I understood this after I once remarked on his using shallots in one of his preparations.

"Shallots?" I asked, exaggeratedly perplexed. "Dario, aren't shallots French?" It was a mischievous query. Dario did not respond well to suggestions that his food was covertly Gallic.

"No!" he boomed. "No! No! No!" According to Dario, shallots were another item introduced *to* the French *by* Italians. "How long have you been here? *Boudin blanc,*" he exclaimed, referring to the French white sausage. "*Boudin noir! La crème caramel! Le soufflé! La crépinette!*" He was shouting. "*Le pâté! La mayonnaise! I salumi—la charcuterie! Canard à l'orange!* These dishes did not *originate* in France! They *arrived* in France!" *Tutta la cucina e arrivata!* "Until Caterina de' Medici, there was no grand French cooking!"

Dario's face was red. I thought of coming clean: "Hey, Dario, just joking!" No chance. He wouldn't be stopped. He cited German dishes, Viennese dishes—"The *Sachertorte?* Eh? From Sicily!" Argentine ones. *Chimichurri*—the country's beef preparation? "Where in the dick do you think that comes from?" Maybe he'd had too much wine at lunch, because he then declared that "most of the world's cooking"—

tutta la cultura della cucina è nata nel Mediterraneo—"comes from the Mediterranean, and most of *that* comes from Tuscany."

I stared at him blankly, taking in the proposition that Tuscans, ultimately, were responsible for all the good cooking everywhere.

(Then again, maybe he was right. I'd been surprised how many items I'd always thought of as French were on a traditional Tuscan menu—like crêpes, *crespelle* in Italian, or flan, called *sformato*.)

This morning, the soppressata reminded Dario of Armandino's stay in the butcher shop. When he'd been here, Armandino had video-recorded everything he was taught so he could reproduce it when he returned to Seattle. But, as Armandino couldn't speak Italian, he had used Faith Willinger as his translator—Mario had introduced the two to each other. During a soppressata-making session, Armandino stood on a stool filming, just over Dario's shoulder, and Willinger provided a steady commentary in English. Suddenly Dario became very upset. Making soppressata involves three people, and, for Dario, those three people had always been his father, his mother, and his grandmother. They are now dead, and it was too much—there were just too many associations—and Dario exploded in a sentimental outburst. "It takes three people to make soppressata! One person can't do it!" He ordered Armandino down from the stool and told Faith to shut up, get dirty, and help.

This time I was the third person, joining Teresa and the Maestro. First I was told to weigh the meat, a pot of leftover pig bits: two hundred pounds of knuckles, heads, toenails, tits, tongues, plus some misshapen parts I couldn't identify. The Renaissance ingredients were added, and it was all boiled slowly until it became a thick, gray sludge, at which time the fire was turned off and the pot was allowed to cool—but only a little. A pig's bony bits are full of gelatin, and they solidify like cement if they reach room temperature.

We began. Teresa worked from the pot, filling a cup with the lumpy mixture and emptying it into a canvas sack, not unlike a coarse sock, which she then handed to me. I tapped it twice, letting the mixture settle, and wiped off the sides—goo seeping through the weave—closed it up, and passed it to the Maestro, who gripped it firmly from the top, his gigantic hand enveloping my puny paw. He then rapidly looped a string around the bundle, like a parcel for the post office.

We established a rhythm. Teresa, the handover to me, the Maestro.

At some point, Teresa started humming. She hummed so much I rarely noticed her humming: it was a background noise of cheerfulness. But the Maestro noticed, and he joined in, whistling. The tune was " 'O Sole Mio."

The three of us continued. Teresa filled a sack, I tapped it, the Maestro tied it. Meanwhile, Teresa hummed, and the Maestro whistled. Then they reached the end of the song. The Maestro cleared his throat.

No, I thought. He wouldn't dare.

"Che bella cosa," he sang. It was an impressive baritone. *"Na jurnata 'e sole."* What a beautiful thing a day in the sun is. I don't think I'd heard the words before. I was impressed that someone knew them. Then again, if anyone was going to know them, he probably would, wouldn't he? (After all, he's Italian.)

Teresa replied. *"N'aria serena,"* she sang. Hers was a perfectly reasonable mezzo-soprano, and I was impressed that she, too, knew the words. She filled up another sack and handed it to me, singing, *"doppo a na tempesta."* In the serene air after a storm.

This was all very sweet. The problem was the song, and the real problem, for me, was that I'd lived in Britain, where a corrupted version was the theme tune in a television advertisement selling a factory-made fake Italian ice cream called a "cornetto": Venice, gondolas, and some guy in a beret singing "Just one more cornetto" to the refrain of " 'O Sole Mio." I was finding these two versions difficult to reconcile: on the one hand, "just one more cornetto," openly accepted as a joke; on the other hand, this Italian hill town, the making of soppressata according to a Renaissance recipe, surrounded by people who were singing this landmark piece of Italian kitsch in earnest. And they knew the words. And it wasn't a joke.

"Pe' ll'aria fresca," the Maestro continued, *"pare già na festa."*

"Che bella cosa na jurnata 'e sole," Teresa replied, and set down her sack. The Maestro put down his as well and took a deep breath. They were preparing for the high notes of the famous refrain.

(No, I found myself saying quietly, Please, don't do it. Aren't you embarrassed? Please stop.)

They didn't stop. They tilted back their heads, projected their voices to the ceiling, and bellowed: " *'O sole mio,"* they sang in unison, *"sta 'nfronte a te! 'O sole, 'o sole mio . . ."*

(I felt so humiliated on their behalf. Didn't they know that this was an ice cream ad?)

When they finished, they were silent. Finally Teresa spoke. "Bravo, Maestro," she said, wiping away a tear.

"Brava, Teresa," the Maestro said, clearing his throat.

The refrain continued in my head as I walked home that night. Who would believe what I'd witnessed? No one would believe it. I'm not sure I believed it, except that I was covered with the evidence. I had soppressata gunk all over me, two fingers were stuck together, and it was going to take some scrubbing before I liberated them. (You've got to wonder: what must your stomach go through before it digests this stuff?) I'd stepped in some as well, scarcely surprising, since, in the three-person handover, there had been soppressata slopping all over the floor. I could hear it: it made a sticky suction-cup sound as my heel pressed into the pavement and tried to come away again. Meanwhile the refrain continued. In fact, I was humming it. It might be kitsch. It might be an ice cream ad. But I had to concede: it was catchy. Also, I couldn't remember another job where people sang while they worked. I liked that they did. I liked that I was here, making this strange food.

21

Dario Cecchini was born on September 10th, 1955, in a house across the street from the butcher shop, now the place where Carlo keeps the books and Lucia arrives every morning to wash and hang out the long aprons soiled from the day before. Dario's father, Tullio, who is still talked about in Panzano with much affection (often in constructions that contrast him favorably with his more histrionic son), was known for his charm, his athleticism, and his winning way with women—which distressed his own father, who, on his deathbed, ordered his son to stop being a ladies' man and settle down. Marry Angelina, he commanded, a local girl, whereupon the father died, and the son, following the deathbed imperative, promptly married Angelina. When Dario talks of his father, he invokes a teacher, often of lessons in how to see: an aesthetic appreciation, an understanding of painting, and a proudly possessive way of viewing the Renaissance, as though its greatest achievements were incontrovertibly Tuscan. The philosophy seems to have been expressed in informal tutorials, father and son at museums together, and went something like this: "You see that statue of David? You see that painting of the Last Supper? They're Tuscan. We did those." What the father did not teach his son was how to prepare meat.

Dario did not want to be a butcher and was resolved to be the first Cecchini, in six centuries, not to be. He also wanted to be the first to have a graduate education and attended the University of Pisa to study veterinary science. "I wanted to cure animals, not butcher them." But in his second year, his sister, Marina, phoned: their father had cancer— very advanced. Dario was summoned to a hospital where his father, dying, confessed to having made a mistake: he had not taught his son

how to butcher. He had thought there would be time. "Go to the Maestro," his father said. "I've spoken to him. He will teach you how to
recognize good meat." Whereupon the father died.

Dario was twenty years old. Following the deathbed imperative,
he abandoned his studies. There was, additionally, a financial imperative: with the father's death, the family, or what was left of it (a grandmother, a sister—Dario's mother had died when he was eleven), had no
money. One day in 1976, Dario paid a visit to the Maestro and asked for
his help, and he agreed to give it.

The village Dario came back to was different from the one he'd
grown up in. Only old people remained, he recalls; everyone else was
leaving (*fuggendo*—fleeing, as though from a pestilence). His father's
customers had lived nearby—*contadini*, tenant farmers and small-plot
holders, who did a type of farming called *agricoltura promiscua*, a
promiscuous mix: they had vines and pasture and olive trees, made wine
and oil, raised livestock, and grew wheat and vegetables. The local cow
was a white breed called a *chianina*, a work animal, distinguished by its
height (it towers over conventional cattle), its size (six-month-old
calves can weigh more than fifteen hundred pounds), and its strength.
Chianine had been here since anyone could remember (*da sempre*, since
forever), and you couldn't cultivate the hilly land without them, normally two at time, yoked together by a wood harness shaped like the
letter "m" to accommodate their thick necks. The older chianine, the
occasional bull, and some of the calves (the *vitelli* surplus to a small
farmer's requirements) were sold off at a weekly livestock market in
Greve, about five miles down the hill. The chianina was prized for its
deep "beefiness"—a unique, complex flavor you get from worked muscles, sometimes tough, rarely fatty, not unlike an animal in the wild. The
bistecca fiorentina is traditionally cut from a chianina. But the mixed
farming had been disappearing.

In 1956, there had been a devastating spring freeze, the worst in two
centuries, which had killed most of the olive trees, including ones that,
hundreds of years old, had seemed capable of living through every
adversity. And the death of the trees, so associated with the area as to
be a symbol or a flag—one that meant permanence and durability—
seemed to kill something of the spirit of the people who cultivated
them. There was another freeze, Dario's first winter back in Panzano,

severe enough to kill off the new plantings. Farmers wanted out. Many abandoned their homes: who wants a stone house with dirt floors, no plumbing, and acres of ruined vegetation? There were other factors (everyone in Panzano has a list), including a bungled effort by an interventionist government to help (too little, too late), followed by an equally bungled effort to get out of the way; the advent of supermarkets; the ubiquity of refrigeration or paved roads or travel agencies or television; the culture of electricity (if only *that* hadn't arrived). In sum, they amounted, for one reason or another (call it "the very late arrival of the twentieth century"), to the end of a long era in rural Tuscany. By 1976, no one wanted to be a farmer. The year Dario embarked on being a butcher, Chianti was desolate.

One afternoon, when the butcher shop was closed, my wife and I joined Dario and Ann Marie at their home, Il Greppo, a stone house like those abandoned by farmers in the seventies. To reach it, you carried on up the steep road by the butcher shop, heading into the wild, uncultivated part of Chianti. On each side, there was a valley. In the direction of Greve, it was rocky and uncleared, and there were herds of sheep. On the other side, it was the big basin kind, a unique piece of geography that gets sun all day called *la conca d'oro*—*conca* like conch, the shellfish, and *oro* like gold: a shell-shaped valley of golden sunshine. Photographs from the 1960s show white cows, high wheat, olive trees, pigpens, some vines. Now you see vines, spreading outward with neoclassical discipline, row after row, a symmetrical aesthetic of spring green, the new leaves having finally unfurled with the warmer weather. There were a few small-plot farmers, but most of the valley was divided between two winemaking families.

One, until 1991, had been headed by Alceo di Napoli, a prince of Naples. (Much of Chianti is owned by people with titles.) Alceo's family has lived in the Castello dei Rampolla, the castle on the far side of the valley, since the 1700s. Accounts of Alceo evoke a determined, nononsense man of aggressive bluntness and worldly smarts, a forthright and charismatic patriarch. Dario describes him, with no small admiration, as "the dickhead of dickheads"—*testa di cazzo*—"the supreme dickhead of dickheads. Il Maestro of dickheads. Always in litigation, always fighting. He was magnificent—*molto bravo!*" During the big freezes and the aftermath, referred to by locals as the "great migration,"

Alceo was living in Brazil. When he returned, his land in neglect, he ripped everything out and planted vines. He produced his first bottle of wine in 1975, Dario's first year back. Alceo went on to make some of the region's most prestigious wines, but when he died in 1991 the family had difficulties running the vineyard without him. One of Alceo's sons, Marco, said to be the most capable, had also been wild and capricious, a rich boy rebel who predeceased his father, when he crashed his helicopter into a mountain. Matteo, the next son, took over, but he overinvested, mismanaged the finances, and disappeared in the aftermath of a tax scandal. The family seemed unable to make a wine that met the standards established by the father (who seemed to linger, like a scolding ghost). Luca, the third son, took over, and the daughter, Maurizia, then helped out. Since 2000, the wine is good again. Their most successful bottling—one Maurizia imagines their father might have made for himself—is called Vigna d'Alceo, Alceo's vine.

Manetti was the valley's other family, headed, until recently, by Dino Manetti, an old Florentine family that has been making terra-cotta tiles since the Renaissance in nearby Impruneta. The Manetti property in Panzano, which the father bought in 1968, included a whole former *borgo*, a little village: several families clustered together, living around a courtyard, with a ninth-century cantina (a combined kitchen, pantry, and cellar) with stalls for the chianine. The borgo had a routine for sharing the domestic duties, including making bread in the borgo's woodburning oven every Saturday morning and only on Saturdays, in part because Tuscan bread, which is made without salt, is believed by many to improve the staler it gets (which might well be possible if only because it tastes of so little when it's fresh). I met the last contadino to have resided at the borgo (in Panzano, you eventually meet everyone), Beppe—a big man, now seventy but seeming much older, with a hefty belly and suspenders to keep his trousers up, long unkempt hair, missing front teeth, and a wild stare. He could be found in the late afternoons in the square where the old men gather. In his time, Beppe had been the animal guy, looking after the chianine needed for the planting and the harvest. Implicit in the arrangement had been a long-standing rural attitude of husbandry: when the animals are so intimately involved in your life, you treat them with the care of a family member—

even if it's one you expect to eat for dinner, and maybe *because* you expect to eat it for dinner.

When Dino Manetti took over the borgo, there were vines everywhere, but they, too, had been neglected, and, like his neighbor, he pulled them out and planted new ones. The effort took four years; he, too, finished in 1975. I never met Dino Manetti; he died weeks before we arrived, although even I, in my ignorance, could feel the loss his death represented. He had been widely adored, something like the unofficial mayor of Panzano, a romantic who had come here, he was quoted as saying, to discover his Chianti roots. Giovanni, his son, who was forty, seemed to be continuing his father's effort by digging deeper to find them. Three months after his father's death, Giovanni began excavating the old borgo. The wood-burning oven had only just appeared underneath what had been a modern floor. From the ridge, you could just see men pulling down rooms, their impromptu partitions, the ad hoc refurbishments: like an archaeological site.

Il Greppo was a three-story stone house, another mile along the ridge, and overlooked a precipitous ravine. Dario bought the building in 1980, when he'd been at the butcher shop five years. It had been a lonely time. One moment, he had been enjoying a student's life, which was novel and diverting and full of promise. "I'd discovered movies." (There are no movies in a Tuscan hill town.) "I had girlfriends, read books, attended gallery openings, went to parties. From there to a butcher shop in Panzano. It was like going to Africa. Africa would have been easier." He lived in the family home, every morning traversing the same piece of earth *("la stessa terra!")* his father had walked on; and his grandfather, and his great-grandfather. The steel Dario used to sharpen his knives had been his father's. So, too, had the counter, where Dario now prepared his meat. He was cutting himself. Incompetence or fear? Both, he said, a debilitating terror. His forearms were covered with scars. Knives frightened him. "In the beginning, I saw only the blade and kept ruining the beef. I hurt myself terribly." He needed to make this new life work for all kinds of reasons he didn't understand. He was in a rush. He wanted to do everything quickly, urgently, even though he knew nothing. The Maestro slowed him down. "You can't do traditional work at a modern pace. Traditional work has traditional rhythms. You need calm. You can be busy, but you must remain calm."

Padre Giovanni, an eighty-two-year-old monk, told Dario about Il Greppo. The monk was a Sanskrit scholar, a poet, a lecturer in dead languages, an alchemist, and for Dario another mentor. Dario wasn't raised religiously. ("A true Tuscan cannot believe in Christ, because a true Tuscan believes only in liberty.") But his father used to take him to see monasteries and churches. ("He wanted me to experience tranquil spaces.") Padre Giovanni seemed to understand Dario, and Dario openly talks about needing male figures—*figuri maschili*—to teach him how to be a man in the aftermath of his father's death: like the Maestro and like Padre Giovanni. Padre Giovanni introduced Dario to the cooking of the Italian Renaissance, the works of the "Glorious Tradition," including Martino, Scappi, and Latini. "Padre Giovanni helped me control my passions. He told me I needed a place to be alone." Dario bought Il Greppo because the monk lived next door. "I didn't see him much, but I was calmer knowing he was nearby."

Dario pointed to a ruin on the facing slope, a stump covered with moss and shrubs. It had been, he said, the ancestral castle of Guido Cavalcanti, the impetuous, reckless father of Italian love poetry and early advocate of the *dolce stil nuovo* (the new sweet style). Cavalcanti had died here, in 1300, while exiled from Florence. In the butcher shop, you need only say *"Donna, me prega"*—woman, ask me—the first words of Cavalcanti's famous love poem, and several people were guaranteed to recite the rest in unison. Cavalcanti had been Dante's best friend, and when Dario mentioned the two men the association called a passage to mind, and he began declaiming the *Inferno,* Canto 10 in fact, where Dante meets the father of the poet in Hell, the none-too-happy Cavalcante Cavalcanti.

Dario's house was like a neglected museum. Apart from an upper floor—where Ann Marie had successfully prevailed upon him to install a working bathroom—the property was largely untouched since its last inhabitants. The ground floor dated from the twelfth century, and most of it was taken up by an open-hearth kitchen. Dario referred to it as *il forno,* which today means oven, and in many ways it was more oven than hearth. It was capacious and accessible—a giant source of heat, a place to cook and be warmed by. Dario grew still. "I don't want to change a thing. I come here to smell. Sometimes I do nothing but sit in a corner and smell." I tried to take in the room's musty history but couldn't stop my mind from recognizing some of the absurdities of where I found myself: are running water, gas, electricity really so evil? Even so, as I stood there, not moving, scrutinizing the silence, I couldn't deny that the room had an eerie power. I walked across the hearth—gray ash rubbed into the clay floor—and looked into the adjoining bedrooms. They were small—space for a bed, not much more. The windows had the original crisscrossing metalwork. During the hot months, they admitted a breeze and summer smells of animals and fruit and olives. In the winter, shutters wouldn't have kept out the cold, and everyone would have gathered round the heat of the forno. I stood in the doorway of one room, lost in a meditation of the house's recurring habits. People had made love here, sweated through pregnancy, gave birth, looked after children, became ill, died, a fire always burning in the kitchen. In this room, the next generation had done the same, the fire still burning. And the next generation, for a thousand years.

It was getting dark. I walked out onto a stone porch to take in the view of the ruined stump that had once been Cavalcanti's home. I couldn't see it. In good light, you had to know it was there to locate it— the outline was apparent in a deeper, more fluorescent shade of green— but now, the sun setting, the outline was gone. It was late, and we were hungry. Dario suggested we get something to eat, perhaps in the nearby village of Lamole.

22

THE RESTAURANT, normally empty at this time of year, was hosting an anniversary party. As we stood at the entrance, an elderly couple were being led up to a small stage to receive their first lessons in karaoke. The owner, the hardworking, thirty-three-year-old English-German-French-speaking Filippo Masini (who, with his brother, had only recently taken over from their father), knew he should be turning us away. His greeting was excessive and full of panic, as though the mayor had just popped in, unannounced. "*Eccolo!*" Filippo cried. "Dario Cecchini. How *very good* to see you! You are so *very* welcome! I am so lucky. The very grand Dario has come to my humble Restaro di Lamole!" But everything else about Filippo's manner was conveying how *bad* it was that Dario had turned up (how, for instance, can you say it's good to see someone without actually smiling?) and that, actually, he was very *un*welcome.

"I want only bistecca, dripping with blood," Dario said as Filippo seated us at a table on the edge of the anniversary party. "A butcher likes raw," he explained to me. "A butcher likes the warm tissue of an animal freshly killed, tasting only of blood. Give me blood!" he boomed to the room and enacted a show of masticating, an exaggerated chomping of his teeth, very big-mouthed. Filippo, standing by the table, taking all this in, was starting to fidget. Dario's display was really a challenge: How good is your bistecca, Filippo? Every Tuscan restaurant has bistecca on the menu, but none of the restaurants in the area offered Dario's meat: it was too expensive and, on some level, just too ideological. Filippo's menu advertised that his came from Gabriella's, a butcher in Greve.

The wine was the first disaster. Filippo was proud of his list, which was many pages long and included all of Tuscany's established names. He handed it to Dario—a large book, which Dario seized, lifted above his head, and hurled to the floor in disgust. The action was startling in the extreme. I looked to Dario for an explanation, but he was staring at Filippo with loathing.

"You know I don't want these wines."

Filippo was baffled.

"Give us a red wine that hasn't been ruined," Dario said.

Filippo mentioned a name, stuttering.

"No!" Dario had attracted the attention of one of the family tables. "You know I don't want a wine made with wood. I want a *real* wine. I want a *simple* wine. I want a wine from here."

Filippo mentioned another name, an inexpensive red from the village.

Dario grunted, an impatient sound, something between a belch and an inadvertent exhale, as though he'd been hit hard on the back. It was Tuscan for "Duh?" Filippo disappeared to retrieve a bottle, distressed and seemingly engaged in an internal debate over how he should deal with this man's very high-handed conduct.

The wine dispute was related to another piece of recent Panzano history and another Dario polemic. Around the time that the Alceos and the Dinos were ripping out the neglected vines and blasted roots of successive agricultural failures, a few local landowners had experimented with making wines in a French style. The results were so successful that others imitated them. By some perversity of cultural logic, the new wines were called not Super French but Super Tuscan. The Vigna d'Alceo, for instance, was made with cabernet sauvignon, the principal grape in a Bordeaux, which, prior to 1975, had never been planted in Chianti soil. Dino Manetti's wines were made with sangiovese, which was a Tuscan grape, but the wine was aged in barriques, small oak barrels, which was very French, although (according to Dario) akin to marinating your wine in a tree.

The menu was the second disaster. On the whole, it was very regional, which also means it was very brown. There is a saying in Italy, *brutto ma buono,* ugly but good, which celebrates the amateurish, often irregular integrity of food made by hand. In Tuscany, the phrase could be *brutto e marrone,* ugly and brown. The local *crostini,* for instance, with every available millimeter smeared with chicken liver pâté, were a brown food. *Pappa al pomodoro,* another local dish, was made from stale bread (the unsalted, flavorless Tuscan kind, so you know it had to be very stale) cooked with overripe leftover tomatoes until it degenerated into a dark brown mush: brown on dark brown. The many varieties of local beans: brown. (Dario once took me to an eleven-course banquet honoring the famous bean of Sorana: beans with veal head, beans with tuna roe, beans with *porchetta,* beans with shrimp, a *torta* of beans—a three-hour celebration of brown on brown, ending with a plate of biscotti and a glass of vin santo, another brownly brown variation.) The soppressata, the sausages, the famous Fiorentina: all brown, without so much as a speck of color. That chopped parsley garnish? A corrupting Italian-American intervention. There was one local pasta, called *pici,* thick, like giant earthworms, which was similar to a pasta the Etruscans had made, although it was a mystery why it hadn't disappeared along with the rest of their civilization: it was inedible if boiled for less than twenty minutes. It was at least chewable if cooked for longer, when it changed color, not to brown, admittedly, but to beige, although the custom was to dress it with the local ragù, which was very brown: a brown-and-beige food. The local vegetables? Green-brown artichokes, green-brown olives, and porcini mushrooms (brown-brown). If indeed Tuscany was responsible for a sizable portion of the world's best cooking, then it must have been the brown part. Filippo had all these Tuscan standards on his menu, printed, naturally enough, on brown paper. In addition, he had a carpaccio of goose. Carpaccio, a way of preserving meat by air-drying, wasn't really a Tuscan preparation; geese, too, weren't very local. There weren't many geese in Chianti. Actually, there were none.

By the time Filippo returned with our wine—chest out and seeming to comport himself with a swagger—Dario had spotted the goose preparation and was looking at Filippo with hyperventilating bafflement. (Poor Filippo, I thought, as he uncorked the bottle. He has no idea what he has returned to.) Dario's stare, which Filippo avoided, was intense and full of rage. "What in the name of my testicles," he said finally, in a low, controlled voice, "is this dish on the menu?"

Filippo glanced casually in Dario's direction. "What in the dick are you talking about?" *(Che cazzo dici?)* he asked lightly, continuing the line of genitalia metaphors that so robustly characterize male Tuscan exchanges.

"You fat head of a penis," Dario said loudly. "Why is *this* on your menu?" He was pointing to the carpaccio of goose. "*Carpaccio di oca?!!*"

Oca means "goose." Dario managed to pronounce the word with an extra long "o"—quiet at first, then much louder—ending it, the "ca" sound, as though he were coughing up his lunch.

"*Oca?*" He repeated.

"Oh, Dario, it's on the menu every year," Filippo said, and then, despite his effort to pretend that none of this mattered, couldn't stop himself from looking over his shoulder, just in case the anniversary party was bearing witness to his humiliation. (In fact, the anniversary party was otherwise engaged: the elderly couple were doing some kind of gyration to what sounded like the Beach Boys in Italian.)

"*Oca?*" Dario repeated. "*Ooooooooohhhh-KA!*"

"The regulars expect it," Filippo persisted. His restaurant had been mentioned in an English walking guide and now had a clientele. "They would be disappointed if they couldn't order their favorite dishes."

"Their favorite dish of ooooooohh-KA!" Dario was persuasively incredulous.

"Perhaps you'd like to try some, Dario," Filippo offered. "It's really very good."

"Filippo, this dish is from Friuli. Friuli is in the north. Near Croatia." Dario could have been talking to a five-year-old. "What are you? Disneyland? There are no geese in Tuscany. You have a panoramic view. How many geese did you see tonight? How many geese, in your dickhead life, have you ever seen? This is fancy food. Like fusion. Fancy Tuscan fusion." He then threw his menu on the floor. "OoooooOOO-KA!"

Filippo picked up the menu and set it back on the table. "Dario, please," he said in a whispery voice.

Dario threw it back down.

Filippo picked it up again. It was a tricky diplomatic moment. He had welcomed the mayor into his restaurant, but the mayor wanted to beat him up. "Dario, Dario, Dario," he said, pleading, and tapped Dario on the head with the menu, an affectionate slap. And expecting a much more aggressive response, Dario flinched, and Filippo, sensing an opportunity, tapped him again: and then again—harder. And then, marginally losing control, he started hitting so hard and fast that Dario had to lift his arms to fend off the menu blows.

A truce had been achieved: somehow Filippo, in unreasonably hitting Dario over the head with a menu, had persuaded him that he had been acting unreasonably. Everyone relaxed—exhaling all at once—and Filippo was finally able to take our order: two and a half kilos of Gabriella's bistecca, Dario said, "barely cooked—so that I can taste the blood."

Relieved, Filippo proceeded through the rituals of ordering a meal, as though he were waiting on a normal table.

"Perhaps an antipasto," he asked, restaurant-like.

"No!" Dario answered, Dario-like. "Like what? *Carpaccio di' oca*? No."

"A primo?" Filippo pressed on, determined.

"No!"

"Maybe a salad, something green."

"No!"

"Oh, come on, Dario," Ann Marie said. It was her first utterance. "Let's get some spinach."

"No!"

"Dario?"

"No!"

"Dario, I'd like some spinach."

"Okay. Spinach. And bread."

Filippo snapped shut his order book and set off for the kitchen. Dario spotted a black bottle on the table. This was the third disaster.

"I don't believe it," Dario said, unscrewing the bottle and pouring some liquid on to his hand. He tasted it. It was balsamic vinegar, which comes from Modena, in Emilia-Romagna, about a hundred miles away.

"Filip-PO!" Dario shouted, doing that irritable last-syllable-stress thing, as though he were in his own butcher shop. Filippo froze—he'd almost got to the kitchen—and turned slowly. Dario locked eyes, extended his arm to the side of our table, vinegar in hand, and upturned the bottle, pouring its contents on the floor.

·   ·   ·

DURING ALL THIS, Annie, after making her pitch for a plate of spinach, said nothing. "What could I have said?" she put to me later. "Ask him to stop being such an asshole? This happens almost every time we go out. All the screaming at the proprietor? It's so bad I hate eating at restaurants."

In effect, Dario had become a food cop, enforcing a law of no change. Dario was trying to stop time. He'd grown up in a region where people had ceased observing the old ways, and he was determined to get everyone back on track before the old ways disappeared entirely. (Historically, time stoppers don't have a great win-loss record, although they score high in the sentimental doing-all-the-wrong-things-for-the-right-reasons stakes.) For Dario, implicit in the old ways was an assumption that the culture of a place was in its language and its art *and* its food—maybe the most direct expression because the habits of cooking and eating arise out of the land itself. What is Tuscan food, precisely? I'd asked Dario earlier at his house, and he'd said something vague, and I'd pressed him, and finally he'd said that true Tuscan food was evoked by the unique fragrance of the wet earth at *that* moment—and he pointed outside where it was still wet after a late-afternoon storm, the grass now glistening in the sun. "The smell of the dirt, here, after a rain," he said. (Which wasn't ultimately illuminating: Tuscan food is mud?)

The final disaster was the meat. It arrived, a steak five inches thick, sitting in a pool of blood. Dario started cutting it up with a pocketknife he carries with him and distributed slices around the table, until he grew impatient and tore off a chunk directly from the serving platter and speared it with his blade and ate it rapidly, re-enacting the evening's earlier furious outsized chomping.

"The meat," he said after taking a deep breath, "is not good." He resumed chewing and speared another chunk. "No. This is not good meat."

It was the first time he'd eaten one of Gabriella's steaks. Gabriella is a rare woman butcher (daughter, granddaughter, great-granddaughter, et cetera, of a family of butchers) whose shop is on the square in Greve. This was where the livestock market had been held, which accounts for the square's curious nonsquare design: narrow at two ends. The chianine used to come in through the entrance at the top—be displayed, win a prize, be sold—and leave by the exit at the bottom, where, after so much public glory, their lives were dispatched into so many dinners. The square is now dominated by tourists, who are Gabriella's principal customers. She is in her sixties; has disconcertingly bleached blond hair (more strawberry than lemon), very thick glasses, and a butcher's outfit that looks like bedtime pajamas. The last time we were in her shop, she had a chicken on a cutting board, its entrails pulled out—she'd started it and forgotten about it—and was hand-feeding raw sausage meat to some queasy Bavarians, barking in Italo-German. *("Molto gut!")*

Dario speared another chunk. "With your tongue," he instructed me, "I want you to touch the roof of your mouth. Do you feel that? It's coated with wax."

I did as he said, and it was true—there was a greasy film. I wondered if the waxiness was so obvious that I would have noticed it without being told about it. I continued rubbing. I wanted to memorize both the slippery sensation and something else—what was it? a taste?—when I was reminded of eating as a child. It was a disconcerting association, rising up ungovernably, and suddenly my mind was entertaining a picture of me at the kitchen table, a child, my father to my right, my mother directly across from me. Where did *that* come from? I continued rubbing. It was this, the residue, that had evoked the memory: the eating of a steak, bought by Mother at a suburban supermarket and characterized by this same quality of fat. There had been a sense of occasion. This, in fact, might have been my first steak, and my father must have been feeling flush enough to buy one. I ate it and thought: This is *it*?

Dario took another bite, chewed, paused. His cheeks puffed out a little, as though they were being punched from the inside: he was trying to identify the source of the meat's sticky cloyingness. "The roof of your mouth should never be waxy," he reflected. "The waxiness betrays what the animal was fed on, which would have been cheap grain, to fatten it up." (And *that's* what I must have been remembering from my first steak—the peculiar qualities of cereal-fattened American beef.) Dario seized another chunk. He was eating with unabated intensity. "This meat will sit heavily on your stomach." He ate another chunk, just to make sure that it would sit heavily on his stomach. "The secret of meat is in its fat," he continued. "When the fat is good, you can eat two kilos without feeling full. But with this, you'll feel full, even though you are not full. All night, you will feel its weight. Here," he said, motioning to the upper part of the stomach. "Like a rock." He grunted and ate, grunted and ate, until he finished the platter.

It was past midnight and time to return home.

In the parking lot, Dario addressed me with great solemnity: "A butcher never sleeps. A butcher works in meat during the day and plays in flesh at night. A true butcher is a disciple of carnality."

The point was a piece of wordplay made possible in Italian. The word for meat and flesh are the same: *carne.* (The line in the Bible about the word being made flesh is, in Italian, the word being made "carne.") Carne, flesh, carnality, sex, meat, skin, dinner, sin, and the word of God or, in the case of the Dante-reciting Dario, that of the Devil: it was one continuous stream of associations.

Dario continued, "You are now a member of the carnal confederation of butchers. You are learning to work with meat like a butcher. You must now make love like a butcher. For the rest of the night, you must enact the dark acts of carnality, a butcher's carnality. And then you will rise in the hours before dawn, smelling of carnality, and unload the meat from the truck, like a butcher."

I didn't know what to say. My boss was telling me that, to do my job, I now needed to go home and have sex. It had already been a long, long day of carnalities. That meat truck was arriving in a few hours. It seemed unlikely that I had the stamina for more carnality *and* making butcher love to my wife for the rest of the night *and* reporting for work before dawn with no sleep. Maybe I didn't have the constitution for this life after all. But, you know, I did the best I could. I didn't want to let the guild down.

23

WHEN DARIO CITED my membership in the guild, he was alluding to a recent breakthrough at the butcher shop. I had convinced him that I could make sausages, had been entrusted with a week's orders, and had acquitted myself well enough.

Never in his life, Dario said, had he seen someone master the craft of handmade sausages so quickly. "You are a natural butcher," he told me. "In the history of your family, there were butchers. It is in your blood."

This was a pleasing thing to be told, and from now on I was officially a butcher in training, although I was skeptical of the role performed by my family blood. Dario never took seriously the time I'd spent at Babbo. But by now I'd been working in a professional kitchen for some time, and—although I didn't have the heart to tell Dario, because I rather liked the butcher-in-the-blood theory—I'd taken a one-day sausage-making course at New York University. Okay: NYU wasn't a Tuscan butcher shop (and I got shit when I returned to my day job smelling of pork fat), but I'd learned some basics.

No matter, I'd been elevated to a new level, and the next morning, after we unloaded the meat, Dario handed me his knife and, recognizing the seriousness of the occasion, gave me a steel glove to protect me from injury, the very thing he had used when he'd started out more than twenty-five years ago. (It was gigantic. I could have fit my head inside—it was more jousting-match body garb than glove—and there was no way I could wear it.) My task, under the supervision of the Maestro, was to bone pigs that would be made into *arista*. *Arista* is a Greek word meaning "the best" and, according to local legend, refers to a preparation first served at a Florentine peace summit in 1439, a convocation of Roman Catholic and Greek Orthodox churches: at the end, the Greek prelates were so satisfied with their meal that they chanted *"Arista, arista, arista"* to express their appreciation. Was there such a chant? I've since discovered the first published mention of arista—in a story, written in 1400, by Franco Sacchetti, which, predating the banquet by nearly forty years, weakens some of the poetic force of the spontaneous Greco-Italo outburst. Whatever its origins, arista appears regularly on Tuscan menus today. In my experience, no two plates are the same, although they usually feature a herbal mix stuffed into the best cut of the pig, what Italians sometimes refer to as the *carré* (the pork equivalent of a rack of lamb).

Dario's arista uses not one cut but nearly half the pig, the torso, which is boned and rolled up with an extravagance of herbs and seasonings: garlic, thyme, fennel pollen, pepper, rosemary, and double-ground sea salt. The logic is that each new item is applied in increasingly larger quantities so that by the time you get to the pepper the meat is covered by a thick black blanket, followed by an abundance of rosemary (a green blanket) and completed by the salt, which, being twice ground, looks like a dollhouse replica of a blizzard. It is then cooked at a high temperature for four hours, emerging from the oven as a noisy sizzling racket, the fat rendered and popping in the roasting tray, trailing a black acrid cloud of smoke, a glistening and rather beautiful thing (brown, of course). When sliced, you get a range of cuts: the carré, tasting like a tender steak; the bacony stomach; and everything in between. But it is an unquiet food, which sends your taste buds in many directions—a slice manages to be both burnt and tender, caramelized and salty, lean and fatty, exploding with both rosemary and fennel—and you can't eat much. After a few bites, your mouth is exhausted from a sensory pounding.

This was what I was to prepare and, at six-fifteen a.m., I stood in front of two halves of a pig cut lengthwise, knife in hand, no mace glove, ready to start. The Maestro was going to show me how to remove the bones from one half; I was going to do the other. He took my knife, and his initial instruction went something like this. *"Guarda!"* (Watch!). "You do this" *(così)*. "You do that" *(così)*. "You cut these"—*tagliale*—"one by one. You work the spine loose, and *basta.*"

He handed me the knife.

"Right," I said, and rehearsed the procedure in a series of kung fu strokes in the air. "I do this. I do that. I cut these one by one. I work lose the spine. And *basta*." (I was talking utter nonsense, of course, and had no idea what I was doing.)

So, first thing: I did *this*. "This" involved working one side of the spine loose, first by pushing the animal up on its side—a hefty, slightly slippery operation—so that the spine was on top. Why? No idea. But the Maestro said to do it this way. Therefore I did.

Second: I did *that*. "That" seemed to involve working loose a rectangular piece of meat, attached to what must have been the little piggy's shoulder. (Shoulder? Neck? Head? This business of figuring out what all the animal bits had once done was a peculiar piece of speculation. If I thought too hard about it, I feared I'd get queasy, or, worse, break down and become a vegetarian. If I thought too little and resisted making the connection between the animal in my hands and its living cousins, like those running around on farms, I wouldn't get the whole picture. My solution was to think of butchery like auto mechanics. This, here, was the axle. That, the drive shaft. The approach was meant to be honest but not too intimate—demystifying the animal but respecting it—and helped me make sense of the fact that I was deep inside it, cutting it up. It occurs to me only now that I never could figure out how a car worked.)

Next: I cut "these" up. "These" were the ribs. To remove a rib, you sliced down one side of it with your blade, sticking close to the bone, constantly aware that every gram of tissue was meat and meat must never be wasted. If you looked up when someone entered the butcher shop, say, and your blade swerved, thereby losing a chunk, you were made to feel very bad. (It wasn't the lost revenue; it was that you'd squandered some animal: the rearing, feeding, cleaning, caring, fattening, slaughtering, transporting, and now butchering, and, at the end of a long, disciplined line of purposefulness, you'd lost your concentration— *Cazzo!* You dick!—and a bit of the animal couldn't be used! How could you? *Non va bene!*) Then, you sliced down the other side of the rib— again, sticking so close that you saw the white of the bone flaking up against your blade. What you were doing was freeing up the rib so that you could then pull it up toward you by the tip, while also trimming the tissue underneath—pulling and trimming, pulling and trimming.

Finally I worked the spine free. This was an early lesson in not using a butcher's knife. I used my fingers instead—along the seams of the muscle—and gravity: that was the point of heaving the pig onto its side, I realized, so that, with prodding, poking, and pushing, the spine might fall away naturally. Then: *basta!* I looked at my watch. It was eight o'clock. Half a pig had taken me one hour and forty-five minutes. There were twelve more to do.

The Maestro came over to inspect my work. "You see that part," he said, standing over me.

"This part?" I said, pointing to the pink meaty rectangle-like steak.

"Yes," he said. "that part. It's the best one of the animal."

"This part," I said, confirming my understanding. I recognized the significance of the exchange. I was being instructed in the art of butchery by no less a teacher than the Maestro himself.

"Exactly," he said. "That part. It is very good."

"This must be the carré," I said, giving the word my best French inflection. I wasn't showing off; I just wanted him to know that I'd put some thought into this enterprise beforehand.

"Bravo," he said. "It's true. Some people call it by the French name."

"Thank you," I said.

"In Italian, it's called the *lonza.*"

I repeated the word and again thanked the Maestro.

He continued, "This is also the tenderest part."

"I see."

"It is also very precious and is, therefore, very expensive. And you have sliced it in half."

"Oh, shit," I said in English. "I did that? Fuck." Then, remembering that I was in Italy, I said (in Italian), "That was a mistake, wasn't it?"

"In fact, that is a very big mistake. That piece here," he said, pointing to the two bits, "is central to the entire preparation. Do you understand?" *(Hai capito?)* "But you've cut it in half. *Non va bene.*"

"I won't do that again," I said, trying to be reassuring.

"Bravo," he said, and resumed his task, which involved a very large thigh.

The next day, May 10th, I returned to New York. I had a commitment there. My wife and I had been in Panzano nearly a month. But I'd been accepted as a butcher in training. I was being instructed by the Maestro himself. How could I stop now?

24

I WAS HOME and wanted a pig.

My friend Paul had a stand called Violet Hill Farm at my local green market and sold chickens, rabbits, and pigs. Paul's pigs were sucklings. I didn't want a suckling. I wanted a proper pig: a big one. I wanted to apply what I'd learned in Italy.

Could Paul get me a pig?

Well, yes, he probably could. His neighbor had big healthy sows, and if I ordered one, while alive, the animal wouldn't have to be approved by the Department of Agriculture. This—an animal's transit from pasture to plate without a USDA stopover—was seen as a good thing. The rustic logic of animal husbandry can seem contradictory and might be summarized thus: anything involving a government agency is an intervention and regarded as bad, even though the agency was established to prevent you from getting ill and dying, which you would have thought was good. In Panzano, for instance, a food store did an under-the-counter trade in *uova proibiti,* illegal eggs, because they came from the grandmother's chickens and hadn't been examined by a European Union official. I bought them and they were good, although I'm not sure whether their appeal was in their flavor or in shells that hadn't been blemished by a bureaucratic stamp.

In my case, there was no need for a USDA inspection, because I was buying a living pig from Paul's neighbor—in effect, purchasing a pet— rather than a dead one from, say, a butcher. But when Jessica and I showed up to pick it up, the animal was definitively dead, wrapped in a transparent plastic sheet and flopped across the back seat of Paul's vehicle: a medium-sized animal, about two hundred and twenty-five pounds, with everything on view—hooves, legs, little piggy tail, head, plus (stuffed in the cavity, Paul told me) the lungs, heart, and liver.

The challenge was getting it into the apartment. The transparent sheet ensured that every passerby knew what I'd bought. It was not your normal parcel of urban shopping. It was not your normal green market purchase either, and many people looked at me as though I were a bad man. There was only so much of this I could take, and I was tempted to prop our pig against the organic wheatgrass stand ("Mind if we leave this here while we finish our shopping?"). A woman was standing in front with her arms folded across her chest in open disapproval.

I had a scooter. Cars are not permitted at my green market, and if I hadn't had a scooter I wonder what I would have done. Hoisted the animal on my shoulder and walked home? Flagged a taxi? I was relieved I could strap my purchase onto my scooter rack, hooves dangling on either side of the front wheel, a pair of ears just underneath the handlebars, my wife on the back. The three of us, precariously poised, puttered home. I parked in front of our building, unloaded my cargo with difficulty, and staggered to the front door, cradling it in my arms, wondering, is there a law against this? Am I allowed in the lobby?

The doorman, Gary Miro, a proud Italian American, greeted me with the enthusiasm of a man who appreciated his meat, and we stepped into the elevator. But before we ascended, a problem appeared in the casual Saturday morning dress of a Wall Street banker who'd followed us in from the street.

"Gary, do we want another passenger?" I was struggling. Two hundred and twenty-five pounds was akin to a big man. What's more, things had shifted in the transporting, and blood was pooling up in a crease of the plastic.

It was a warm summer day in a small elevator. There were the doorman and the Wall Street banker and, just behind, my wife and me and my pig. The Wall Street banker turned. I don't know why. Maybe he smelled something, although the smell, as these things go, wasn't bad. He saw what was in my arms. His eyes conducted a rapid inventory of the details apparent in the plastic sheet, and when the door opened he exited with unusual speed.

"Did you hear the sound he made?" the doorman asked with a meat lover's sadistic glee. I had heard it, and I was distressed. I had been uncomfortable in the green market. Now I'd made my neighbor sick.

I deposited my pig on the breakfast table and got ready. I emptied out the refrigerator and washed down the counters. I sharpened my new boning knife—short, thin, and stiff. (The Maestro had mocked a long floppy one I'd brought from New York—*Che cazzo fai con questo?* What in the dick are you going to do with this?) I then reflected on the difficulty of a pig at home. I hadn't wanted to upset my neighbor. I didn't know him well but suspected, and later confirmed, that he was a meat eater. The ironies are familiar enough. My pig was just a more elementary form of things he'd been eating for years. The implication confirmed what I knew but was reluctant to acknowledge: people don't want to know what meat is. For my neighbor (and my friends and me, too, for most of my life), meat wasn't meat: it was an abstraction. People don't think of an animal when they use the word; they think of an element in a meal. ("What I want tonight is a cheeseburger!")

I wasn't a proselytizer. Meat, for me, had never been a cause. I didn't feel as strongly about it as Dario, who banishes vegetarians from his shop and tells them to go to hell. To my mind, vegetarians are among the few people who actually think about meat—at least *they* know what it is. I just believed people should know what they're eating. After all, at the green market, you overheard discussions about fertilizers and organic soils and how much freedom a chicken needs before it's free range. Wouldn't it follow that you'd want to know what your meat is? And that's what I thought I was doing. I had brought home a recently killed animal, healthier, fresher, and better raised than anything at a store, and, in preparing it, I was hoping to rediscover old-fashioned ways of making food. This, I felt, could only be a positive thing. But I was sure getting a lot of shit for it.

I got to work.

I began by cutting an arc around the hips to remove the hind legs— the prosciutti. In Italian, a prosciutto is both the limb and the preparation, the tasty salt-cured ham you see hanging from deli ceilings. I wasn't going to cure these—a long, ritualized business that, like Miriam's culatello, is traditionally done in January—but do something I regarded as "Dario's summertime pig." Dario had learned the recipe from an elderly contadino, who in turn had learned it from his father on his deathbed. The father had ordered him to convey the recipe to some-one at the Cecchini butcher shop: not Dario, because he wouldn't have been born yet, but probably Dario's father. The contadino wasn't sure why it had taken him so long, apart from his rarely coming to Panzano and not knowing how to drive. But he was happy to have fulfilled his father's wish and passed on an old Chianti preparation into the appro-priate hands before it disappeared.

The recipe was really just an elevated way of incinerating a piece of meat (and everything else residing in it) without actually torching it. First you broke the legs down into what Marco Pierre White calls "the cushions." The Maestro had taken me through the process and created a road map of sorts, going through each muscle, using gravity and your fingers to find "the seam." The result was a bowl of pork pieces—around a dozen.

Next, you brined them. For the brine, I tipped a bag of salt into a bucket, added water, and swirled until the salt was half dissolved. After a day or two, you removed the pieces, put them in a pot filled with white wine, cooked them for a few hours, and left them to cool overnight. In the morning they were done and could be stored in olive oil. The pieces, half cured by the brining, flavored by the wine, and now submerged in oil, keep for a year.

I now understand that the method was devised to clean up pork that the contadino hadn't got around to dealing with during the hot months. In general, you don't kill pigs in the summer unless something has gone wrong, and Dario had once let slip that the contadino had used the recipe for his sick pigs, not the kind of information nugget a butcher forthrightly shares with his customers: Here, try this, a bit of diseased pork I hammered. In the event, what Dario did or didn't say was imma-terial because, for several years, no one bought it. Who wants fat (pork) in fat (oil)? But the meat was actually lean, with the texture of fish, and in a moment of marketing clarity he renamed it *tonno* (tuna) *del Chi-anti.* Now it is the most popular item in the shop. In 2001, the European Union recognized it as a food unique to the region and, giving it an offi-cial designation, ordered that the recipe be preserved as a monument of Tuscan culture. I like it with beans, parsley, lemon, and olive oil—like tuna.

· · ·

ON THE SECOND day of my pig, I addressed the front, removing the forelegs and boning them. These are Mario's unsung heroes, tough and supposedly flavorful and good for slow braising (or rather, good *only* for slow braising), although I was going to use them in sausages.

When I made these at the butcher shop, people often ate the meat raw, straight from the bowl, while I was preparing it, which—I don't know, call me old-fashioned—just seemed wrong. But it illustrated an attitude toward good meat, if you're lucky enough to get it: don't mess with it. The shop followed the recipe (to the extent that one existed—everything was pretty much eyeballed) of three parts meat to one part fat, the rich back fat from the top of the pig, all ground up together, plus garlic, pepper, and salt: that was it. You mushed it all together until it became an emulsified pinkish goop, which you then stuffed into a canister that looked a like a giant bullet. At one end of the canister was a spout: this was where you slipped on the casing, about twenty feet of pork intestines, which the meat mix went into. The task of getting the intestines onto the spout, which was not unlike putting on a condom the length of an African serpent, involved a universally recognized hand movement, and, alas, predictable Tuscan jokes were had at my expense (at which point I tended to fall into a Freudian state of mind and wonder softly to myself what humor tells us of a culture).

Tuscan sausages are smaller than their American cousins, and each one is demarcated with a string, a graceful loop drawn tightly into a knot—looping and tightening, looping and tightening, a symmetrically floppy, aesthetically appealing rhythm. At the butcher shop, I made sausages in the lower room, and visitors came down to watch. "Aaaah," they'd say, "so that's the way it's done." One man, his voice cracking, whispered, "This is how my grandfather made them." Sometimes the visitors would want to chat, a dodgy moment (How could I chat? What came out of my mouth would have blown my cover), which I survived by limiting my replies.

"*Salsicce?*" someone would always ask, rather redundantly.

"*Sì,*" I'd answer forcefully, in what I believed to be an imitation of a singsongy Panzano rhythm, packing in all the notes that the locals seemed to get into a one-beat word like "*sì.*"

"*Di maiale?*" (pork?) they asked next, with tautological tenacity.

"*Sì,*" I replied again, impatiently this time so they understood I was very busy.

Once I got in a jam. "What herbs do you use?" a visitor asked.

I panicked. This was the kind of question I avoided. "*Sì!*" I said inexplicably. I couldn't bear the prospect of his realizing he'd been duped: the romance, the history, the handmade integrity of it all, only to discover that an American was the sausage maker.

MY PIG was now legless, but there was one more cut, just between the shoulders, that I was hoping to have for dinner on the third day. This was the meat encased by the first four ribs, the "eye" of the chops. In Italian, this is called the *coppa* or *capocollo*—*capo* means head and *collo* means "neck"; the capocollo starts at the top of the neck. When it's cured and aged, it makes for the lean salumi that was served to the Nashville diners. The preparation was associated with Bologna and was therefore one you rarely saw in Tuscany, where the coppa is normally sold fresh, not cured, and broken down into the chops. When it is roasted whole, it is called something else again: a *rosticiana,* the best meal in the house. I cooked one on the bone, in a hot oven for about thirty-five minutes, and contemplated how brief the journey can be from the very raw to the only-just-been-cooked.

On the fourth day I made arista. I sawed the torso in two, boned each half according to the Maestro's instructions, and added the ingredients in Dario's order: garlic, thyme, the fennel pollen (which I'd stashed into my suitcase; everyone else was smuggling it—why not me?), the black blanket of pepper, the green blanket of rosemary, and the salt blizzard. I rolled it up into a giant Christmas log, cut lines along the skin to render the fat, tied it up, and cooked it until it was crispy and blackly smoking.

On the fifth day, I made a ragù—enough for two hundred people. A pig was turning out to be a pig of work.

On the sixth, I made headcheese, boiling the head until the meaty bits come loose and set in their own gelatin.

On the seventh day, I contemplated the lungs, tempted by a recipe I had found in Apicius, who recommends soaking them overnight in milk, filling each cavity with two eggs and some honey (what, when you think about it, could be simpler?), sealing them back up and boiling them until ready, the lungs bobbing like pool toys. He doesn't say when a lung is cooked, but I concluded that the virtue of having two is that if the first lung isn't quite ready you know to wait a little longer for the second. In the end, I didn't cook the lungs. It was hard to throw them away. It seemed so wasteful—why buy a whole pig if you're going to throw away the lungs?—but I'd been working on this pig for a long time. It was the seventh day. I needed a rest.

We had many meals. By my reckoning my green-market pig generated four hundred and fifty servings of food and worked out to less than fifty cents a plate. But the lesson wasn't in the pig's economy but in its variety and abundance: okay, I admit, maybe over-abundance, because pretty early on my wife and I discovered we'd had rather a lot of pig. We'd eaten our way from its snout (which went into the sausages) to its tail (which I added to the ragù). We were sick of pig. I badly needed to return to Italy. It was time to learn beef.

Tuscan Butcher

It is important that children make their own decisions about what they will and won't eat, whether this is on moral or taste grounds. It should be our responsibility as parents to make sure they have all the information they need. We must not pass on any of our own eating hang-ups. I have always made our children aware that when they are eating beef, for example, they are actually eating a cow. There is nothing wrong with this as long as the animal has led a good, healthy life and has been killed humanely. The quality of the meat is directly influenced by the quality of life of the animal itself. After all, evolution has designed us to be carnivorous both in the way we eat and the way we process our food.

Unfortunately supermarket price wars have resulted in all food prices coming down, including those of meat. If we would only stop to think: how is this possible? Land and property values and wages have been increasing. Inflation still exists. How then can meat and poultry prices fall?

—HESTON BLUMENTHAL, *Family Food*

25

T HE MAESTRO GREETED me on my first morning. "So you've returned to resume your instruction in the thigh." Of course I'd returned. How could I not?

Dario, weirdly, was expecting me. What had taken so long? he asked. How did he know?

He answered by telling me about a man from New Jersey. The man had come to San Gimignano, the famous town of towers about an hour away, to learn how to make bread. At the end of his stay, he packed his bags and went to Pisa to catch his flight home. He couldn't leave. He couldn't walk down the gangway to the airplane. So he tore up his ticket. "He has been here twenty-two years. He is a very good baker," Dario said in that imperious, this-is-God-speaking tone. "You, too, can tear up your ticket." (My wife, standing beside me, shuffled anxiously: she knew I didn't even have a return ticket.)

Without my fully realizing it, my mission had changed. When I'd begun this whole business—what I'd come to regard as my excursion into the underworld of the professional kitchen—I'd been a visitor. I'd been a tourist, and, like many tourists, I'd been able to throw myself into my journey with such abandon because I knew it would end. At Babbo, I seemed to endure abuse more easily than others because this wasn't my life. Now I wondered: had I stayed too long? Mario once said that to learn a kitchen properly you should spend a year in it, cooking your way through the seasons, and I'd thought: I can do that. So I was at Babbo from January 2002 until March 2003 (minus the time I took off for my office job when I had one). Mario said that if you want to master Italian cooking you should learn the language and work in Italy, and I'd thought: I can do that, too. This, apparently, wasn't sufficient, because I then got it into my head that I should undergo a miniversion of Mario's own culinary education: knowing-the-man-by-knowing-his-teachers. Thus my time with Marco Pierre White (Mario's first teacher) and the weeks spent with Betta and Gianni (Mario's pasta teachers). And while Mario had never worked for Dario Cecchini, Mario's father had: not an exact fit but close enough.

Then I had crossed over. I was no longer on the outside looking in. I stopped being an author writing about the experience of the kitchen. I was a member of it. The crossover was obvious to the people around me—my wife, long-sufferingly, had quietly identified in me the traits commonly described as an obsessive's (mania, a lack of perspective, an inability to recognize limits)—but hadn't been evident to me, even when I'd woken up in New York with this resolve to return to Panzano. Did I need to come back? Of course not. But I'd been unable to forget the often repeated aphorism, occasioned by Mario's trashing of Nick after he'd got homesick in Milan: one might never have the opportunity to learn so much again. Dario Cecchini had trusted me with a blade. He'd asked the Maestro, his *own* maestro, to teach me. How could I stop?

So, yes, Maestro, I was back to resume my instruction with the thigh.

The thigh was a cow's, and mastering it was a crucial credential in being a Tuscan butcher. On my last day of my first stay, just before returning to New York, I'd given it a try, the Maestro by my side, but I'd made a mess of it. No matter: the Maestro, ever patient, had assumed we had weeks of instruction ahead. I hadn't said anything about having to go home, and he had been genuinely uncomprehending when I told him the news.

"What are you talking about? How can you leave, just when you need to try again with the thigh?" He'd shaken his head in bafflement. I felt as if I had been acting in bad faith: that by *pretending* to be a Tuscan butcher—in effect, by being a tourist—I had tricked the Maestro into giving me a thigh lesson.

I put on an apron and went back to work and had what I now regard as a symbolic exchange. A Japanese family appeared in the butcher's shop, clustered round their English-speaking, enthusiastic mother. ("Oh, my god, is that Dario Cecchini? Is this real Chianti in my glass?") They took many pictures. They then came downstairs and took pictures of me, knife in hand, my floor-length apron already bloodied. The crossover was complete. I was no longer a tourist. I was an attraction.

As I UNDERSTOOD my schooling, I'd studied a range of things during my first stint but had majored in pig. Now, during my more studious second stint (I thought of it as graduate butcher school), I'd be taught cow. Pig was easy; cow was complex. Pig was very Italian; you can find lots of people who know pig. But few know cow. Cow was Tuscan, and knowing cow was at the heart of what it meant to be of Panzano.

Giovanni Manetti had explained this to me when my wife and I had called on him. We'd wanted to see his wine-making operation, the vast Fontodi estate in the conca d'oro, acres and acres of vines, now droopy with swollen, purple fruit, but had been warned beforehand by his younger sister Giovanna (an acquaintance of my wife, who had to do something during the day and so befriended the nine hundred inhabitants of Panzano) that he might use our visit to show off his cows. The cows, four young, bright-white chianine known as "the girls," had been an impulse acquisition (Giovanni was still in a discover-my-Chianti-roots frenzy) and were kept in a pen at the bottom of the valley. For Italians, no image is more evocative of Chianti than a chianina. The word "Chianti" seems buried inside it. Every cliché about the region is in this animal: all that rugged, stone-house, beef-eating, peasant authenticity. Unfortunately, you don't see them anymore. Actually, apart from Giovanni's, I'd seen none. Giovanni, trying to raise his girls, was involved in a major task ("I know I'm crazy, everyone in Panzano laughs at me"): rescuing the Chianti heritage from tourists and paved roads and electricity, and reintroducing to the land the famous cow that had once worked it.

"They have delicate constitutions," Giovanni said, staring into the pen, his forehead pressed against a slat of wood. "It's said they get colds easily."

I looked. They didn't seem fragile. They were giants, by far the biggest cows I'd ever seen.

"Look at their legs!" (*"Ecco le gambe!"*) "So long, so graceful, so beautifully shaped. Really, they're like fashion models." He sighed.

I studied them. They looked nothing like fashion models. They looked like cows. True, they were unusual cows. Very white and very tall. They were also leaner than a normal cow, and not as wide. Most cows are basically round. These—if you squinted to take them in—were like rectangles: not much across, but more (much more) from top to bottom.

I then glimpsed the traditional bistecca fiorentina in their shape—the height, the narrow spine. I don't know how this happened: probably a symptom of the time I'd spent in a butcher shop. But once I'd seen the steak in the animals, the steak was the only thing I saw. A fiorentina looks like a triangle—analogous to a T-bone but gigantic and more geometrically defined. To make one, I now saw, you split the animal's spine (cows arrive already cleaved at the butcher shop), which was then the bottom of the steak—in effect, the base of the triangle. The meat was in the two muscles attached to it: the backstrap (the same one you have on both sides of your own spine) and the tenderloin, the smaller one underneath. A classic bistecca fiorentina was a rather beautiful thing.

I expressed my observation—that the girls would produce steaks like works of art. Giovanni visibly flinched.

"We won't eat these animals. They are for lovemaking." The idea was that if Giovanni capriciously bought a bull as well (and, with prodding, he admitted he had his eye on a boyish ribbon winner) these four beauties would be breeders. The first generation of their offspring would also be breeders, until, eventually, the herd would be big enough to slaughter some for meat.

Giovanni remained staring at his animals. The thing about Giovanni was that, in most things, he was really quite worldly—even a familiar type. In vintners' circles, he was a celebrity: savvy, easy with journalists, sound-bite fluent, comfortable in a business dominated by image making. He was handsome, with dark hair and classical features, meticulously dressed, overwhelmingly courteous, and had a reassuringly normal set of narcissistic concerns: he worried about his weight, for instance (unnecessarily); he fussed with his hair; if he had lived in a city, he would have belonged to a gym. You did not expect him to be smitten by a cow.

"If you're Tuscan, you love beef," he explained. "Every family prizes it, knows where to find it, has a butcher who is like next of kin." You would never find a tortellini recipe among the Manetti family recipes; instead, you'd find a knowledge of what to do with different cuts—the cheek, tongue, shoulder, stomach, breast, haunch, tail—although the most prized was always the bistecca. "For us, the bistecca is a spiritual food," Giovanni said. "It is one of three elements"—the others being Tuscan bread and a red wine made with the local sangiovese grape—"which, when combined in one meal, makes for an experience that is almost mystical." (Bad bread, good wine, great steak—a happy repast, and every Chianti restaurant offers up its version: not a lot of veggies, of course, but I'd accepted that Tuscans don't like green, and none of them had grown up with parents' urging them to eat their greens; their mothers had obviously said, "Eat your browns.") "Beef speaks to our souls. I don't know how else to explain it. It's in our DNA, this appetite—this need—for beef. It's what makes us Tuscan."

This was pretty heady stuff, but okay, I'd go along with it—beef as Tuscan soul food—even though I'd done my own research, inspired by a clever piece of analysis by a medieval historian named Giovanni Rebora. It was based on an obvious but seldom recognized fact that, until recently, there had always been plenty of meat: that in the long era of human history before rubber, plastic, and the use of freon as cooling agent, meat was consumed in quantities that, to us, seems excessive. It was also cheap. Meat was so available because farm animals were, in the pre-plastic days, essential for many other things besides dinner: like leather for belts, boots, helmets, and the adornments required by Europe's vast armies. These other needs—wool for the English garment industry, say, or goatskins for Spanish winemakers—could be, at any point, the "dominant" one of the animal: if you had to fight the Austrians yet again, and your army wanted a lot of saddles urgently, and you were prepared to pay whatever it cost to get some hides, there was going to be a lot of meat around afterwards. The analysis is known as "the dominant demand food theory." I liked it because it made sense of something that had always seemed more than a local coincidence: that Florence, the historic capital of European leather making, was only twenty miles from Panzano, in the historic heartland of the Italian cow. Even today Florentine guides urge tourists to buy leather shoes in the morning and have a Florentine steak for lunch, without anyone observing the relationship. Now I understood it. According to the dominant demand food theory, a chianina cow would have been prized for many qualities, including its strength, a boon to the farmer in a hilly landscape, and the very thing that Giovanni believed made them so beautiful: being tall, they had more hide than most other breeds.

I stared at Giovanni and rehearsed in my mind how I might advance my theory. But I couldn't. You don't tell a romantic that it can all be explained by economics—especially when the romantic is your host. What's more, the romantic might be right: maybe it wasn't all economics. Maybe economics itself was a metaphor, a pseudo-scientific way of accounting for something much more mysterious, this profound, dark thing Giovanni referred to as the Tuscan soul. Maybe, on balance, the economic theory was plain wrong. So I said nothing about my theory. In fact, I abandoned it. I thanked Giovanni and told him that I now understood Chianti much better.

THE MAESTRO began with names.

"Oh, this," he explained, manifestly pleased, "is very dear," and, from somewhere inside a thigh, he pulled out a small cut about eight inches long, tapered at both ends. I was standing next to him but missed where it came from and looked back inside the leg to see if I could locate the spot. I couldn't, of course. My assumption had been that an animal must be like a jigsaw puzzle and would have one obvious piece not there. (Actually, that's still my assumption, and I have no idea why I couldn't locate the spot, apart from everything being big and complex and maybe a little scary.)

The Maestro held up the cut. It had no fat or connective tissue and had a grain like a piece of wood. I touched it. It was soft. In fact, if you hadn't known better, you'd think it was fillet, except you'd never find a fillet in the leg.

"This is one of my favorites," the Maestro said. "It's called the *campanello*."

I repeated the word and wrote it in my notebook.

"It's very tender. So tender you can eat it raw—served with lemon and olive oil. But," the Maestro said, lecturing me with his long finger, "the olive oil must be very good. Do you understand? The olive oil is important."

He seemed about to describe the campanello's other qualities when he stopped himself, smiled broadly, and pulled out something else. "Aah, but this, too, is special." This one was more substantial. He trimmed it. It was a pinkish eighteen-inch-long cylinder, also a single muscle, very uniform in texture.

"This is called the *girello*. You can do many things with the girello. It's not as tender—the tissue is more compressed—but it is still very good." He stared at the meat happily. "Here in Chianti, the girello is cooked whole in olive oil with shards of garlic poked inside and served rare with peas. In Umbria, you eat it with fava beans." And the way he described these distinctions—the authority of them, their absoluteness—I knew that if I was in Panzano, I'd never eat a girello with fava beans.

The Maestro returned to the leg, working his knife, a rhythmic series of small strokes, until he'd extracted another piece, the largest so far. "The *sottofesa*," he said. *Fesa* means "rump." *Sotto* means "underneath." This was the cut below the rump. It was a hefty, worked muscle, as you'd expect it to be. A cow butt is a big thing.

"Some butchers slice this and sell the slices as steaks." The Maestro shook his head disapprovingly. "*Non va bene*. It is too tough." In the Maestro's eyes, passing off a piece of cow butt as a steak came close to shady trading. "I prefer to braise it with olive oil, tomatoes, and rosemary. That's called *stracotto*." *Cotto* means "cooked," *stra* is an intensifier—in effect, directions for beef stew.

That night, I went home with three new words—*campanello, girello,* and *sottofesa:* a very tender piece, a less tender piece, and one that wasn't tender at all. Actually, that's not true. I went home with about thirty new words, but these three were ones I understood and wanted to know more about.

I didn't find them in my Italian-English dictionary. I then flipped through Artusi's *The Art of Eating Well,* where I came upon an instance of *girello* but none of the others. The next morning, in the butcher shop, I consulted other texts, including some translations. Again, I found only *girello,* several instances of it, but each time it seemed to be defined differently. In one, an American edition of Artusi, a girello was described as a "rump roast." In a different book, it was a "top round." In a third, published in England, it was a "silverside." These were cuts from a cow's hindquarters, but none were what the Maestro had held in his hand.

Instead they were complex pieces that had to be roasted slowly before they would be edible. The Maestro's was a simple cut, which cooked uniformly and quickly.

The discovery led to a modest epiphany. Until now, I'd assumed that there was a universal lexicon of meat terms (after all, a leg is a leg is a leg), which, like any other piece of language, could be translated from one country to the next. The belief, I was now realizing, had been encouraged by those diagrams of a cow cut in half, the kind you sometimes see in cookbooks telling you what a thing is in France, England, and America. These early lessons with the Maestro taught me that a cow was not knowable in this way. One day, wanting to confirm a spelling, I consulted an Italian food encyclopedia from Dario's bookshelves and discovered (under *bovino*) not three or four diagrams but pages of them, thirty in all, none in French or English but only Italian, broken down by region, each one different, no two cuts alike, with few shared terms. The Tuscan chart was dizzying. Every single tissue seemed to be identified. The thigh was a maze, like a road map of an impenetrable medieval city, with more names than there was space on the two-dimensional representational leg to accommodate. I understood why there were no obvious translations of *girello, campanello,* or *sottofesa:* because, outside Italy, they don't exist. Outside Tuscany, they rarely exist. I remembered how I'd researched the short rib and been surprised that the terms my butcher in New York used were so different from the ones known to a butcher in Edinburgh or Paris. But I'd understood only half of it: every country—and in Italy, every region and, sometimes, every town—has its own unique way of breaking an animal down into dinner-sized portions. Finally, I was getting it: there is no universal butcher language; *none* of it is translatable.

It gave me pause. Who would ever know what I was talking about?

MOST OF WHAT I learned from the Maestro was indirect instruction. I got it by being there: like the smell of good meat, which has little smell, but what little there is, even in its rawness, makes you want to eat it. Frequently, I'd take one of the Maestro's cuts, another favorite piece, and bring it right up to my nose. Because I knew the animals had fed on grass, I expected something like a football field after it had been mowed and found instead that I was thinking of roast beef: useless information (akin to wondering what a flower smells like and concluding, "Yes, that's it! It smells like a flower!"), except that the association was so explicitly appetizing. Good raw meat calls to mind a good plate of the cooked. The color was also telling: more rosé than red (again, uselessly, I want to say that the color was of health). There were a few occasions when the animal had been ill or injured. One had a broken shoulder; another had a trapped nerve; one, alas, had been killed badly. In these instances, the meat was more red than rosé—it conveyed adrenaline or unease.

According to Dario, the most valuable thing he'd got from the Maestro was how to judge meat: that was the Maestro's gift, the facility for knowing what was good. Naturally, I wanted some of that gift for myself and had been informally bringing in pieces for the Maestro to assess, samples that I'd doggy-bagged from a restaurant or another butcher. The Maestro was irritated by the practice, but it was always illuminating. "It is difficult to judge a meat that has been cooked," he would protest, nevertheless chewing meditatively on what I'd given him. "When it's raw," he'd add plaintively, "you learn more about the animal. You can tell how it was raised, what it ate, and what its life was like." He'd sigh—cooked meat made him grumpy—and then make his pronouncement: this was from a French cow, or this was aged too long, or this was from an animal that had grown up on too narrow a diet, probably grain.

One day, I brought a sample I was sure would be very good—half of a chianina bistecca. I'd enjoyed the other half the night before. I unwrapped it solemnly and handed it to the Maestro. He chewed for some time. He was concentrating and seeming to analyze the meat's texture, rubbing its fibers against the roof of his mouth. Then he had it.

"You were deceived. This is not a chianina." He chewed some more. "But it is not bad. It is from a cow in the Maremma, the one that grazes near the beach, called a *maremmana*." Like a chianina, the maremmana was a white cow, but not as tall or as temperamental: a sturdy animal with big horns, like those in the cowboy movies. I'd seen small herds of them, roaming the hills by the sea.

.   .   .

KNIFE SKILLS were next. I'd learned some already during my time at
Babbo, but the skills the Maestro taught me were of a different order—
more like a branch of metaphysics.

The most philosophically interesting was one I call the "point cut,"
which involved using a knife like a small paintbrush: no blade, only the
tip. The point cut was for separating biggish muscles. You "brushed" the
seam between them, tearing ever so slightly a clear, almost liquid film
holding the muscles together. Then, effortlessly and rather miraculously, they peeled away from each other. At least that was the idea.

"Lightly," the Maestro would say, looking over my shoulder. "The
knife must be free in your hand, never exercised, so that it can discover
the lines of the meat." He had become the Zen master of sharpness.
"Elegantly," he would say, "the knife should be easy. *It* is doing the
work, not *you*. Your hand has disappeared into the knife."

Right! I'd say, and repeat the instruction: "My hand has disappeared." Then I'd think: How is that helpful? My hand hasn't gone anywhere. I was sweating, because I always sweated whenever the Maestro
stood so close, and I was afflicted, in addition, by an acute pain radiating
tightly from my lower back, because I would tense up as well, while
determined to keep all this bad feeling hidden from my hand, because I
knew it wouldn't do my hand any good. "Relax, hand," I'd say, coaxing it
along. "Remember, this is your day off. You're not doing the work. That
sharp thing is."

There was the "dagger cut," an aggressive piece of business, looking
like the bad guy in a silent movie, holding a blade high above the head
and plunging it. The dagger cut was for removing tenaciously adhering
meat from a bone. I had practiced a version when I made arista, holding
the blade like Jack the Ripper and scraping it against the ribs until they
flaked white. But that had been pig; this was a cow, and cow is different
because a cow is so big. Let's say you're working on a rump. You've done
your point cut, and two beautiful muscles have cleaved like water,
revealing a gigantic Fred Flintstone–like bone underneath, the femur,
which the two muscles are still very stuck to, clinging to it by a thick
membrane. To remove the muscles, you've got to get underneath that
membrane (jam the knife in there!), and, once in position, you *rip* across

the bone. It was a violent moment, and people stood back when they saw it coming.

"You must not fear the knife," the Maestro commanded. "You can't be hesitant. You are one with the knife: attack!"

I did my best, but it was tricky. One moment, the knife was a paint-brush, which I couldn't feel because I had no hand. The next moment, it was an assault weapon.

There was the "silver sliver" to get rid of the "silver skin." (Okay, so maybe the names were a little goofy, but no one else seems to have come up with anything like them. The truth is much of the time I was lost. I remember writing a friend, Pete de Bolla, the son of a butcher, thinking he'd understand when I said that, often, when I was deep inside these giant thighs, I had no idea where I was. These names—they're what my brain devised, like a map.) Silver skin is a shiny coating of inedible white stuff ruining what would otherwise be a beautiful piece of meat. If you don't know it, you'll recognize it the next time you buy an expensive cut from your butcher, take it home, and find a silvery bit you can't pull off: it isn't fat, it isn't a tendon, and it isn't going to do your meal any good. The trick is to slip your knife underneath and drag the blade down its length. If you're the Maestro, the silver skin comes off in one long piece, and the meat is pure and pink. If you're me, the sil-ver skin comes off in eighteen bits of knotty string, and the meat has more or less survived. The implications are in the silver skin's texture: once you realize how hard it is—that it's like plastic and you can push your blade right up against it—you're ready for the next technique: the "scrape and slice."

I don't know why I had such trouble nailing the scrape and slice, but I spent hours on it, watching the Maestro like a movie, hoping to commit his movements so deeply into my brain that I'd be able to imitate them without thinking. The approach was used on stumpy scraps—the stuff that's left over after you've trimmed up your choice cuts—and is based on your perfecting a lateral flick with the side of your knife, a flick-flick-*slice* sort of thing, to push off any ugliness. In my first week, pre-dictably, that last flick flicked off the meat entirely and caught a knuckle on the index finger of my other hand, which I kept forgetting was in the vicinity and which then beaded up redly. This was the same knuckle I'd lacerated when looking for duck oysters in the Babbo prep kitchen. By now, you would have thought I'd known it was there.

You use the scrape and slice when it doesn't matter what the meat looks like. Marco Pierre White had used the Harrogate version when he'd been ordered to pick up the scraps from his butcher and make a meat pasty from them. Dario used it to make terrines or ragù or *peposo*, now my favorite winter preparation and one that cooks so long you could also toss in a sneaker and no one would notice.

Peposo is a traditional, slow-cooked beef shank, surrounded by a typically Italian debate about its origins. According to one theory, the dish comes from Versilia, on the northern Tuscan coast, although that recipe—with a familiar French medley of finely chopped vegetables, plus the stand-in herbs (rosemary, thyme, bay leaf), a broth, and even a pig's foot—is more like a boeuf bourguignon than anything served in Panzano. There people believe the dish came from Impruneta, halfway to Florence, where the furnaces of Giovanni Manetti's family have been preparing red terra-cotta tiles for seven centuries. The conceit is that pots of peposo were always being cooked by the same fires baking the tiles. Dario is confident the dish was devised in the fifteenth century by the architect Filippo Brunelleschi to feed artisans employed to work through the night constructing the dome of the Santa Maria del Fiore Cathedral, further proof of Brunelleschi's genius, that he came up with the first great dome *and* the first peposo.

Besides the beef, the dish has four ingredients—pepper, garlic, salt, and a bottle of Chianti—and a simple instruction: put everything in a pot, stick it in the oven before you go to bed, take it out when you wake up. Beef cooked in red wine is ubiquitous, and every European country has its version, but nowhere will you find one more elementary. It helps to recognize what's *not* in it: there are no sauce-enhancing vegetables (no carrots, celery, or onions), no broth, no herbs. There is no water. There is no fat—not even olive oil. There are no salty intensifiers like bacon or pancetta or olives. There is no orange zest. There is no browning of the meat. It is five ingredients plopped into a pot and cooked all night. (Thus the name: *peposo notturno*—"pepperiness by night.")

The secret is in the cut, the shin, which you prepare by using all the knife techniques taught to me by the Maestro: the point cut, to separate the major muscles; the dagger cut, to remove the shinbone; the silver sliver, to eliminate the gnarly stuff; and the scrape-and-slice, to reduce the connective tissue. At home, I cook two shanks at once and use four heaping tablespoons of coarsely ground pepper. (Dario uses more, but his peposo is so peppery it makes Teresa cry.) I add a tablespoon of sea salt, plus a bulb of garlic, start the oven hot and turn it down to two hundred degrees. After two hours, the meat is cooked. After four, it has the chewy mouth-feel of a stew. Over the course of the next eight hours, the dish gets darker and the smaller bits break down into a thick sauce, until, finally, at a point between a solid and a liquid, it is peposo. It smells of wine and lean meat and pepper. You serve it with a rustic white bread and a glass of a simple red, preferably the one you cooked with—once again, the three elements of Giovanni Manetti's Tuscan soul: the beef, the bread, the wine. The taste is a revelation: it seems impossible that something so deeply flavored can be made with so little. When I eat it, I find myself using words like "clean," "natural," or "healthy"—none of which is among conventional descriptions of meat. In this dish, I redis-covered a commonplace that I've long heard but never really believed: that the most worked muscles have the most flavor, provided you learn how to cook them.

26

IN THE MAESTRO, I found a tranquillity I hadn't witnessed before: a patience, a sense of order, a stable relationship to a world that was old and trustworthy. This was new to me. It was also very different from the rest of the butcher shop. At the best of times, Dario was not one of the planet's more serene individuals. ("It is my affliction, I have too much passion, I don't know how to control it.") As it happens, he was, on my return, even more unstable than normal. He and Ann Marie had split up, and Dario was either sullen and morose or unpredictable and manic. He seemed to be heartbroken. Then he seemed to be newly in love. He was probably both. At dawn, just after the meat was delivered, he would sit outside on a curb, memorizing poetry. When he finally entered the shop, it was to play Elvis love songs. Every day began with "Love Me Tender." Actually, there were many "Love Me Tender"s in a row, sometimes a whole uninterrupted morning of "Love Me Tender"s, before he would relent and move on to "It's Now or Never."

"Melancholy," the Maestro said without explanation.

Dario's condition was hard on customers. One day, he wanted to show off his horns, including a multivalved instrument that played the three-note siren of an Italian emergency vehicle. The last time he'd used it was on a visit to Grossetto, in southern Tuscany, to see a friend, Simon (a characteristic Dario charity case, a middle-aged man with the emotional age of a child, living in an assisted care accommodation). After lunch, Dario led Simon out into the main piazza, and they played police cars, the two of them alternating blowing into the siren instrument, until the real police showed up and told them to stop.

Dario blew into the instrument. It was loud and sounded so siren-like that it provoked in me a feeling of panic, as though I needed to get out of the way quickly. Dario's eyes were glistening. He'd had, I suppose, a tad too much red wine at the family meal. There was a bottle of Jack Daniel's on a shelf. He drank bountifully from it and walked outside.

Panzano is too small to have a police force, so when Dario blew his siren there was no official to stop him. So he didn't stop. People appeared in the street, summoned by the urgent blaring. Dario blew and drank some more Jack Daniel's and didn't notice a man trying to get his attention. The man was in his sixties—wool trousers, a matching jacket, good shoes—with a moustache and a civilized manner. He made an effort to be noticed, but Dario was noticing nothing. In his excitement, he was probably blind. He blew, drank more Jack Daniel's, and blew again.

"Please," the man said, and stepped forthrightly in front of Dario. "You are Dario Cecchini, are you not? May I introduce myself? I have driven from Monaco to see you." Monaco was a long way away.

Dario nodded vaguely and took a hit of the bourbon.

"You are very famous. Did you know that there was a long article about you in *Le Figaro*?"

Dario shrugged. "It's possible," he said and turned slightly. The man was in Dario's way. He blew, drank, and wiped his mouth with his sleeve.

"*Le Figaro* says you are very good," the man persisted. "It says you are the best butcher in the world. That's why I've driven all this way. To meet the best butcher in the world."

Dario dropped his siren instrument to his side and stared at the man with blurry intensity. Then he laughed. "Ha! Ha! Ha!" It was more a coarse bellow than a laugh, inches from the man's face. "Ha! Ha! Ha! Ha! Ha! Ha!" He turned to me and said, "I am a nightmare!" He looked back at the man and blew into the siren instrument.

The man retreated, disappointed, and walked back to his car.

One busy Saturday, Dario was serving a woman about to purchase her first bistecca who then asked him if the meat was good.

"*E' buona?*" Dario said, his voice rising theatrically with exaggerated indignation. "*Non lo so. Proviamo.*" (I don't know—let's find out.) So he took a bite—the woman's raw purchase—chewed it melodramatically, swallowed, said, "Yes, it's good," wrapped it up, and gave the woman her change. The woman, aghast, took her package and fled. The consequence was that several people asked Dario if he would take a bite out of their steaks as well—as though his teeth marks were an auto-graph. "Please," one man said, "it's for my wife."

When the atmosphere was jovial, exchanges like this could be jolly. But there could be real tension. Twice, I feared a fight. "No! No! No!" Dario shouted at a man who had wanted a smaller piece of meat than what had been offered him. "What's for sale is what's on view, and if you don't like what you see you can go. You are in my territory. You are not welcome. In fact, you should leave. Good-bye." I had to remind myself I was in a food shop. Even in New York (once famous for its rudeness, now stuck in a condition of permanent impatience), I had never seen anything like it. There, a retailer, however jaded, still pre-tends to honor the shopkeeper's code that a customer is always right. Dario followed a much blunter, take-no-prisoners philosophy that actu-ally the customer is a dick.

ONE DAY, I was looking at Dario's display case ("what's for sale is what you see") and realized there were no lamb chops. There were also no birds, not even a chicken. There was no meat for stewing. There was no wild boar or rabbit or hare, although Tuscany was known for its game. For the first time, I saw that most of the items you go to a butcher shop to buy weren't there. I don't know why I hadn't noticed this until now except (as my Babbo polenta lesson had taught me) you sometimes have to be in a place a long time before you see it.

What I saw now was what Dario called "my works" *(le mie opere),* which I'd been reluctant to acknowledge because it sounded so preten-tious. But that was what you got: a butcher and his works. I remembered the earful I'd got when I'd suggested that the butcher shop was a business—an innocent enough assumption when you think about it. What I had actually said was a question: What will happen when Dario dies? It had probably come out wrong. I wasn't meaning to dwell on Dario's dying. The point was theoretical: a feature of a good business, in the United States anyway, was its ability to function without the main guy.

Dario exploded. "What are you talking about? I don't have a good bizzzness. I have a bad bizzzness. I am not interested in a good bizzzness." "Business" in Italian is *commercio,* but Dario preferred his own mutilation of the English, with its corrupting sense of foreignness, hissing the sibilants as though he were about to spit. "I do not want to be Mario Batali," he said, punching the "B" in Batali like an air bag. "I am repelled by marketing. I am an artisan. I work with my hands. My model is from the Renaissance. The bodega. The artist workshop. Giotto. Raphael. Michelangelo. These are my inspirations. Do you think they were interested in bizzzness?"

By now, I'd eaten all of Dario's meat, and I can testify: it is very good. It is the best meat I've eaten. But it is not a painting by Michelangelo. It's dinner. You eat it; it's gone.

And yet as I stood there, suddenly taking in the display case, I had to admit that the food had something of an artist's purposefulness. Every item there made a point. Some foods had long and complex preparations, like the red pepper mostarda, which took a whole day to make, or the beef "sushi" (a raw beef preparation made with "very good olive oil"), which took a morning, or the "Tuscan tuna," which took nearly a week. But every item *really* was a "work," even ones that seemed very simple.

There was no ham or pork loin, for instance, but you could always buy a pork chop. Why? Because the chop was covered with fennel pollen. (Pork chop—*no*; pork chop with intense expression of nearby hills, according to a classic combination, now seldom seen— *yes.*) You couldn't buy a leg of lamb, but at Easter you could get a baby lamb's shoulder—delicate, the color of a pink flower, boned and rolled up with rosemary and pecorino, the local cheese made with sheep's milk: "the milk of the mother with the meat of the child" seeming to violate some unspoken code of meat eating but, according to Dario, a Roman preparation as old as the Mediterranean. (Conventional lamb cut—*no*; neglected cut plus unique ingredient, according to ancient recipe—*yes.*) In northern Italy, you see *polpettone* everywhere: a meat loaf cooked in a bread tray and made from a fatty cut. Dario's was different. The meat was the shank (once again), ground fine, mixed with red onion, garlic, and egg, and rolled into a large ball: in fact, it was gigantic. Why? Once, making it with Dario, I overheard his muttering, "It's a family dish, a family dish, it has to look like the family bread loaf." He had a picture in his mind, a family supper served at the end of the week: that's when you ate your polpettone, because Tuscan bread was normally baked at the beginning of the week, and this used the leftovers. And, apart from the shank, the essential ingredient was that stale bread: lots of it, crushed and smacked into the meatball, slapped, spanked, thwacked, until the crumbs formed a thick yeasty skin. The result, when "baked," looked like a peasant loaf: round, brown, and crusty. (Conventional polpettone—*no*; rustic, mutant dinosaur egg evocative of country living—*yes*.)

One night, Dario woke up troubled by the thought that his message was not getting across. It was cold, he said, three in the morning, with an icy light from a full moon filling up the bedroom of Il Greppo. He got up as though summoned and began writing. "I am not an author, but there are things people should understand." He made a list of his twenty most important works and wrote a page about each. He called the collection a *Breviario,* an ecclesiastical word used to describe a book of prayers. "It should be small enough to fit in your back pocket." Dario can't type; his letters are done by Miriam (a "retired poetess," another charity, the one who is paid to come in to read the newspapers); and after Miriam had typed Dario's text she gave me a copy. It was, predictably enough, informed by a high sense of purpose: dedicated to the Maestro ("who taught me the quality of meat and . . . made me into a man"), it opens with a declaration of principles ("I am an artisan!"), and concludes with a promise to the reader that, in eating these dishes, "your life will be improved."

It is not a recipe book and only intermittently describes the dishes. Instead, it is a defense, an apologia for why each one matters. The accounts have a tendency to wax a little purple (the herbal salt, "the perfume of Chianti," expresses, in its heady fragrances, "the roots of our soil" and "the love that moves the sun and stars"). Some are more personal (the polpettone is cooked according to "the rhythm of bread"—an elegant invocation of a village's baking routine—and was first made for Dario by his Aunt Tosca). Much of it is characteristically brazen: for those who can't endure the unmitigated carnality of Dario's braised shank (the bone is removed and replaced by the marrow and cooked in a pot of caramelizing shallots), Dario sanctifies it by splashing it with vin santo—Tuscany's sweet "sacred" wine. In fact, the book isn't really about the food of the butcher shop but about how to visit it. It was a user's guide, addressed to strangers, the uninitiated who came to Panzano expecting a butcher.

I wondered if I was glimpsing Dario's secret. Fundamentally, he didn't want to be a butcher, and therefore if he had to be one—because of patrimony or family or simply because he had no choice—then he would be unlike any butcher you'd ever met. His was a calling, not a trade—he was an artisan, not a laborer—and his "works" were about history and self and being Tuscan and only indirectly about dinner. They amounted, ultimately, to a tortured response to grief, and the "works" had become Dario's way of remaining in touch, physically (those giant hands), with those who are no longer with him. When you came to his shop, he didn't want you to see a butcher—and wouldn't be able to say why—but he knew what you should see instead: an artist, whose subject was loss.

I THINK OF PANZANO as a village of dead fathers. In the beginning, I regarded them as ghosts—like so many Hamlet seniors rising from their graves, urging their sons to swear oaths of revenge or continuity, some business left undone. And, like Hamlet junior, I couldn't tell if they were good ghosts or bad ones. Now, after nearly six months in the place, I saw them as neither good nor bad, just irritating doddering presences: pushy patriarchs refusing to accept they were dead. Bugger off, you creepy old bastards. Stay in your graves and let your children get on with it.

Dario put them in my mind. So did Giovanni Manetti, who, continuing his father's search for his Chianti heritage, had gone ahead and bought that bull. For two weeks, it was what people talked about.

"Did you hear? Giovanni bought the bull!"

"Boy, that lad is going to have a good time"—nudge, nudge, wink, wink—"one bull and four wives."

"The bull arrives next week."

"No, he doesn't, he arrives tomorrow."

"You're out of your mind. Giovanni is in New York. No bull is arriving when he's not here."

Giovanni was in New York selling his wine. As it happened, Dario was in the Veneto, at a conference promoting his meat. The two men should have been friends, each committed to continuing traditions of Panzano, red wine and beef being at the heart of the place, as each man, separately, had urged me to understand. I liked them both. But they didn't get on. They came from such different backgrounds. Giovanni was the son of a father proud of his family name and its long history. Dario was the son of a father proud to be a member of a line of men who worked with their hands and their long history. But the most divisive issue was a matter of honor, involving a love affair, and the culture of omnipresent patriarchs: Giovanni's younger sister, Giovanna, and the Maestro's son, Enrico, had fallen in love.

Enrico was thirty, a tall, gangly, dark-haired version of his silvered father, with a clay-like nose, an easy smile, mischievously expressive brown eyes, a voice so deeply baritone that it seemed contrived, and many of the Maestro's rhythms of speech and manner, including that way of leaning back, slightly, to make a point and emphasizing it with his hands, his (also) long fingers emphatically drawn together. Enrico made the "very good olive oil" that Dario used. He also made the vin santo splashed onto Dario's beef shanks. And he was also accomplished at plant grafting—the meticulous science of manipulating nature—in which capacity he had been hired, seven years earlier, by Dino Manetti, to work the Fontodi vines, and had met Giovanna. The two had fallen in love, transgressing boundaries that most modern societies no longer recognize. But Giovanna's father seems to have recognized them, and when he discovered the relationship he was not happy. According to Dario, Enrico was fired, Giovanna was ordered never to see him again, and she obeyed because that's what the children of Panzano fathers do: they obey. (Giovanna, for her part, insists that Enrico left on his own accord, and that in any case, it was a youthful folly—she'd been nineteen and, like so many children growing up on Italian hilltops, sheltered from the ways of the world.) But Enrico's sudden disappearance, however it might be described (*he* believes he was fired), was real and public enough—in Dario's eyes, an outspoken how-dare-you? rebuke—and Dario, indignant on behalf of the indignity suffered by his own surrogate father ("What? A son of the Maestro, *my* Maestro, is not good enough for a Manetti?"), was in a rage, a rage that continues to this day. When Dino Manetti died, Dario refused to go to the memorial service, attended by hundreds (the man was much loved by everyone else in the world), which was some kind of public protest, probably comprehensible only to Dario, because later that day he attended the burial, a small affair, and the distinction was important: even in his rage, Dario couldn't fail to attend the burial. The death of a father was still the weightiest event in a Panzano son's life. Dario claims that the condolences he then conveyed, and Giovanni's expression of gratitude, were the first words spoken between them in ten years.

At the end of the summer, my wife and I were on the square when Dario and Giovanni ran into each other: by Dario's reckoning, the second time in ten years; Giovanni, for his part, wasn't aware that the two of them hadn't been speaking, which might well be true: sometimes Dario's rages were very private affairs. The occasion was an annual wine festival, held at harvesttime, when Panzano's eighteen winemakers (mainly sons and daughters of recently departed patriarchs) set up stalls and offered tastings. Dario, objecting to the fact that most Panzano wines are aged in wood barrels, normally boycotted the event, but he had a new love in his life, Kim, and she wanted to attend. The two of them showed up late, Dario in his look-at-me party clothes, a linen blowsy shirt, a leather cowboy vest, and brightly red-striped trousers. Giovanni, in a dark blue silk suit with a light blue shirt and tie and brown leather shoes, was returning from a proprietors' dinner, another harvest ritual, and had stopped by the Fontodi stand. Dario spotted him.

"*Eccolo!*" he boomed, so loudly that people stopped what they were doing. "There he is!"

Giovanni bowed.

Dario bowed.

So they're friends after all, I thought, until I realized that the display was the kind of over-the-top friendliness you see only between people who are not really friendly. At a safe-seeming twenty feet apart, they were never in danger of having to shake hands, for instance. A frantic moment followed as each one tried to think of a nice, vacuous thing to say to avoid an act of *brutta figura*.

Dario bowed again and cleared his throat.

Giovanni bowed, too.

Dario grinned.

Finally, in an effort at grace, Giovanni mentioned that he'd seen Dario's meat on the menu of Da Caino, where he'd had dinner "only last week!" Restaurants that buy Dario's meat cite the butcher shop—an honor, and a way, too, of explaining the price; Da Caino was the famous southern Tuscan restaurant that did not teach me how to make pasta.

Dario said, "It's true, Da Caino orders my meat," and bowed again, accepting the compliment. (There were multiple ironies: Giovanni did not say he had actually eaten the meat, and, in any case, he had no need to travel a hundred miles either to see or eat it; the butcher shop was around the corner. But Giovanni didn't buy his meat from Dario; he patronized the other butcher shop, the one run by Filippo and *his* father.)

The men remained thus—was Dario humming?—surrounded by a dozen or so onlookers who all sensed the prospect of a terrible spectacle and couldn't stop staring. I counted myself a member of that voyeuristic audience. I had a camera in my pocket and, recognizing the fear-and-awe uniqueness of the encounter, wanted a picture. But how to take it? The two men were standing so far apart I couldn't get them into a frame, but I didn't dare ask them to move. I couldn't even summon the courage to tell them to stand still (Giovanni was shuffling), until finally I gave up. My pulling the camera out might have acted as a trigger, and the frightful thing would happen, whatever it was—Zeus zapping me with a thunderbolt, probably. Finally, they parted.

"Well," Dario said.

"Well," Giovanni said.

Dario whipped round a hundred eighty degrees and walked off, Kim tagging along behind, trying to keep up. Giovanni turned round as well, and walked off in exactly the opposite direction. I'm not sure they knew where they were going. Both men seemed to have had different destinations in mind when they ran into each other. Because of the hasty spin-and-flight, their backs were simultaneously on view. I saw it first—a thing clinging to the back of Dario's neck. I saw that Giovanni had one, too. I elbowed my wife, standing next to me, and pointed, and she gasped but then wasn't sure she had seen it. "Look again," I said. "Giovanni doesn't know it's there." He was easing into the evening's shadowy darkness, just outside the range of the wine festival's night lights, but he seemed so preoccupied (by the harvest he now had to deal with or the exchange he'd just had or maybe the regret that he hadn't ordered a steak at Da Caino) that he appeared wholly oblivious to the thing—a tiny, wizened figure, looking something like an old man, hanging on with a bony clutch.

27

THE DELIVERY of Giovanni's bull—for eventually it arrived, on a Wednesday, when the butcher shop was closed, and my wife and I had rushed down the valley to watch—turned out to be one of the most illuminating pieces of theater I had seen in some time. No one was ready for the animal. I now suspect that, on an unspoken but profound level, people didn't believe the beast actually existed until they could see it with their own eyes.

The beast in question was pacing back and forth on a flatbed truck. Vineyard workers were running around confused and frantic. Some were putting posts in the ground—a fence was required, rather urgently: no fence, no pasture, and no one wanted a giant white bull roaming around the open valley. A manger was also being built, and you could hear the frenzied hammering of a half-dozen carpenters just over the crest of a hill. The bull's four wives needed moving as well: they had been in a smaller pasture with another breed, a French one, locally called *la rossa*. But the vineyard workers had no idea how to persuade a cow to move.

All and all, there was a lot to do, and the driver of the flatbed truck was in a condition of utter incomprehension. "I don't believe this. You knew I was coming, didn't you?" (He, too, was unlike anything anyone had seen before. He resembled a large frog—head like a bullet, no neck, and a very croak-capable-seeming belly—and was wearing a T-shirt the size of a military tent, probably because it was one of the few garments that could cover his girth. Until this moment, I'd never contemplated the kind of person who delivers bulls, but if I had, I'm sure I would have pictured someone exactly like this man.)

The principal difficulty was the bull's four wives. They were really not cooperating. The workers shouted at them and made cowboy sounds and chased the animals with branches of wood. The effect was animals in panic. They sprinted, they jumped, they dodged: they could have been a species of white antelope. I had to remind myself that they had been docile, passive animals. Until now, the most movement I'd seen was in their chewing.

"Why do I let you guys bust my balls?" the frog man shouted. "I'm coming back in the morning."

A worker undid his belt, swung it above his head, and charged, something the cows interpreted as an even more pressing danger to their well-being, and they sprinted in four directions. There was now a cow in each corner of the pasture. Two workers had given up. They were leaning together against a post, their shirts dark with sweat, their chests heaving. A cow stood nearby, eyeing them.

I don't know why they had taken it upon themselves to move the cows in the first place. Beppe was supposed to be in charge. Beppe was the gap-toothed geezer from the town square—the one with the incomprehensible rustic accent who had grown up in the Fontodi borgo. When Giovanni had decided to raise his own chianine, he'd put the word out that he needed someone. "Everyone wanted the job," he told me, "but there was only one position. So I asked them to pick the most qualified person among them." Keeping their own animals was central to how Tuscan men of a certain generation liked to think of themselves, but almost none of them had done it. In fact, of all the men in the village, Beppe was the only one with any experience. And, of course, in hiring Beppe, Giovanni had completed a circle.

Beppe was sitting on a stump. The vineyard workers had irritated him. It seems that, in their excitement at the bull's arriving, they'd rushed out like film extras on a western.

"What do those guys know?" Beppe asked. "They're grape pickers. They know dirt. They don't know animals. Beppe knows animals. You can't make animals do what they don't want to do."

The frog driver shouted. "I'm going to put the bull into that pasture. *That* will chase out the cows." He laughed heartily, and the laughter moved like a wave across his massive cotton T-shirt. "He's coming!" The driver made to open the gate at the back of the truck. "He's coming!"

"Patience," someone shouted.

"Patience?" the driver said and spat. "Don't talk to me about patience. I could write a book about patience, and the first chapter would be about you dickheads." He waddled over to the side of the truck and shook the slats. The bull stopped pacing and stomped. Why would he provoke a bull he was about to release?

"I can't keep him back any longer. He's so horny he's dangerous."

Beppe chuckled. "The bull is going to have a good life." He was staring unapologetically at my wife's thighs. ("Maybe," she said later, "it was a mistake to wear shorts.") "Tonight he'll have four women."

Then, one by one, the vineyard workers gave up. And, as though their collapse were a cue, Beppe shuffled over to a makeshift shed, poured out some grain, and with food and gentle words coaxed the cows into the next pasture.

"*Finalmente,*" the driver said and opened the gate at the back of the truck.

The bull was indeed a powerful animal. He also had a distinctly youthful face. We all stared at him. He was a boy—a large, muscular boy. He was bigger than the girls and had defined muscles, especially around the shoulders, and a body that tapered in the back, like a cartoon of masculinity. My wife and I watched from behind a rock, as though it would protect us if the bull charged. We were joined by the vineyard workers, just behind us, who seemed to believe that we would protect them.

"He's beautiful," someone said.

"Mythic."

"But the pressure is on. He does it now or"—a vineyard worker made a slashing movement across his own throat—"he gets sent home. He knows his job."

I'm pretty sure the bull didn't know he had one. He seemed interested in more elementary questions, like why he was here, standing at the back of a truck in front of an audience eager to watch him have sex with strange cows he hadn't met. He looked left, right, left. He stomped, he snorted. He seemed to want to be bull-like. Then he spotted the girls, gave up the routine, trotted down the ramp, and joined them, as easily as old friends meeting up after an absence. In less than a minute—and who knows? maybe instantly—he assumed his role as bull, pushed the girls out of the way, and positioned himself in front. He then led his little herd on an inspection of their new home.

For the next hour, the onlookers remained, waiting for the bull to get to work. But he didn't seem to understand the terms of his employment. There was some excitement when a cow became interested in his genitalia and poked her head between his legs.

"She's ready," a workman whispered.

"*Toro*—what are you waiting for?"

"Four wives. Really!" *Veramente!* "Does it get any better?"

But the bull just carried on. Every now and then he'd stop, and that one eager cow, seeing an opportunity, would pop down and give him another lick. The bull couldn't have been more indifferent. That cow's friendly tongue on his testicles could have been a gnat.

THE BULL, I understood now, was as exotic to everyone in Panzano as he was to me, and for some time he was what people talked about: Has he scored yet? Does he need instruction? Is he a homosexual? The only place where he wasn't mentioned was at Dario's. This was not unusual. The shop was like a foreign country inside Panzano, with its own laws and head of state (not unlike the Vatican, if the Vatican were a giant butcher shop). But the concerns raised by the bull—chianine! Tuscan beef! the Tuscan soul!—put me in mind of something I need to come clean about: something I had been unprepared for when I discovered it and that took weeks of the Maestro's tutorials for me to understand. Ever since I had made the discovery, I'd wondered how I'd convey its magnitude. Actually, I don't know what to do except offer up the bare fact: the meat sold by Dario Cecchini—the most famous butcher in Italy, possibly the most famous living Tuscan—is Spanish.

No butcher, I should clarify, slaughters his own animals, a common misconception, especially in Italy, where the word for "butcher," *macellaio*, comes from the one for slaughter, *macello*. A butcher's job is about mastering the thigh, in all its implications, and, in Chianti, that thigh, for a millennium or two, came from a local cow: one you saw on your way home every night. Dario's came from a Spanish cow, raised a thousand miles away on a small farm on the Costa Brava and delivered in a truck that left Spain every Thursday and arrived in Panzano on Friday, long before anyone else in the village was up, except for the dedicated

staff at a bar called La Curva, who opened at six and prepared a cappuc-
cino for Dario, the Maestro, and me minutes after we finished unload-
ing. For a while, I wondered if this was why the deliveries came before
dawn—so no one would see the Spanish plates on the vehicle.

My suspicion arose when I was boning a pig and noticed a stamp on
the belly: *Hecho en España*. Made in Spain? This was puzzling. I took
my boned sides to Dario and stood nearby as he prepared arista. Then,
before rolling it up like a log, Dario examined the outside for blemishes,
including the "Hecho en España" stamp, which he lopped off with a
knife. To hide the evidence?

My suspicions were misplaced. Dario would never deny where his
meat was from. You ask him, he'll tell you. But he wasn't going out of
his way to advertise it.

"It comes from *where?*" *(Viene di DOVE?)* asks a voice rising melodramatically in mounting incredulity.

This is the first part of an exchange familiar to everyone in the
butcher shop. A man—in his middle years, professional, educated, committed to the elusive relationship between food and culture and national
identity—has driven many hours, a road map of Tuscany on the seat
next to him, found a parking place, asked the old geezers on the square
for directions, and entered the famous butcher shop. For a moment,
he takes it all in: the display case, the aesthetic presentation, the loud
music. (And the tune might be anything but, toward the end of
my stay, was finally—"At last!" young Riccardo declared—no longer
Elvis. Dario had returned to Mozart, particularly *Don Giovanni*, and
every morning played Leporello's inventory song, the one cataloguing
Don Giovanni's sexual conquests. "Happier," the Maestro observed,
without explanation.) The man steps up to the counter and shouts the
words that will result in his banishment: *"Una bistecca di chianina, per
favore!"*

Dario turns down the music.

No, he cannot give the man a bistecca from a chianina cow, he says
(the voice, a monotone, bored, oppressed; the eyelids, heavy), because he
does not have a chianina cow to sell.

"Oh," the man says, "what kind of cow do you have?"

Dario tells him. If the man's mind is of an inquisitive nature, he will
say, "Oh, how interesting." A simple sentence, which, in my time at the

butcher shop, was uttered by only two people, who were both instantly rewarded by a bistecca, even when the allocation had been spoken for. If his mind is characterized more by respect than by curiosity, he will say, "Oh. Why's that?" He won't get a bistecca but will be able to reserve one. Things get nasty if the stranger is an inflexible, even if highly romantic, believer in the correctness of things. A man of this sort invariably poses the aforementioned question ("Your meat comes from WHERE?"), although its force is more declarative than interrogative. What the question is actually saying is: "I have taken time out of my precious life, driven to this godforsaken village on a windy road to visit hill people like you in order to have an authentic Tuscan experience, and you're telling me I might as well have gone to Barcelona?"

The man is about to be ordered out, but before his exit and his journey home, when he will reflect nostalgically on the evanescence of Italianness, he will be told there is no chianina because the chianina is now not good. It's actually a lecture—everyone gets it—delivered in a fast I've-said-it-once-I've-said-it-a-million-times tone. "The chianina is now not good because it is fundamentally banal. It is a name. Prada is a name. Versace is a name. Armani is a name. Chianina is a name. If I sold it, which I do not, I would be selling a name. Would I make money selling a name? Certainly. Would it be good for bizzzness? Certainly. But bizzzness does not interest me. Names do not interest me. Meat interests me. That's why I sell meat, not names. Besides," Dario adds, in a final flourish, "I don't believe in the purity of races. You, evidently, believe in the purity of races. So did Hitler. But Hitler, in *my* view, was wrong." That legendary white cow is now an Aryan Nazi cow, and the stranger is a Fascist and a traitor to the cause of Italian nationalism. That's when he is invited to leave.

Of all the tensions in the butcher shop between customer and proprietor, of all the flame-ups and flare-outs, the chianina issue was the most contentious. I knew, watching Dario during these encounters—his face stiffening, his head dropping before the speech, the weariness of the same message—that, secretly, he longed to serve a meat that came from an animal raised nearby. He hated being a myth destroyer, especially because he, too, was living some version of the myth, knew how pervasive it was and how tenaciously it was clung to. After all, the man who had driven through the hills for his Tuscan experience believed in it so absolutely that it had rendered him blind: it never occurred to him that he hadn't seen a single cow on his journey to Panzano (and, swearing at Dario on the way back, would fail to realize that he still wasn't seeing one). Once, when I visited Porretta for one of my tortellini lessons and mentioned casually to Gianni that Dario's beef was Spanish, Gianni gripped the table—a telling gesture, as though the earth were unstable—stopped me midsentence, and declared that he was devastated: "From this moment on, I have no more illusions."

I WENT TO the Maestro for an explanation.

"In the seventies," he said, "the chianine were good. They tasted of the hillsides and clean air. They ate grass and had acres to roam in, and, because they were work animals, they were exercised constantly. The meat was firm and pure. It might take two weeks before it softened up." He was alluding to the meat's aging. I used to watch the process in the walk-in: each day, a piece would yield a little more to a prod from my finger. "Today, the chianine do not have hillsides to roam in, because they are covered with vines. The chianine are not exercised, because you use a tractor to work vines, not an animal. And instead of grass, they eat cereals, grains, and protein pellets: *mush*." He used the English word, with its irresistible onomatopoeic veracity. "They eat *mush*. They taste of *mush*. And after the animal is slaughtered, the meat behaves like *mush*: it disintegrates in days. A chianina is a thing to flee from!" *(Da sfugire!)*

In the butcher shop, the Maestro was everyone's senior, but he had the innocence of a younger man—a lack of guile. He had no campaigns or polemics. He never made speeches about Hitler or marketing. "I have no enemies," he said during a family meal, after an oblique reference was made to the terminated romance between his son Enrico and Giovanna Manetti. "I have no grudges." So when the Maestro uttered a judgment you didn't think twice about it, and if he said chianina was now bad I stopped going out of my way to find some. "You should always listen to the Maestro when he speaks," Dario told me, "because he doesn't speak much. Six, maybe eight sentences a month. But the sentences have the weight of thought." (I knew enough to listen to the Maestro, but I don't know where this six-to-eight-times-a-month masculine taciturnity thing came from. My suspicion was that Dario and the Maestro didn't spend a lot of time alone together anymore, except at five in the morning, waiting for the meat truck to arrive from Spain: at that hour, I, too, would be lucky to get out six to eight sentences a month.)

"When I was young," the Maestro recalled one day, "there was one kind of prosciutto. It was made in the winter, by hand, and aged for two years. It was sweet when you smelled it. A profound perfume. Unmistakable. To age a prosciutto is a subtle business. If it's too warm, the aging process never begins. The meat spoils. If it's too dry, the meat is ruined. It needs to be damp but cool." *Umido ma freddo.* "The summer is too hot. In the winter—that's when you make salumi. Your prosciutto. Your soppressata. Your sausages."

The Maestro suddenly put me in mind of Miriam—I don't know why I hadn't seen the connection before—and her insistence on making culatello only in January, because that's when you make your meat. Both were members of the old-way-is-the-best-way-because-it-is-the-old-way school.

"When I was young," the Maestro continued, "there were no supermarkets. Now there are many. They're able to sell more prosciutti than it is possible to make. So they invented new kinds. In addition to a prosciutto that's aged for two years, you can now get a cheaper one-year kind, a cheaper six-month kind, and a very cheap three-month variety. They are made all year round, in prosciutto factories. The truth is, there is only one kind of prosciutto, and it is made in the winter, by hand and not in a factory, and aged for two years. These new varieties are not good. They do not smell sweet. They are bad."

What the Maestro was describing was the familiar, sad history of animal husbandry since World War II, an Italian history, but also a European and American one. In the event, I don't know if supermarkets are to blame—they're too easy a target and, like bad newspapers, wouldn't exist if people didn't want them. But something, somehow (call it, once again, the twentieth century) went badly wrong, almost everywhere, as though great stretches of the globe had been inexplicably afflicted by a gastronomic amnesia and forgot that beef came from a cow, an animal that, like all animals, needed to be treated well.

"Everyone in Italy likes steak," the Maestro said, "and the supermarkets have always been able to sell more than they could get. You see the problem." In the Maestro's history, the supermarkets were unable to invent new varieties of steak, like so many different kinds of prosciutti. The challenge, therefore, was to produce industrial quantities of steak, faster and cheaper; the rest of the animal could be sold off as meat product. "Someone came up with the idea of feeding the animals fish meal." *Farina di pesce;* ground-up fish. "It was cheap and high in protein, and the cows fattened up quickly. But the meat tasted of fish. Next they tried feeding them a manufactured protein mix, made with the remains of the animal itself. The meat no longer tasted of fish, but it wasn't correct." This was high-tech cannibalism with famously disastrous consequences: bovine spongiform encephalopathy, or mad cows. "Now," the Maestro sighed, "well . . ." His voice drifted off. I braced myself: any moment, he was going to declare he'd become a vegetarian.

"You see why Dario doesn't sell chianina. The breed doesn't matter. This Spanish meat: it happens to come from a white cow. It's not a chianina. But it doesn't matter. It could be an American cow or a French one. It's not the breed. It's the breeding."

The Spanish meat came from an out-of-the-way rustic farm: backwards, family-run, ideologically tiny, incapable of becoming bigger unless Dad wins the lottery and buys the next mountain. The family knows what it can do with its land and that it can't do more. In the world according to the Maestro, the most important knowledge is understanding what you can't do. Most of the great meat producers are, in the Maestro's view, small and old-fashioned and philosophically conservative.

"Very good beef in Namibia," he said one day.

Christ, I'd think, *Namibia!* Do I have to go to Namibia to get a good steak?

"Yugoslavia—very good beef there as well."

Argentina, he said another day. "Very, very good beef. Probably the best in the world. It tastes of the open air and long grass and wild hills. In Argentina, that's where you'll discover Tuscan meat of thirty years ago." He stopped what he was doing and pointed his long finger at me. "Billy"—he'd taken to calling me by my diminutive, because it seemed more Italian—"you have to go to Argentina. For the beef." He paused, enjoying the memory of something cooked over an open fire and smiled. "And when you're there, you can also eat exceptionally good goat."

And I found myself writing in my notebook, "Don't forget—when in Argentina, eat the goat."

In fact, every place cited by the Maestro was provincial and unmodern, with one exception: Denmark. "I can't explain it," the Maestro confessed, "but in Denmark you can get very good meat."

"Not the breed but the breeding"—it was the secret password of the butcher shop.

28

ONE FRIDAY in September, I walked to Panzano's oldest church, La Pieve di San Leolino. I'd been in Panzano nearly seven months and hadn't seen it. It was on a high hill, along a dirt ridge near the cemetery, and was known for the best view of the area. The church was something of a puzzle: erected in the 900s, destroyed soon after (when the valley was a Florentine-Sienese war zone), rebuilt in the 1100s, and now a Romanesque mishmash: a square building with old bits attached, tipping precariously. To complicate its genealogy, a stone remnant had been dug up nearby, with an incomprehensible Etruscan text around the perimeter, dating from five centuries before Christ. People have been enjoying the view for a long time.

Dario describes this valley as among the oldest cultivated lands on the planet. After the Etruscans, the Romans moved in (a grain tower remains—built for livestock fodder); a few centuries later, they were chased out by the Lombards, the so-called northern barbarians of history, who were then converted by Christians in the 700s. For centuries, the tenants changed but the valley didn't, each occupier taking over from the one before, assuming agriculture routines that have continued without interruption since the invention of the hoe. The routines are implicit in a thirteenth-century letter by Luca di Matteo, a landowner, written in the aftermath of the valley's being ravaged by Sienese troops. Soldiers had burned huts and homes (*chapane e chase*, in di Matteo's old Italian), killed cows and livestock *(perduti buoi e bestiame)*, and everyone would be without grain or fodder for a year *(un anno senza richore grano e biade)*. The letter is revealing for what's not said. Amid so much destruction, there is no mention of an olive tree, a grapevine, or wheat, although I'm sure all would have been features of the landscape.

After church and home, what mattered was the cows *(buoi)* and the fodder *(biade)* to feed them. Dario might be correct, that this land has been long cultivated, but if so it has been cultivated for raising livestock. Cows have been here as long as people.

From where I stood, I could see Giovanni's little herd. The young bull turned out to be neither homosexual nor ignorant. Just shy. "A nighttime lover," Beppe said when I saw him on the square. "He injured his shoulder." Beppe then made a universally recognized hip-swiveling movement. The bull had fallen awkwardly in midmount, although not before scoring. All four wives had missed their periods. So Giovanni had succeeded, and chianine would be returning to the Chianti hills. It was a curious thing to contemplate. History always teaches us we can't turn back the clock, but I seemed to have been surrounded by people who kept trying.

It was the first day of autumn, and the weather had got hot again. The vineyard workers were coming in for lunch and wouldn't be back in the afternoon. When grapes overheat, they behave unpredictably, and the practice is to hope for cooler temperatures in the morning. Giovanni was ahead of the others, and most of his sangiovese had been picked. Buckets of it were being dumped into a small truck, with dry ice poured on top to prevent the fruit from stewing. For Giovanni, the grape was another item essential to his Tuscan identity, and his making a wine from it connected him to the soil's history. "Everyone knows that sangiovese has been here since Roman times," he told me once. "It's in the name: *sangue*, blood, plus Jove. But few people believe the Romans introduced it. We think it had been here already." Like raising cows, growing sangiovese grapes was, in Giovanni's view, just another one of the practices that the new tenants always appropriated: that, ever since these valleys have been inhabited, people have been drinking a version of a god's blood.

On the far side of the valley was Castello dei Rampolla. There the grapes were the smaller, darker Bordeaux varieties planted by Alceo, another ghostly patriarch, although I couldn't tell the difference from where I stood. I saw only symmetrical leafy green lines, with slumping, tired people walking up the hill between them. My wife and I had recently been received by Alceo's daughter, Maurizia—wispy, evanescent, in her late forties, with a Bohemian's baggy dress sense and an intellectual's no-nonsense manner, living with her brother in the windy castello. She normally refused visitors and rarely ventured out, even to promote her own wine, drinking it only "every now and then, when in Florence, perhaps," professing to like its Bordeaux perfume more than its taste. "At our family meals," she confessed, "we preferred milk." Unlike every other winemaker in Chianti, she hadn't been worried by the brutal summer (her grapes will do well or they won't), because she was philosophically indifferent to the extremes of weather ("Let nature do what nature does"). She harvested by phases of the moon, unless instructed by certain configurations of the stars, and rejected any practice that seemed too obviously modern: like the use of refrigeration or pumps or air-conditioning or filtering, although one night my wife and I were convinced that, looking across the valley at the castello, we spotted electric lights. At the end of our visit, Maurizia took us into the family's famous cellar, where wines have completed their fermentation for more than 1,100 years. The cellar, built in the 900s, was the same age as the church.

I have been toying with a theory, one being played out now in this valley. It had originally been put in my mind by Enrico, the Maestro's son. Enrico occasionally stopped by the butcher shop, but I never had a conversation with him until we attended an event in Montaperti, not far from Siena, to celebrate the anniversary of a battle fought there on September 4th, 1260. Until the advent of firearms, it ranked as one of the Italian peninsula's most devastating days of war. Ten thousand Florentines were killed, one by one, a detail that Dario relishes with a butcher's enthusiasm for knives. Dario was the guest of honor. The event featured a lot of Dante, recited in Dario's gaslight, vaudeville manner to uproarious applause. There was also a performance by one of the last practitioners of a mournful, singsongy troubadour-like bellowing. The bellower was from Pistoia and pretended to make it up as he went along: a "spontaneous" two-line rhyme, followed by a new couplet and then the original rhyme. The structure was something like this:

> *I am an old man who is very boring,*
> *I know you know this because you're snoring,*
> *What can I do? This is my medium,*
> *Which seems like a poem but is actually tedium,*

Besides, this is no game, with lots of scoring,
Just a drunk old man who is very, very boring.

The evening was interminable and I remember little about it, except for a brief exchange with Enrico about his olive oil. I wanted to know why it was so good.

"There are two reasons," Enrico said. "*When* I pick and *what* I pick. Nothing else matters."

Enrico begins his harvest in September, when common sense suggests that your trees should be left alone. In September, the olives are green and hard. Most people pick in late November or December. "Ten to twelve weeks later, the olives are swollen and full of juice. The more juice you get, the more oil you can bottle, the more money you make," Enrico said. "But for me, the olive is bloated. It is pulpy and full of water." The fruit is like "mush," his father's word. "As a result, the oil is thin. You have volume, but no intensity. For me, intensity is everything. For me, less is more. My oil is very, very intense."

Enrico has a thousand trees, but he picks only half of them. "The others are too young." He sells off the olives from the younger trees or lets them fall and rot, but his tone said that only a contemptuous sniveling snail of a human being, without pride or dignity, and not a true Tuscan, would make oil from a young tree. "I'm not making oil to make money," Enrico said.

(I wonder if I need to stop here and acknowledge that exchanges of this sort were becoming fairly familiar. I quote Enrico as though he were a perfectly normal human being. But occasionally, as I nodded in a socially affirmative way, saying nothing, patiently listening to sentiments of this kind—like, "I'm not interested in bizzzness," or "I don't care if the weather ruins my grapes" or "I do this only for the smell"—I had to hit an imaginary pause button, as I've just done now, and admit to myself that there was nothing normal about what I was hearing. Sometimes when I was having these pause-button-like reflections, I wondered what made these people into hill-poet freaks. Was it not eating enough vegetables when children? An excess of protein? I wanted to scream: Hey, you there, Enrico! Don't you like island holidays and flat-screen televisions? Don't you like money?)

Enrico's olive oil, I can testify, is very good, but there are a lot of good olive oils, made by other nutty earth artists with no interest in money, obsessed with smell, looking over their shoulders to make sure they're the first on their mountain to pick their greenly pungent unripe olives, squeezing the tiniest amount of intense juice from their oldest trees. The viscous, gold-green liquid that dribbles out from their stone-like fruit is unlike any other oil I have tasted, and the makers chauvinistically boast that none of it leaves Italy.

For me, these oils have qualities that you also find in the region's good wines (and there are plenty of good wines—in Chianti, it's hard to go to bed sober). Giovanni's best bottling (his Flacianello, named after the Roman village by the old church) is made from old, gnarly, tree trunk–sized, unproductive vines. Like old olive trees, old vines make less fruit, but the grapes produced by them have a grapiness (again *that* intensity) that you don't get from younger vines. Giovanni's riserva is very good, but for me the olive oil is the precious thing. Unlike an expensive bottle of wine, a good oil doesn't improve with age. It is most vibrant just after the olives are crushed. Then its vibrancy dissipates, ineluctably, minute by minute, until it is gone: evanescent, like a season.

My theory is one of smallness. Smallness is now my measure: a variation on all the phrases I'd be hearing, like the Maestro's "it's not in the breed but the breeding" or Enrico's "less is more." As theories go, mine is pretty crude. Small food—good. Big food—bad. For me, the language we use to talk about modern food isn't quite accurate or at least doesn't account for how this Italian valley has taught me to think. The metaphor is usually one of speed: fast food has ruined our culture; slow food will save it (and is the rallying manifesto for the movement of the same name, based in Bra, in northern Italy). You see the metaphor's appeal. But it obscures a fundamental problem, which has little to do with speed and everything to do with size. Fast food did not ruin our culture. The problem was already in place, systemic in fact, and began the moment food was treated like an inanimate object—like any other commodity—that could be manufactured in increasing numbers to satisfy a market. In effect, the two essential players in the food chain (those who make the food and those who buy it) swapped roles. One moment the producer (the guy who knew his cows or the woman who prepared culatello only in January or the old young man who picks his olives in September) determined what was available and how it was made. The next moment it was the consumer. The Maestro blames the supermarkets, but the supermarkets are just a symptom. (Or, to invoke a familiar piece of retail philosophy: the world changed when the food business agreed that the customer was right, when, as we all know, the customer is actually—well, not always right.) What happened in the food business has occurred in every aspect of modern life, and the change has produced many benefits. I like island holidays and flat-screen televisions and have no argument with global market economics, except in this respect—in what it has done to food.

The watery eggs Gianni bought when he fell asleep after lunch: big food. Granny's eggs sold under the counter to Panzano regulars: small food. The pig I brought home on my scooter: small food, even if it was in such big food quantities I couldn't finish it. A ham from a chemically treated animal that has spent its life indoors in a scientifically controlled no-movement pen (every cut perfectly identical as though made by a machine): big food. The so-called ricotta in a supermarket: big food, don't touch it. The ricotta in Lou di Palo's shop in New York's Little Italy—cheaper than the supermarket stuff, but because Lou is in the back making it and not at the counter serving you'll have to wait an hour before you get any: small food. (Even in New York there are a few people in no hurry because you're just a customer and therefore a dickhead.) Actually, Lou's cheese is both small food and slow food; in fact, very, very slow food. But these are exceptions.

Italians have a word, *casalinga,* homemade, although its primary sense is "made by hand." My theory is just a variant of casalinga. (Small food: by hand and therefore precious, hard to find. Big food: from a factory and therefore cheap, abundant.) Just about every preparation I learned in Italy was handmade *and* involved my learning how to use my own hands differently. My hands were trained to roll out dough, to use a knife to break down a thigh, to make sausage or lardo or polpettone. With some techniques, I had to make my hands small, like Betta's. With others, I made them big, like the Maestro's. The hands, Dario says, are everything. With them, cooks express themselves, like artists. With them, they make food that people use their hands to eat. With the hands, Dario passes on to me what he learned from his father. With the hands, Betta gives me her aunts. The hands of Miriam's mother, her grandmothers. The hands of Dario's grandfather, the great-grandfather he never met, except indirectly, in what was passed on through his hands.

Miriam, who can't get a pastina to roll out the dough, no longer makes handmade pasta. When her daughter takes over, will she roll it out by hand? In Tuscany, you can't get the meat at the heart of the region's cooking, so Dario and the Maestro found a small farm that reproduces the intensity of flavor they grew up with. How long will that taste memory last? The Maestro will die. Dario will die. I will die. The memory will die. Food made by hand is an act of defiance and runs contrary to everything in our modernity. Find it; eat it; it will go. It has been around for millennia. Now it is evanescent, like a season.

I HAD SOUGHT out the old church because I knew I'd be leaving. I felt I had probably learned enough, finally, although I didn't know how to articulate what I had learned until I visited the butcher shop for the last time. By now, Dario was like a brother, and he wasn't going to be easy to leave. And the Maestro?

I gave myself a purpose: I was going to give the Maestro my steel— the thing you sharpen your knife against. It was an inside joke. The Maestro sharpens his knife five hundred times a day. It was the rhythm of his labor. His knife was very sharp. But his steel was very dull, and at some point he had taken to using mine: he hadn't asked, he'd just taken it. I was flattered by this. I'm not sure why. Maybe it was a way of showing trust: yes, you're making a mess of everything, but it's going to be okay.

"Maestro. Here. For your knives." I shoved the steel in his direction.

He stared at it for a long time. When he looked up, the rims around his eyes had welled up with tears. I stuttered pathetically, thinking: How do I say good-bye to these people? I will never leave.

Then he exploded. "No!" he said. That familiar injunction. I'd heard it so many times. "No. I cannot take this steel. It would not be correct." He opened his knife drawer. "It goes here," he said, "until you return."

(That's how you leave: by never saying good-bye.)

And I learned that: to return. I came back the following year and the year after that. I hope to return every year (after all, I may never have the chance to learn so much), until I have no one to return to.

Dinner with Mario

~~~~~~~~~~~~~~~~~~~~~~~~~~~~~~~~~~~~~

The primary requisite for writing well about food is a good appetite. Without this, it is impossible to accumulate, within the allotted span, enough experience of eating to have anything worth setting down. Each day brings only two opportunities for field work, and they are not to be wasted minimizing the intake of cholesterol. They are indispensable, like a prizefighter's hours on the road. (I have read that the late French professional gourmand Maurice Curnonsky ate but one meal a day—dinner. But that was late in his life, and I have always suspected his attainments anyway; so many mediocre witticisms are attributed to him that he could not have had much time for eating.) A good appetite gives an eater room to turn around in.

—A J. Liebling, *Between Meals*

NEW YORK, AUGUST 1998. The *New York Times* review that awarded Babbo its three stars, written by the paper's restaurant critic, Ruth Reichl, was variations on the theme that here, at last, was a place prepared to take risks. The service was described as attentive but eccentric. Reichl was particularly taken by Joe's table-breadcrumb removal technique, using a spoon, which he defended by saying that this was how crumbs were dealt with in Italy and, besides, "I like the way it looks." The wine list was uncompromisingly Italian. "Try it and if you still don't want it," Mario was quoted as saying, advocating a bottle by an unknown maker, "I'll drink it myself." And the menu was "loaded with dishes that Americans are not supposed to like" (Reichl cited headcheese, octopus, beef cheeks, lamb's tongue, and calf brains). Her favorite dish was a "spicy, robust" squid preparation called a "Two-minute calamari, Sicilian lifeguard style." "Eating it, I always imagine myself on a wind-swept beach in Sicily," Reichl wrote—an elegant adverbial touch: the critic not only liked the food but was already a regular.

She had also been a target. When Reichl had showed up, she wasn't to know how dedicatedly everyone had been preparing for her. Until her review was published, the restaurant's second floor was closed; the bar accepted no more than six people; the maximum seating was restricted to eleven tables; and, by the end of the night, there were no more than fifty covers. (Today, Babbo does as many as three hundred and fifty.) When there, Reichl had the most experienced waiter, plus a backup waiter, a floor manager, and two runners. The music was either calculatedly purposeful—on Reichl's first visit, a selection of Bob Marley tunes, to whom Mario had heard she was particularly partial—or else studiously atmospheric: a languid compilation of opera arias, say (and all of it very different from what you'd hear now, a motley miscellany, circa Rutgers class of '82, of Moby, the Jayhawks, Squeeze, R.E.M., and the early Stones, intended solely to entertain the proprietor chef while he's knocking back glasses of white wine at the bar, the high-volume message being that this is my house and I'll play what I want to).

All in all, the strategies built round Reichl's visit call to mind a coach preparing for a big game. They also created an illusion of dining room serenity and a genuine serenity in the kitchen. Was her food different as well? There is no way of knowing, but its preparation was certainly more orderly than the normal high-stress frenzy. Elisa remembers that the whole restaurant (she was then making the starters) was in a condition of constant dress rehearsal—waiting for Ruth. Joe was in the front, overseeing the service. Mario was in the kitchen, whispering every order and inspecting it before it went out. Even Andy was cooking. He was working the grill and wasn't allowed to expedite until *after* Reichl's review.

Reichl came to Babbo five times and ate everything on offer. The *Times* encourages its critics to make an effort at being anonymous. Reichl, with a head of black hair, was known to wear a blond wig and wouldn't have made the reservation under her own name. But the practical truth is that a critic, after only a handful of reviews, is spotted by the people who worry about this sort of thing. Mario knew she'd be there long before she arrived.

The importance attached to the review now seems exaggerated but was a symptom of the ambitions of the new restaurant: Mario and Joe wanted those three stars. (Before Otto opened, they went through a similar drill; the hope then was for a more modest two stars, which it duly received, a more than honorable laurel for a pizza joint.) But I was mystified by the stories—the stratagems, the clandestine preparations—and asked Mario if, knowing a critic was in the house, he could make the meal better than what otherwise might be served. Wasn't the point of the kitchen consistency—a dish was a dish was a dish?

"Trust me," he said. "Our knowing makes a difference."

Reichl left the *Times* in 1999 and was replaced by William Grimes, who was the critic for the next five years. (Grimes gave Otto its two stars.) At the beginning of Grimes's tenure, Mario was convinced that

Babbo would be reappraised. The worry informed that first instruction on my first day: be prepared—the critics will be back. Mario never mentioned the concern again. Instead it became Frankie's paranoiac refrain (the you-guys-are-doing-this-deliberately-so-that-Babbo-will-lose-its-three-stars-and-I'll-be-fucking-fired refrain). When Grimes left, the spot was filled by Amanda Hesser, an accomplished food journalist and, it seemed, a friend of the Batali-Bastianich approach. I didn't know there was a unifying methodology, but Mario seemed to believe in one: "She *loves* us," he told me one day, citing her enthusiasm for Lupa, their Roman-inspired trattoria not far from Babbo, and the implication was that since she liked Lupa she'd like everything else. But Hesser didn't take up the position permanently; it remained unfilled for another five months.

At the time, I was grateful for my casual affiliation with the food trade because it provided me with a glimpse of what this period was like among the restaurateurs I happened to meet: the speculation was constant, and underlying it all was a legitimate business concern. New York is different from most European cities, which often have several upmarket newspapers competing for an upmarket audience, the kind that tends to support high-end restaurants. New York has one, the *Times*, and its critic, in the view of many proprietors, can make or break a business. The fear isn't that a critic might have a personal agenda; it is merely that judgment is unpredictable and sometimes arbitrary, even if its consequences can be absolute: if your restaurant gets trashed, for whatever reason, your trade will suffer, and, if it survives the trashing, you may not have another chance to prove yourself.

One Saturday night in June, I was meant to have dinner with Mario but he canceled at the last minute. He had just learned that the *Times* had filled the vacancy left by Grimes. The new guy was Frank Bruni, who had been the paper's bureau chief in Rome. Without anyone's realizing, Bruni had dined at Babbo several times during the preceding month. *(Holy fuck!)* It was only on his last visit that he was finally spotted. His debut review would be of Babbo, and, this time, the critic had genuinely eaten his way through the menu anonymously. Mario had canceled our dinner in the hope that Bruni might return. He didn't. He didn't need to. His review was already written: it would appear on the following Wednesday.

There was to be a preview on a local television news station: the practice was that the critic reads the review on New York One at nine-fifteen the night before it's published (in shadows, to preserve his anonymity). On the afternoon of the broadcast, my wife, walking past Babbo, spotted John Mainieri, the maître d', standing outside with a gaggle of the staff, smoking furiously (John doesn't normally smoke), his shirt soaked through with sweat. "Come back in the evening," he urged. "We'll be celebrating or mourning, because our future is on the line."

"How am I?" Mario asked, rhetorically repeating the question I'd put to him. "I'll tell you tomorrow. The whole year could be ruined."

My wife and I spent the evening in the restaurant, enduring the countdown as well as continuous displays of self-doubt. Martin Gobbee, who'd happened to wait on Bruni's table on his last three visits, was rehearsing the exchanges he'd had with the man. Another waiter confessed that he'd just bought an apartment in Brooklyn ("Christ, I've taken on a mortgage!"). The wife of David Lynch, the wine steward, was pregnant ("Because, you know, we thought the future was solid"). Mario wasn't around.

There were two fears. One pertained to the critic. Only one thing was known about him: that he'd been previously based in Rome. This Bruni fellow actually knew Italian food. It followed that Babbo would be judged not simply against other New York restaurants but also against those from the old country. No other New York critic had that kind of knowledge.

The other fear was Frankie.

Frankie continued to have difficulties settling in, which was scarcely surprising, since almost the entire kitchen staff had resigned. Meanwhile, he had fired the new sous-chef and hired another. And then, with a day's notice, Abelardo, from the prep kitchen, had been promoted to the pasta station, the most difficult in the kitchen. Mario was now having to be at Babbo every night. In addition, there had been some pejorative word-of-mouth patter. A Babbo regular, a writer and occasional food journalist, had eaten a bad meal—"my lamb was overcooked, and the squab was raw"—and had told so many people about his leaden lamb and his pink pigeon ("Was it because Andy is no longer there?") that it became a public refrain, one that was regularly reaching Joe and Mario. The fear was that the patter would provoke a reappraisal—ironic now, since a reappraisal was already in the works. "This is what happens with regulars," Joe told me, the sour word-of-mouth report circulating unstoppably. "They all self-destruct. They expect too much. They forget that it's a business. You can never make them happy. All regulars crash and burn." I had never seen Joe so angry.

Recently, I contacted Frank Bruni. I had obvious questions—about the Italianness of Babbo's cooking and how it compared to what he'd been eating in Italy—but what really interested me were more prurient preoccupations: Did he realize his review had put everyone in a panic? Did he have any idea that he represented what everyone feared, a reappraisal, at a time when the kitchen was in upheaval? Mario had been at the restaurant every time Bruni ate there: did he really think that was normal?

Bruni admitted he'd been surprised that no one had caught on that he was there as a critic, especially after getting the same waiter three times in a row. And, no, he hadn't thought that the kitchen's performance was uneven, over and above the normal (and considerable) "disruptive feeling" of the whole place. And, no, he hadn't picked Babbo for its Italianness, although, it's true, he had found himself judging the food against what he'd been eating in Rome. ("Babbo is too elaborate to be genuinely Italian. Italian cooking is simple. Babbo is not simple. Italy is a starting point.") Mainly, he was astonished that anyone would have been nervous. He explained that before he had taken up his position he had sought out the best the city had to offer. He spent four weeks eating at great New York restaurants and then considered where he'd had the most fun. "This review was my first time out, and I wanted it to be about the joy of dining in New York. It wasn't scientific. I just liked Babbo a lot. It has a consistency of deliciousness that I knew I'd enjoy describing."

The review was a rave. Mario walked in, just after nine-thirty, with an enlarged photocopy (the text had appeared on a Web site). "Among the restaurants that make my stomach do a special jig," Bruni wrote, "Babbo ranks near the top, and that's one reason a fresh review appears today, six years after Babbo opened and received a three-star rating from Ruth Reichl." Bruni confirmed the restaurant's three-star status but suggested he'd wanted to give it a fourth star. At present, he pointed out, there were five four-star restaurants, and all of them were French.

Was there a reason that an Italian restaurant was not among them? "Why not Babbo?"

"There is a short, emblematic answer: the music. On the first of my recent visits to Babbo, what thundered—and I do mean thundered—from the sound system was relatively hard rock. Bucatini with the Black Crowes? ('Their second album!' a waiter proudly informed us.) Linguine with Led Zeppelin?"

It was the perfect Batali review: the food was so good it could have been French; the food was so good it could have got the city's highest accolade; but, in the final reckoning, the place was too rock 'n' roll, a rebel without a fourth star.

It was also a vindication of Frankie. I went back and found him leaning against the pass, reading the enlarged photocopy. He had been running the kitchen for half a year. He'd gained weight (the butter) and lost hair (his dark Italian-American curls receding to reveal an older man's sage forehead). And he had a calmness I'd never seen. Ever since I'd met Frankie, he had been preparing for this day—when a critic would wander in and judge his cooking. The day had come, and Frankie had acquitted himself: he was running a four-star kitchen, marred only by the music tastes of his boss. In fact, if Mario hadn't been here, worrying about Frankie's kitchen, the music wouldn't have been so loud—only Mario jacks up the volume so high that everyone in the restaurant is compelled to listen. Was it possible that Frankie, on his own, would have got the fourth star? Frankie chuckled. "I'm happy," he said. We embraced. What can I say? He's a dickhead, but a dickhead with talent, although I will always be mystified by the complicated process of restaurant pedagogy, the one where Mario learned so many things from Marco Pierre White, including not to be like Marco, and that then continued into the next generation, where Frankie learned so many things from Mario, including how to be like Marco Pierre White.

I lingered, relishing Frankie's day, this once-in-a-lifetime moment, a culmination of years in hot kitchens, the hours of learning, perfecting, memorizing, until finally you reach a point where you've learned enough. Mario's story came to mind—surviving that London pub, the humiliations of Italy, the failure of Rocco. It takes a long time. It had taken Andy a long time. And now Frankie: he had arrived.

29

S o," Mario asked me, "what about your own restaurant? Say, a small place in Italy, maybe in the hills. Italian for the Italians. A few tables. Open only on weekends. Completely authentic. Jessica in front, you in the back. Or," he paused theatrically, "you could do something here." He wiggled his eyebrows. "We have the means . . ."

It was a ridiculous suggestion, but I accepted it as a flattering indication of how much I'd learned. I had no idea how much that was until I sat down with Mario and jabbered away about the girello, speculated on what could be done with the sottofesa, enumerated the miracles that can be performed on a shank. I'd assumed anyone who had spent time in Italy knew this stuff. I hadn't recognized that not even most Italians didn't.

"Please," Mario said. "I have no idea what you're talking about."

Wow. In this small area of expertise, I know more than Mario. The apprentice has become a disciple has become a—what? Something: if nothing else, the Maestro's student, and Dario's, as well as Betta's. (It's only now that I realize I'd forgotten an important lesson from the butcher shop: that when I got home no one would know what I was talking about.) Even so, against my better judgment, my mind wandered, contemplating Mario's suggestion, preparing food that was genuinely Italian and genuinely simple. Could "simple" work in New York? Or a version of the macelleria? I pictured the display case, the eccentric opening times, the hours I'd put in memorizing Dante: *"Nel mezzo del cammin di nostra vita."* Midway through my life, once again.

The occasion was a debriefing dinner—postponed by Mario (because of Bruni), although, post-Bruni, Mario no longer had the high-testosterone swagger I had known him by but something bigger:

omnipotence, perhaps. Our evening had begun on the stoop, where Mario hangs out and summons waiters by cell phone to keep his wine glass refreshed. He had emerged in something of a sprint, customers grabbing him until he was out the door. ("Kathleen Turner just gave me tongue," he said breathlessly, having been stopped by the actress before he escaped and who, rather than peck him on the cheek, had slipped in a wetty. "I hate it when people do that, especially with her husband staring at me.") Mario was bearing two bottles of white wine, which disappeared so fast I don't remember drinking them. ("Hey, Lynchy," he said, phoning the wine steward, "bring us two more bottles along with your two best Mexican prostitutes.") Those downed, we set out for Lupa, but not before dispatching three cops to Otto. They'd chatted with us on the stoop, tolerantly watching us slowly lose our ability to watch them. "Hey, Amanda," Mario said, phoning the manager, "give them the corner table and lose the bill."

At Lupa, we had a Vernaccia di San Gimignano (bottle number five), and thirty-five different dishes, many composed on the spot by the restaurant's genius chef, Mark Ladner—a spread that, before my Italian experiences, I would have considered excessive, but now seemed perfectly reasonable: after all, compared with Scappi's 1,347-plate pranzo, what's thirty-five little plates? There were cured things, fried things, and vegetable things, including stuffed zucchini flowers deep-fried in a mix of olive oil and butter, which, according to the chef, made for a more interesting texture than normal peanut oil, a detail that fascinated me so much I wrote it in my notebook, believing I'd be scoping out the green market in the morning for zucchini flowers. (In the event, I missed the morning.)

We were on to reds, two bottles of Giovanni Manetti's Flacianello, the one made from the very vines I'd seen from that ridge by the old church in Panzano. Those finished, Mario and I passed the half-case point, a full case in watery view. By the time pastas appeared (I hadn't realized that the first thirty-five dishes were starters), my notes grew less reliable. According to one entry, there were eight pastas, but what I wrote seems incomplete: "ramps, breadcrumbs, spaghetti, wife" (when did she arrive?) followed by an instruction to her from Mario—"You will eat your pasta or I will rub the shrimp across your breasts"—which is confusing because I don't remember any shrimp. By now, we'd had, by my count, forty-three plates of food, although I feel compelled to add that the plates really were very small. Main courses arrived. And more wine. ("Bricco dell' Uccellone," my notes say. Three bottles, which brought our tally to ten, mitigated by the presence of a third drinker, my wife— if she was drinking. If she was there.) I remember pork and oxtail stew and an uproar following the appearance of a swordfish. "It's perfectly nice," Mario protested, "but, hey, it's a fish. It's from under the sea. Who wants fish?" After this, who knows? For a start, my notes are upside down (never reassuring), and what means this remark—"Let's push the envelope a little"? Or Mario's request of the waitress: "It's not fair I have this view all to myself when you bend over. For dessert, would you take off your blouse for the others?" (Lucky woman—she works for the guy.) Or this: "Two thirty; exterminator here." To disinfect the restaurant or us? Alarmingly, we then left to get something to drink (Mario was parched), when he put the question to me again: so, a restaurant?

And I realized: no. I did not want a restaurant.

When I started, I hadn't wanted a restaurant. What I wanted was the know-how of people who ran restaurants. I didn't want to be a chef, just a cook. And my experiences in Italy had taught me why. For millennia, people have known how to make their food. They have understood animals and what to do with them, have cooked with the seasons and had a farmer's knowledge of the way the planet works. They have preserved traditions of preparing food, handed down through generations, and have come to know them as expressions of their families. People don't have this kind of knowledge today, even though it seems as fundamental as the earth, and, it's true, those who do have it tend to be professionals— like chefs. But I didn't want this knowledge in order to be a professional; just to be more human.

I also had a piece of unfinished business I didn't think Mario would understand. For more than a year, I'd been thinking of Caterina de' Medici.

The Medici story was the one told endlessly in the butcher shop, although I'd heard it elsewhere as well; Gianni, in Porretta, for instance, repeated it as often as Dario. A beloved member of Tuscany's favorite family crosses the Alps to become the queen of France and gives away Italy's secrets. Thus ends Italian gastronomy; thus begins the French. Outside Tuscany, of course, no one believes it. *The Oxford Companion to Food* lists it among history's most foolish food fables in an entry headed "culinary mythology" and describes how it is routinely demolished by historians who point out that Caterina was never meant to be a queen, but only a princess. What's more, she was only fourteen at the time, so what would she have known about food? Besides, she probably didn't cross the Alps but arrived by boat in Marseilles (ergo, no pack animals full of goodies) and for the next ten years was in the doghouse (fertility issues), anyway. And, finally, a codified French cuisine didn't emerge for at least another century, long after she was dead.

I've got to admit it's a persuasive list of objections, but does it mean the story was made up? Okay, so Tuscans give Caterina too much credit—can you blame them? They're Tuscans. But would this be the first time that modern historians, working in the established niche of myth bashing, had gone too far?

The queen, we know, was living in rough times. She didn't have her first child until she was nearly thirty (downright old age in the sixteenth century) but then, getting the hang of it, had five in quick succession. The king turned out to be a philandering scumbag with a mindless penchant for running around in armor (he died in a jousting match, when the queen, now Catherine, was forty). The country was on the verge of civil war (Catholics and Huguenots), and there wasn't a lot of time to think about lunch. But the most telling episode in Catherine de Médicis's culinary life occurred in the 1560s, when she was not fourteen but well into her forties and, with her sad-sack king husband gone, had become the most influential woman in France. To create unity at a time of factional fighting and to engender respect for the monarch (and for the reign of her three sons), she, as queen regent, mounted an extraordinary campaign. With an entourage of eight thousand horses, soldiers, and attendants, plus the royal chef, along with his extensive staffs of cooks, carvers, scalcos, and servers, she embarked on a two-year culinary tour of France, setting up banquets and festivals and regal entertainments in what amounted to a sixteenth-century royal road show. For two years, she sought to consolidate the monarchy in a way that an Italian would understand: by feeding people.

Where else, in the 1560s, was anyone in Europe preparing lavish, elaborate banquets with many courses? Not in France or England or the German countries. But an eight-course Italian *pranzo* comes to mind, one with 1,347 different dishes, made by Bartolomeo Scappi. The menu was undated—that was part of its rhetorical force when it was included in Scappi's 1570 edition of his works—but was almost certainly prepared during the preceding decade. Such a banquet, or something like it, was surely one of the models for Catherine de Médicis's road show: a Renaissance Italian feast.

But even this speculation misses the point. I am not persuaded that Catherine de Médicis taught the French how to cook, but I now believe she was one of several important culinary influences. By the sixteenth century, many in France recognized that Italian cooking had been enjoying a long renaissance—a sideshow beside the flourishing of the Renaissance itself. In 1505, Platina's account of the Maestro Martino was translated into French and became widely popular. Ten years later, Giovanni Rosselli located the Maestro's own manuscript (the one Platina plagiarized), claimed it as his own, and published it under the title of *Epulario:* this, too, was immediately translated. The papal courts in Avignon had Italian cooks, as did Catherine's father-in-law. Rabelais had already written about his three trips to the Italian peninsula; Montaigne was about to embark on his own journey. Did Catherine single-handedly change French cooking? No. But she was clearly the culmination of a trend that had been well under way by the time she crossed the Alps (or the Mediterranean).

This was no time for me to open a restaurant. When I thought back on what I'd learned in Italy—the fifteenth-century arista, the Mediccan terrines and ragùs, the thigh, the Renaissance ravioli, the recipes of Martino—I saw that I'd mastered food in one tradition (I'll call it the Florentine-Tuscan-late-Renaissance tradition) up to a certain point: when Caterina became Catherine and crossed the Alps (or the Mediterranean) into France.

I'm not ready, I told Mario. There is still much to learn, and I may never have this opportunity again. I want to follow Catherine de Médicis. If I'm really to understand Italian cooking, I need to cross the Alps and learn what happened next. I have to go to France.

Acknowledgments

The reference to the first use of "pasta," in Cagliari, in 1351, is from *Pasta: The Story of a Universal Food* by Silvano Serventi and Fransoise Sabban, translated by Antony Shugaar (2000). The reference to the first published account of a corn polenta in Italy is from *Italian Cuisine: A Cultural History* by Alberto Capatti and Massimo Montanari, translated by Aine O'Healy (1999). *Italian Cuisine* also describes the autobiography of Antonio Latini. The dominant demand food theory is described in *Culture of the Fork: A Brief History of Food in Europe* by Giovanni Rebora, translated by Albert Sonnenfeld (1998).

In addition to the obvious texts, the following books were especially useful: *On Food and Cooking: The Science and Lore of the Kitchen* (1984, and the revised and enlarged edition of 2004) by Harold McGee; *Platina, On Right Pleasure and Good Health,* edited and translated by Mary Ella Milham (1998); and *Apicius, Cookery and Dining in Imperial Rome,* edited and translated by Joseph Dommers Vehling. In addition, several Italian texts were essential, including the two-volume collection *Arte della Cucina, Libri di recette testi sopra lo scalco, il trinciante, and i vini,* edited by Emilio Faccioli (1966); the facsimile edition of the 1692 text of *Lo scalo alla moderna, overo l'arte di ben disporre i conviti* by Antonio Latini (1993); *Ne pomodoro ne pasta, 150 piatti napoletani del seicento,* edited by Claudio Novelli (2003); and the facsimile edition of the 1570 text of *Opera dell'arte del cucinare* by Bartolomeo Scappi (2002).

I am very grateful for the advice and comments of those who read the manuscript: Leyla Aker, Jessica Green, Austin Kelley,

Cressida Leyshon, David Remnick, and Andrew Wylie, and my two book editors, Dan Franklin in London and Sonny Mehta in New York.

This book would not have been possible, in any shape, without the support, tolerance, encouragement, instruction, and friend-ship of Mario Batali. A proper expression of my gratitude could fill another tome.

About the Author

Bill Buford is a staff writer for *The New Yorker*, where he was the fiction editor for eight years. He was the founding editor of *Granta* magazine and was also the publisher of Granta Books. He is the author of *Among the Thugs*, a non-fiction account of crowd violence and British soccer hooliganism. He lives in New York City with his wife, Jessica Green, and their two sons.

About the Type

The text of this book was set in Aldus, a typeface
designed by the celebrated typographer Hermann Zapf
in 1952–1953. Based on the classical proportion of the
popular Palatino type family, Aldus was originally intended as
a slightly lighter version that would read better in smaller
sizes. Hermann Zapf was born in Nuremberg, Germany, in
1918. He has created many other well known typefaces
including Comenius, Hunt Roman, Marconi, Melior,
Michelangelo, Optima, Saphir, Sistina,
Zapf Book, and Zapf Chancery.

Composed by Creative Graphics,
Allentown, Pennsylvania
Printed and bound by Berryville Graphics,
Berryville, Virginia
Designed by Anthea Lingeman